ONE IN FIVE

ONE IN FIVE

How We're Fighting for

Our Dyslexic Kids

in a System That's Failing Them

BY MICKI BOAS

TILLER PRESS

New York   London   Toronto   Sydney   New Delhi

TILLER PRESS

An Imprint of Simon & Schuster, Inc.
1230 Avenue of the Americas
New York, NY 10020

First Tiller Press hardcover edition August 2020

TILLER PRESS and colophon are trademarks of Simon & Schuster, Inc.

For information about special discounts for bulk purchases, please
contact Simon & Schuster Special Sales at 1-866-506-1949
or business@simonandschuster.com.

The Simon & Schuster Speakers Bureau can bring authors to your live event.
For more information or to book an event, contact the Simon & Schuster Speakers
Bureau at 1-866-248-3049 or visit our website at www.simonspeakers.com.

Interior design by Laura Levatino

Manufactured in the United States of America

1   3   5   7   9   10   8   6   4   2

Library of Congress Cataloging-in-Publication Data
Names: Boas, Micki, author.
Title: One in five : how we're fighting for our dyslexic kids in a system
that's failing them / by Micki Boas.
Description: First Tiller Press hardcover edition. | New York : Tiller
Press, 2020. | Includes bibliographical references.
Identifiers: LCCN 2020009757 (print) | LCCN 2020009758 (ebook) |
ISBN 9781982130602 (hardcover) | ISBN 9781982130619 (ebook)
Subjects: LCSH: Dyslexic children—Education—United States. | Parents of dyslexic
children—United States. | Dyslexia—United States.
Classification: LCC LC4709 .B63 2020 (print) | LCC LC4709 (ebook) | DDC 371.91/44—dc23
LC record available at https://lccn.loc.gov/2020009757
LC ebook record available at https://lccn.loc.gov/2020009758

ISBN 978-1-9821-3060-2
ISBN 978-1-9821-3061-9 (ebook)

For My Boys,
Fede, Matias, and Oliver

TABLE OF CONTENTS

Preface   1

Section I: How Did We Get Here?   5

Section II: The Story of My Son's Dyslexia Journey   21

Section III: The Outrageous Highlights Reel   79

Section IV: Savvy Solutions to Persistent Problems   193

Epilogue: One Last Fight: My Second Son's Story   237

Acknowledgments   247

Endnotes   251

ONE IN FIVE

PREFACE

Three months after giving birth to my first son, Matias, it was time to go back to work. I felt the dread and the separation anxiety every mother feels when the short maternity leave was up. Each night, I rushed home to give him his last feeding before bed. Between being a first-time mother and being entranced with every move, giggle, and twitch my precious firstborn made, I didn't realize that he was not progressing the way he should.

He never crawled.

He had sensory issues.

His speech was delayed.

Now I wish I'd paid more attention and had known what these signs meant. But like all parents, I simply wanted my son to have a happy, uncomplicated childhood.

As early as two and a half years old, when he began school, Matias struggled to learn the alphabet. He steadily fell further behind his classmates in reading, spelling, and comprehension. Yet whenever I asked about his progress, his teachers assured me that Matias was "within range" developmentally.

Far from being any kind of children's expert, I chose to believe them.

Looking back, I was mired in denial. Why did it take me so long to admit that Matias needed help? What was I thinking?

Choosing to listen to the "experts" at school meant not having to acknowledge that he might fall through the cracks of the educational system and ultimately face a tough road ahead, not just in school but in life itself.

By first grade, the thought of going to class tormented Matias so much that he resisted going. After the hour-long struggle of getting him to school, he did everything he could to avoid reading in front of the class.

It took all of the courage my little guy had in him to bravely raise his hand for help. He asked for support so many times that his teacher and classmates gave him an unfortunate nickname: "The Statue of Liberty."

Perhaps my son's pediatrician might have identified Matias as a child who would need early intervention and special services in school if she'd had more time to see him, but given the way our health-care providers are pressured by insurance companies, one out of three well-child doctor visits are 10 minutes or less.[1] To our doctor, Matias seemed healthy and happy—and of course, in most ways he was.

The teachers should have been my allies in spotting Matias's academic problems and addressing them. I knew they cared about my son. But the sad truth is that many schools have an approach of "don't ask, don't tell" when it comes to identifying and providing services for children with dyslexia, largely because they know they don't have the funding to provide specialized teachers or extra resources.

If you're reading this book, my guess is that you or someone you care about is trying to support a child with dyslexia and have been met with untrained teachers, staff, school district officials, and a child study team (CST) that delay or deny student evaluations, and provide infinite mountains of paperwork. And, inevitably, your money and your patience runs out.

I call this complex ribbon of obstacles "the invisible red tape." It exists almost everywhere in America, and it threatens to wind itself around us until we're mummified and silent. Now that you've encountered it, you're probably angry and desperately seeking tools you can use to slash through it and get the help your child needs.

Looking back, I wish I'd trusted my maternal instincts and gotten angry sooner. Maybe then I would have pushed for earlier interventions to keep Matias on track. At age three, your child's brain is only 80 percent the size it will be at adulthood.[2] Researchers agree that how you nourish and care for your child during the first thousand days of life—from conception until age three—has a profound impact on how your child will develop and learn.

I wrote this book to help frustrated parents like me, not just get by, but also to have your child with dyslexia thrive in spite of all the internal and external obstacles that come their way. I'm sharing not only the shortcuts, tricks, and inside information I used to cut through that invisible red tape, but also solutions and hacks from more than two hundred other parents and experts I spoke to over the course of writing this book.

In the first section, "How Did We Get Here?," I offer the startling facts about dyslexia and frame the problems we face in educating children affected by this invisible learning difference. The second section, "The Story of My Son's Dyslexia Journey," details my own personal story as a mom who started out denying that my son had learning issues, but who gradually became a fierce advocate pushing for changes in how our government and schools educate all children with dyslexia.

The third section of the book offers you an "Outrageous Highlights Reel" of parent stories I've collected from across the country. Federal and state education laws are implemented at the local level, so I made a point of engaging with parents from distinct geographic regions, as well as from different educational backgrounds, income levels, and professions, to see how these factors impacted their journeys. Some of the stories are infuriating, like the one about a mom who was told by a school district attorney that it was fine if her son didn't reach his full potential, "because we need more janitors." Others, like the stories of children so shamed and depressed by their school experiences that they wanted to kill themselves, will surely break your heart.

And in the final section of this book, "Savvy Solutions to Persistent Problems," I offer some measure of hope. I spoke to teachers, principals, school superintendents, psychologists, and researchers about the most common challenges parents face in having our children properly identified and served with the resources they need to learn, including early intervention, specialized teacher training, and adequate funding. Happily, many of them spoke frankly with me about the view from the other side, and I share their thoughts here, because the more you know, the better you can fight. I also outline simple, pragmatic steps you can take right now to ensure that your children receive the education they deserve.

By the time you finish reading this book, you will have enough knowledge to have the confidence to trust your instincts and know when your child needs help. Even when school officials tell you that your child is "within range." Even when they say they're "doing everything possible to help." You will be able to recognize when your child's teacher isn't cutting it. When your child is not receiving the right interventions. Finally, you will be able to spot and call out gaps in services your child misses out on due to lack of educational funding.

Most important, you will have the tools you need to cut through whatever invisible red tape is keeping your child from learning. I invite you to join me in becoming a force for change.

SECTION I

HOW DID WE GET HERE?

FRAMING THE PROBLEM

Imagine a child, five or six years old, who has been invited to meet the family in a house down the road. His parents tell him he'll love it, because this family has lots of nice children, and he's excited to go.

However, when the child arrives, the house is completely dark. He can't find the light switches, despite people telling him where they are. The longer he stays in this dark house, the more frustrated and frightened he feels—especially since the other children seem to have no problem navigating the rooms.

That's what it's like when a child with dyslexia is trying to learn how to read. As neuroscientist Sally Shaywitz, MD, points out in her groundbreaking book, *Overcoming Dyslexia*, "Most children look forward to learning to read and, in fact, do so quickly. For children with dyslexia, however, the experience is very different: For them, reading, which seems to come effortlessly for everyone else, appears to be beyond their grasp. These children, who understand the spoken word and love to listen to stories, cannot decipher the same words when they are written on a page. They grow frustrated and disappointed."[1]

Dyslexia is referred to as a hidden or "invisible" disability that often goes undiagnosed, simply swept under the rug. Unlike students with obvious physical disabilities, attention deficit issues, or behavioral problems that impact learning, many children with dyslexia develop coping strategies to fit in with their classmates, like memorizing or guessing words based on context. Teachers—especially those with little training in identifying dyslexia, or those overburdened by too many children in class—may chalk up a child's failure to read as laziness, or as the child just being "slow."

School districts often resist identifying children with dyslexia because they lack the specialized staff and reading programs necessary to help them. As a school administrator in Chicago admitted, "I barely have enough money in my budget to get kids to school and feed them. How am I going to educate a kid like yours, who needs more resources?"

I was floored. I couldn't believe the scope of budget crises that schools like this are facing. Yet I also knew that we have no choice but to keep fighting for all our children—not just the lucky few who get the proper support. Dyslexia is the most common of all neurobiological disorders, affecting up to 20 percent of our population and up to 90 percent of all those with learning disabilities, according to the Yale Center for Dyslexia & Creativity.[2]

* * *

That's right: *One out of every five people in the U.S. has dyslexia.*[3]

* * *

To put dyslexia into context, it falls under the specific learning disability category (SLD), which is by far the largest of any category in the thirteen categories covered by the Individuals with Disabilities Education Act (IDEA). These numbers are too large to be ignored.

If those numbers are still too abstract, consider this: The average national class size is just over twenty students. Given what we know about dyslexia, twenty percent of that classroom will be impacted by this invisible disability because they aren't seen or diagnosed in time or don't receive appropriate interventions and instruction.

This isn't a blip. This is a massive problem, and we need to solve it.

DEFINING DYSLEXIA

DYSLEXIA is a brain-based type of learning disability that specifically impairs a person's ability to read. These individuals typically read at levels significantly lower than expected, despite having normal intelligence. Although the disorder varies from person to person, common characteristics among people with dyslexia are difficulty with phonological processing (the manipulation of sounds), spelling, and/or rapid visual-verbal responding. —National Institute of Neurological Disorders and Stroke.[4]

NOT EXACTLY FUN FACTS

- According to the International Dyslexia Association, the exact causes of dyslexia are still not completely clear, but anatomical and brain imagery studies show differences in the way the brain of a person with dyslexia develops and functions. Moreover, most people with dyslexia have been found to have difficulties with identifying the separate speech sounds within a word and/or learning how letters represent those sounds, a key factor in their reading difficulties. Dyslexia is not due to either lack of intelligence or a desire to learn; with appropriate teaching methods, students with dyslexia can learn successfully.

- Dyslexia occurs in people of all backgrounds and intellectual levels. People with dyslexia can be very bright. They are often capable or even gifted in areas such as art, computer science, design, drama, electronics, math, mechanics, music, physics, sales, and sports.
- Dyslexia can be inherited in some families, and recent studies have identified a number of genes that may predispose an individual to developing dyslexia.[5]

GLOSSARY OF TERMS

504 Plan: Provides accommodations and related services to general education students who are identified with a disability but who don't need specialized instruction.

CST: A Child Study Team is a multidisciplinary group of professionals typically employed by the board of education to provide parents and teachers with a variety of learning related services.[6]

CTOPP: The Comprehensive Test of Phonological Processing helps evaluate phonological processing abilities as a prerequisite to reading fluency.[7]

EIP: An Early Intervention Program is the term used to describe the services and supports that are available to babies and young children with developmental delays and disabilities, and their families. These may include speech therapy, physical therapy, and other types of services based on the needs of the child and family.[8]

IEP: An Individualized Education Program provides specially designed instructions, accommodations, modifications, and related services, such as speech-language therapy, to students who qualify for special education.

OHI: Other Health Impairments is the term used to cover several impairments or disorders that limit a student's ability to learn. Whether a condition falls under OHI depends on the limitations the condition places on the student in three different areas: alertness, strength, and vitality. This category includes health conditions like diabetes and asthma, as well as attention disorders like attention deficit hyperactivity disorder (ADHD).[9]

RTI: Response to intervention is a systematic way of identifying struggling students and giving them extra help.[10]

Science of Reading: Includes all methods or approaches that have been found, through research, to teach kids how to read.[11]

SLD: Specific Learning Disabilities is the umbrella term the federal government uses to describe one or more of the basic barriers involved in understanding or using spoken or written language. According to federal guidelines, in order to qualify for an IEP, a specific disability must be identified.[12]

Three Tiers of Response to Intervention Support

Tier 1: The Whole Class Intervention: Teachers do their best to give the kids instruction that fits their skill levels and how they learn best in a general education classroom

Tier 2: Small Group Intervention: Fewer students in a group, more deliberate, direct and explicit in how students are taught and how feedback is modeled, with details provided

Tier 3: Intensive Intervention: Intensive instruction, including the introduction of a specialist with specific expertise to weigh in on the situation[13]

LAWS THAT SHOULD WORK, BUT DON'T

Students with dyslexia have the same basic civil rights to an education as the rest of the population, thanks to the Individuals with Disabilities Education Act of 1975 (IDEA), section 504 of the Rehabilitation Act of 1973, and the Americans with Disabilities Act of 1990 (ADA). These laws define the rights of students with dyslexia and other specific learning disabilities, and legally entitle them to special services designed to help them overcome and accommodate their learning differences, including tailored educational programs.

According to a report by the National Center for Learning Disabilities (NCLD), "students identified by schools as having a disability may qualify for one of two types of assistance. An IEP has specifically designed services and a 504 plan has accommodations for those in general education."[14]

Sounds good, right? There's just one problem: None of these laws are working.

Of course, everyone agrees that early identification and intervention are key to helping students with dyslexia learn to read by that critical third-grade year—when all children are expected to read fluently enough to comprehend and retain content.[15] Only 6.6 percent of students in special education are typically identified with specific learning disabilities (SLD) by age six, and the achievement gap can be seen by first grade; it doesn't all of a sudden appear in third grade. Yet by age ten, the percentage increases to just over 40 percent of students identified.[16]

What's wrong with this picture?

It's either ignorance or pure denial. As I discovered while interviewing parents around the country, many students don't receive an "official" evaluation and diagnosis for dyslexia until third grade or beyond. This puts them at risk for academic difficulties. At the very least, students with SLD who aren't identified or don't receive the services they need in time are likely to enter middle and high school without essential literacy skills. Children who experience reading difficulties by third grade are four times more likely to leave school without a regular diploma compared to proficient readers, according to a study by the Annie E. Casey Foundation.[17] Children with dyslexia are twice as likely to drop out than the general population.[18] A study out of Northeastern University found that "high school dropouts cost taxpayers $292,000 over the course of their lives."[19] This means that if we are proactive and provide literary services to kids earlier, we could prevent the reliance on social services later. There is a small window of opportunity that the "let's wait and see" approach is not addressing.

However, it's no stretch to suggest that there's a link between children with undiagnosed dyslexia—or those who are identified as having dyslexia but are never given the appropriate interventions—and our prison population. The Literacy Project reports that three out of five people in U.S. prisons can't read, and 85 percent of juvenile offenders have trouble reading.[20]

On the other hand, 35 percent of entreprenuers define themselves as dyslexic in the U.S.[21] Some had the advantage of being given the help they needed early and others were able to develop coping mechanisms to use their big-picture, problem-solving skills. According to Made By Dyslexia, a global charity, 70 percent of successful people with dyslexia had a "champion" who recognized their potential.[22] The organization has launched an awareness campaign to help the public better understand dyslexia by encouraging people to speak openly about it, featuring a number of celebrities, including Orlando Bloom, Richard Branson, Kate Griggs, and Keira Knightley, discussing their triumphs and struggles.

There is proof that investing in early childhood can have a huge impact, not only on individual children, but on our nation. As Nobel Memorial Prize winner James Heckman explains in the Heckman Equation, every child needs effective early childhood development to be successful, but disadvantaged children are least likely to get it. Professor Heckman has proven that investing in early childhood development, especially among disadvantaged children, produces great benefits across education, health, economic, and social outcomes. Investing early in education produces high returns in a cost benefit analysis; for every $1 invested, it produces $6.30 worth of benefits for society.[23] So why aren't we being more proactive about helping all children develop and learn?

THE SYSTEM IS BROKEN

If we have the laws in place, why aren't children with dyslexia being identified earlier and receiving the education they need—and deserve?

The answer is complicated. It starts with the fact that many of us are hesitant to "label" our children as different. We're also too willing to believe what teachers and school districts are telling us, rather than trusting our own instincts. This naivete allows schools to be resistant when it comes to providing special education services.

I did not struggle in school, and expected the same of my children. By the time Matias was only eighteen months old, I begrudgingly admitted that there were concerns, thanks to nudging from my mother and husband. However, I still resisted applying for government-funded early intervention services because I didn't want my son to be labeled as "less than." If he had a label, I was afraid that Matias wouldn't have access to the same things other kids did in school.

I'm not the only parent to deny that my child needed help. In fact, even when educators do recommend that children be evaluated for special education services, the NCLD estimates that parents follow their recommendations only 56 percent of the time.[24]

Federal laws like Child Find, part of IDEA, require schools to identify and evaluate all children who have a disability and who may be entitled to special education services. When this law is implemented, states are required to identify and evaluate students at no cost to the parents. Here lies the problem: States look the other way in implementing these laws because of lack of consistent oversight from the federal government. Fundamentally, the finances and extra effort needed are standing in the way of helping our kids early. You will see these reasons as the crux of the issue in the stories to follow.

In order to standardize and monitor the states' implementation of Child Find, parent-led grassroots organizations have been involved. Grassroots groups like Decoding Dyslexia now claim chapters in all 50 states. Forty-six states have laws supporting dyslexic students that put an emphasis on early screening for dyslexia and teaching that includes phonics instruction and phonemic awareness, according to the International Dyslexia Association.[25] However, even with these laws in place, schools still find ways to skirt them, claiming they don't know what tools to use or saying that they have budget constraints in regards to screening.

As a result the onus is still on parents to push for screening, evaluations, and interventions, often paying out of pocket for those expenses, even though most can't spare the money (or time).

There are many caring teachers, but they're caught up in a broken system too. In my interviews with parents across the country, I heard over and over again about teachers who approached parents to suggest that their child should be identified for educational services, then quickly said, "But you didn't hear it from me," or, "But of course we can't say the word 'dyslexia' here."

There seems to be a gray area among parents and teachers to use the word "dyslexia," as it is a diagnostic term and they are not in the position to diagnose them. However, if we don't speak more often about dyslexia, it propagates the taboo. The schools don't want to say the word, because if they do, they need to have resources to support it, which they don't. So *shhh*.

Finally, in 2016, parents began to gather on Capitol Hill every July for a SayDyslexia Rally to bring awareness to the issues at local schools to the national capital to create change.

Why are teachers sometimes reluctant to raise red flags when a child needs an evaluation or special services? Because those services cost money, and in many districts, teachers fear retaliation by administrators for speaking up. For instance, the SEEK CT survey of teachers in Connecticut reported that 65 percent of staff said "they would likely be reprimanded or punished if they openly spoke with parents about what their child needs related to special education."[26]

Of course, many teachers also lack the specialized training they need to identify children with special needs. Many parents I spoke with were told their children were just "slow" in reading, and that nothing more could be done to help them. One mom was even advised to "use kind words with staff" in an IEP meeting with teachers and school administrators when she lost her temper, "because we're doing all we can to help your child read."

THE READING WARS ARE STILL A THING

Of course, when I was a new mom, I didn't know this basic fact: Reading doesn't come naturally to all children. I assumed that my son's teachers would show him how to read, and eventually he'd pick it up. That's a myth. According to Dr. Louisa Moats and Dr. Carol Tolman's 2009 work, *The Challenge of Learning to Read*, "The attainment of reading skill has fascinated psychologists and invited more study than any other aspect of human cognition because of its social importance and complexity."[27] The truth is that children with dyslexia must have a specific type of reading instruction in order to learn how to read, but most schools don't have these methods of instruction in place.

Over the past forty years, there has been a battle in the classroom over two basic types of reading instruction: phonics versus whole language. One approach assumes you know what you're seeing is a "CAR" and the other explains all the parts that makes up the *C-A-R*.

In simple terms, phonics-based reading instruction breaks written language down into simple components, using letter sounds and letter symbols. Phonics-based reading utilizes decoding, where children identify and break down the letter sounds within a word and then piece the sounds together. "When using the phonics method, kids see a new word, take what they know about what sounds each letter makes, and then put those letter sounds together to sound out the word. It allows a child to do things like switch out a *c* with an *h* to get either 'cow' or 'how,' or to put those two consonants together to read the word 'chow.'"[28]

In the whole-language approach, kids are expected to draw from their prior experiences, and the framework around a word, instead of breaking down the sounds. The idea is that if a child sees the word "cat" written enough times alongside a picture of a cat, he/she can associate the whole word with that picture and will know how to read it.

Schools typically are using whichever reading instruction materials their districts provide, varying greatly based on the knowledge of those making the decisions. Emily Hanford, a senior education correspondent and producer with American Public Media (APM), has done extensive reporting on dyslexia and other problems with reading. As she reported in the *Hard Words* podcast, most teachers today, except recent graduates, are convinced that the whole-language reading approach is the best, since that's what they were taught and have used thus far in their careers.[29] But according to the current research, phonics is essential for all children when learning how to read. And Hanford has reported that only four in ten current teacher-preparation programs nationwide train future teachers on the reading components that have been identified by research to be the most effective.[30] We can see why this is a root cause of education inequality for children with dyslexia.

INADEQUATE SPECIAL SERVICES

When Matias started school, I trusted the teachers to educate him. If he struggled, I assumed that the school would find ways to help him catch up with his peers and succeed academically.

That's when I snagged on another bit of invisible red tape: In addition to not being screened early or thoroughly enough, most children with dyslexia are not given the appropriate services due to the reading wars.

For example, many children with reading problems and other academic issues are held back in school so that they'll "catch up" with their peers. According to the National Center for Learning Disabilities (NCLD), "1.22 million students repeated a grade, yet 76 percent of those were general education students who hadn't yet been identified as having a disability."[31] Here's the thing: If children with dyslexia are held back without being properly evaluated, or if they are identified but don't receive appropriate reading strategies to teach them to decode words, holding them back will do nothing to help. They'll still be fumbling for light switches in that dark house.

If you or your child's teachers suspect something might be going on with your child, you're most likely to hear the phrase "response to intervention," or RTI. That, too, is problematic.

RTI is loosely defined as a framework for teaching elementary school students who need a bit more support in areas such as reading. It has been adopted in more than 70 percent of school districts across the country, making it more of a general education approach than a special education strategy. RTI calls for schools to identify learning problems early, and to adopt interventions—according to the *Education Week* article, "Study: RTI Practice Falls Short of Promise."[32] Students who need more reading intervention strategies receive a Tier 2 level of additional supports.

Sounds good, right? However, sometimes schools use RTI "incorrectly to delay or deny a timely evaluation for students suspected of having a disability," according to the NCLD. In addition, if your school says, "We aren't putting your child on a 504 plan or an IEP because we're giving him RTI," that means that your child's teacher and school are adopting intervention strategies that they think will help your child—but you have no say in the approach they will take, nor any way to measure if their interventions are working, because there's no formal "program" that the school is being held accountable for following. I experienced the RTI debacle with my younger son.

One article in *Education Week* reveals that RTI may actually hold back some children it was originally designed to help. For instance, first graders who received reading interventions without an appropriate evaluation actually did worse than "virtually identical peers" who didn't get more targeted assistance, according to a study released in November 2015 by the National Center for Education Evaluation and Regional Assistance.

To complicate matters, if your child has another, more visible problem, like ADHD (attention-deficit/hyperactivity disorder), which coexists with dyslexia 30 percent of the time, your child may be "diagnosed" as having behavioral problems that interfere with learning.[33] If that's the case, the onus will be placed on you to improve your child's behavior with some combination of medication and behavioral interventions, often without your child being evaluated for other learning issues that might also be causing him or her to act out.

And finally, if your child does end up being evaluated by the school district and qualifies for special services, those services will likely be "pull out" sessions, where your child will see a special education teacher for small group help sessions. The first problem with that is, schools don't have enough qualified special education teachers trained in the science of reading to go around. The country as a whole is facing a teaching shortage, according to the Economic Policy Institute, particularly in science, math, and special education.[34] In fact, some school districts are so desperate that they're importing special education teachers from countries abroad, because American-trained teachers are often reluctant to go into that particular discipline. And why wouldn't they be? In addition to low pay, emphasizing testing over teaching, and tying teacher performance to test scores, SPED teachers are also grappling with serious issues.

Problem number two is that those pull-out sessions are not synced with general education scheduling. Thus support services often take place while important content is being taught in your child's regular classroom—so your child will fall further behind in those subjects.

Finally, the pull-out sessions will likely include groups of children with various kinds of learning issues. Most special education teachers are either not trained in the specific type of reading instruction recommended for children with dyslexia, or are forced to accommodate many different learning disabilities, with different recommended approaches, at the same time.

There's got to be a better way, right? There is, and we'll get to that in the final section of this book, "Savvy Solutions to Persistent Problems."

FUNDING: WHERE IT ALL BEGINS

Even for children who are identified early on as dyslexic, the outcomes aren't always great. The bottom line is that most schools don't have the budget for special reading programs and other resources dictated in their IEPs, 504 plans, or RTI interventions.

For example, in the charter school my younger son, Oliver, attends, there are around six hundred students. Despite the statistics I've cited above, only about thirty-five of these students have been identified as having learning issues that qualify them for IEPs. That's less than 6 percent of the entire school population, which suggests that a heck of a lot of students there are coping with unidentified issues. However, Oliver's school is lucky to have a highly trained literacy specialist on staff. Other schools have the specialists travel around the district for support. How is it humanly possible to serve kids with up to thirteen different types of needs, all grouped together in the same session?

It isn't.

The thing is, when it comes to dyslexia, we know a lot. Research has identified specific, structured literacy programs that can teach a child with dyslexia how to read, including the Orton-Gillingham Approach, the Barton Reading and Spelling System, and the Wilson Reading System.

But despite this wealth of knowledge, there is a resource gap. Only 12 percent of teachers and parents internationally in a Made By Dyslexia Global survey stated it was very easy to spot dsylexia in their schools.[35] Even fewer are trained in Orton-Gillingham and related programs. According to the National Council on Teacher Quality, only 37 percent of elementary and special education programs appear to be teaching scientifically based reading methods to preservice teachers.[36]

Given the funding crisis in our schools, we aren't likely to see this change anytime soon—unless we keep making noise. (More on how we can do that later, in the "Savvy Solutions to Persistent Problems" section.)

It costs twice as much to educate a child with special needs versus a general education student.[37] With too little help from the federal government in funding, it leaves a gap for the state and local goverments to fill out of their already strained budgets.

The reality? That's not happening either.

The federal government is currently picking up only 15 percent of the shortfall, not the mandated 40 percent excess cost per general education student, which means that, nationwide, states and local school districts are struggling when it comes to providing appropriate resources for children identified with special needs.[38] Hence the "don't ask, don't tell" policy adhered to by so many school districts.

However, there are glimmers of hope, which we'll discuss in the final section of this book. I'll highlight examples of innovation in the form of dyslexic charter schools, microschools, and private schools focused on language-based learning differences. Optimism also lies in uncovering new solutions. The Research Excellence and Advancements for Dyslexia Act (READ) was signed into law in 2016 with a sunset provision for 2021, which means that the National Science Foundation must spend at least five million dollars per year on SLD research. What's more, half of this funding must be spent on dyslexia.

With this research effort and the raised outcry of parents across the country, hopefully we can look forward to a time when we will see the following solutions:

- We will identify dyslexia earlier, with better screening methods.
- We will provide science of reading training to teachers to better understand and instruct students with dyslexia and other SLD.
- We will create and implement more effective educational tools for children with dyslexia and SLD.
- We will scale successful models of dyslexia intervention.

To offer children with dyslexia an equal opportunity at education, we must keep finding that invisible red tape and hacking through it whenever schools are being resistant or opaque about policies or funding. Only by vigilantly advocating for our children, and for all children who need an extra hand to succeed in school, will we make education truly equal in this country.

SECTION II

THE STORY OF MY SON'S DYSLEXIA JOURNEY

3 15.02.
Those five numbers may not mean much to the average person, but to me, they were everything, because that's the DSM-V code used by mental health professionals to diagnose dyslexia. I had been working and waiting almost five years to get that diagnostic classification for my son so that we could put those numbers on his records once and for all.

Selfishly, it felt good to prove all the doubters wrong, but for him, I thought it would be much more than that. I was naive enough to think that getting the 315.02 designation on his IEP would magically unlock an infinite amount of resources located behind door number three. Unfortunately, it was not. Instead, getting the code turned out to just be the first move in what ultimately became a much longer game than I could've ever anticipated.

Like most parents, I lacked the ample time and patience required to navigate the early years of a child's education. But let's back up. I'd like to share a few moments from my story to help you understand how I formed my belief system, and what inspired me to write this book.

I was raised by two parents from the Midwest, who moved to Tampa when I was one. My mom was the only girl in her family, and her mother believed in the generational bias that boys were breadwinners and women should marry well. Her brothers went to medical school due to the emphasis on a career. My mom wanted to go to medical school as well but wasn't encouraged to do so. She did not want to be dependent on a man for income so she went to school to become a speech pathologist. She vowed that she would raise her two daughters differently, giving them the opportunities that she never had. Blessed with a strong entrepreneurial spirit and work ethic, she ran two successful comprehensive speech centers while also raising us.

My dad is an engineer by training, and financial adviser by trade. Stoic and stable, he is very analytical and amazing with numbers. "Dad, what are you up to today?" I would ask on a Saturday morning.

"Oh, the usual," he'd answer. "Just got your mom some flowers, watching a few football games, spent some time at the puzzle table, and off to dinner with friends somewhere your mom picked." He's very predictable, a creature of habit. I tell him everything, because he never judges me—just gives me the space to figure out how to proceed.

It was always a fun ride between the poles of my mom's creative drive and entrepreneurial spirit, and my dad's calm and predictable ways. I became sort of an amalgam of both of them. My sister sits firmly in the middle, the unofficial mediator, a skill she honed during her time as a social worker and now applies to her work as a human resources director.

My friends have always described me as a bold, provocative, creative spirit. I plead guilty as charged. I believe that taking an unconventional approach to life allows us to have more fun, have greater life experiences, tell better stories, gain wisdom, and be better equipped to solve the complex problems that life throws our way. I learned this at at a young age.

I started to question authority out of the womb. Surface answers never satisfied me. I wanted to understand the context, the anthropology, behind the answers.

My mom saw this and felt very strongly that I should have a progressive education to encourage this curiosity, so I started out in the Montessori system, then transitioned to public schools in the fifth grade. But learning was not a breeze for me, in any environment. I was in gifted classes and could take in information easily, but I struggled with attention issues. I could never finish long books (and I still can't believe I'm writing one now!). To this day, I prefer audio formats, where the voice sticks in my head easily. (If you're like me you're probably listening to the audio version of this book.)

I tried to apply my creative, inquisitive approach with the popular crew in my new public school. They were not big fans of it. On the first day, I jumped on the bus with my bright yellow glasses and began asking what fueled their souls. All they wanted to know was what material items my family had access to that might up their status. My cool style and big mouth was enough to be tolerated, but I always felt most at home with freaks and geeks. Studying people made me happy, and I quickly learned what made them tick.

I continued to study foreign cultures in college, where I minored in Japanese language and lived for a semester in Japan. I actually majored in advertising at the University of Florida, because I had a hunch my interest in people and cultures could help me create more compelling, relevant, and resonant themes for products and services.

This led to a career as a strategic planner for ad agencies. For twenty years I helped companies figure out what drives their audiences, so creatives could craft meaningful campaigns. I learned how to navigate the corporate waters by working with brands like Budweiser, Britney Spears, Samsung, Coca-Cola, and Procter & Gamble. Then I took a big risk when I was at the top of my game at a chief strategy officer level in advertising and decided I needed to leave the world better for my kids, so I turned my skills to focusing on mission-driven projects such as the ACLU, Fusion Media Group, and the United Nations.

I call this "positive defiance." This means breaking rules in a constructive way to fix what's not working. I'm hoping that the skills I've developed in my career as a passionate, curious storyteller will come in handy now as I tell the most important story of my life.

THE BIG PICTURE

My husband, Federico, has been my patient partner on this crazy journey. It is important to understand all the amazing talents he brings to our story. His passion for life is contagious. He is a great observer, a common trait of those with dyslexia. These genes allowed him to see the signs of Matias's dyslexia early on, well before I wanted to hear it.

He grew up in a family of eight in the south of Argentina. Little was known about dyslexia at the time, and certainly, no one was being diagnosed as dyslexic. His parents couldn't understand how he was so bright, yet struggling in school. They tried to figure out the best environment for him to learn in, sending him to four schools in five years. However, none of these options worked without a proper diagnosis and the accompanying support that might have showcased his brilliant mind. His struggles in school seriously impacted his self-esteem.

But by the age of seventeen, the frustration between him and his parents had reached a tipping point. He moved out of his parents' house to live alone in an abandoned building. It was not an ideal solution, but the only one he could think of to mitigate the situation. With his newfound sense of freedom and control, he dropped out of high school and began working at a variety of jobs in town. Through these experiences, he confirmed that he was a great observer and a people person. And that he probably wasn't suited for a traditional career.

When he started to think about what would come next, he headed to Buenos Aires and then turned his sights toward the United States, where he saw the potential for a better life.

I'm so lucky he did, because it led him to me, on a beach in Coney Island a few years after he arrived. Five years later we welcomed our first son, Matias, who shares his father's passion, observation skills, and learning style. I'm so proud of my husband, whose skill at seeing the big picture and capturing moments helped fuel his entrepreneurial path as a photojournalist and a coffee shop owner, bringing a whole neighborhood together.

HELPFUL HINT: BEFORE GETTING PREGNANT

Do you know that dyslexia is a neurobiological condition, and can therefore be inherited?

If one parent has it, there is a 40–60 percent chance that one or more of their children will be dyslexic.[1] If you suspect that you or your partner might have struggled with learning issues, talk about it. You might ultimately want to consider raising the child in a school district or area that is supportive of learning differences and willing to direct resources toward them.

MEET MATIAS:
A DIFFICULT ENTRY INTO THIS WORLD

I had an easy pregnancy. Everything seemed to go by the book. Matias even arrived on his exact due date.

However, the birth experience was not what I had expected at all. He got stuck in my birth canal, my blood pressure began to drop, and he was breech, with his butt positioned to come out first. After twenty-four hours of painful and difficult labor, I was rushed into an emergency C-section, where Matias and I almost didn't make it.

His Apgar scores were fine, so there was no permanent damage done. I am thankful for an ob-gyn intern who was on standby, but jumped into the leading role and saved him as the doctors were reaching their breaking point.

HELPFUL HINT

Start keeping all of your health records starting from your delivery. You will be asked for them multiple times during the intake and IEP processes.

---

* * *

I was finally healed from the surgery and enjoying all the firsts in the comfort of my home. We quickly achieved some predictability. Matias was as steady as a clock. Sleeping like a champ, eating with gusto, and a smile so big it was contagious. I couldn't believe how lucky I was to have such a gift.

Three months later I was back to work, forced to contain my excitement about being a new mom in an industry that was not welcoming to such "distractions." It's kind of ironic that I worked at one of the largest advertising agencies, on one of the biggest mom brands in the country, and I was told to keep my own "kid moments" at bay because my colleagues feared it might derail my career. One boss of mine, with no trace of irony, told me, "Moms don't come back to work; they stay at home where they should be." And when I got pregnant with my second baby at another agency, I was fired upon telling them. These companies did not have an environment that was open to women seeking to grow their families.

Given my stark work enviornment, the bright spot of my day was when I could return to my family. Every night I would rush to seek the comforts of home, to bond with my baby, give him his last feeding, and eat up that big smile.

I was so immersed in his preciousness that I failed to note some obvious delays. I wish I had paid more attention.

THE MISSED MILESTONES

I shared with our pediatrician my husband's family history with learning disabilities and my concerns over Matias's missing milestones. She brushed off my worries and told me he was within range of normal. But how is it normal for your child to never crawl, speak almost six months late, and struggle with an overresponsive sensory system that triggered an averse reaction to getting dressed?

Of course, I wasn't alone in living in the ignorance of these delays. As new parents, most of us want to enjoy all the firsts, but children with special needs typically miss developmental milestones, and parents wait an average of nine months from when they first sense something is off before seeking an evaluation.[2]

I don't think my pediatrician wanted to worry me. In retrospect, I'm upset that we didn't have more meaningful dialogue, but how is that supposed to happen when one third of all well-child visits are under 10 minutes?[3] How can pediatricians (or RNs, or physicians' assistants) diagnose developmental delays in this time? One in four children are at risk for developmental delays before the age of five, when they are easy to address—if spotted.[4] But given the insurance companies' mandate to be efficient and effective, we all lose.

> ## HELPFUL HINT: USE A MILESTONE TRACKER
> ## AS A TALKING POINT WITH YOUR DOCTOR
>
> The CDC's Milestone Tracker app is one of your choices. It helps you keep track of how your child is progressing developmentally. This is not meant to be used in an obsessive manner but simply to see where your child falls along the spectrum of development for their age. It's an easy way to calm (or ignite!) your fears, using real-time data.

EARLY INTERVENTION:
WHY DOES IT SOUND SO SCARY?

After a bit of prodding from my mom and husband, I decided to take matters into my own hands. I asked my friends how their children measured up, and their answers confirmed my fears. But I still didn't want to deal with all the known and unknown obstacles we were about to face in dealing with government services to get my son the help he needed. I wasn't alone. Unsurprisingly, up to one-third of parents with kids with learning disabilities don't feel prepared to take on the challenges.

While I saw his challenges, I didn't want them to officially show up on paper, and I fought to keep it that way. That is, until my mom visited when Matias was two and a half, and forced me to confront the issue, giving me a list of phone numbers and websites for free resources and support from the government. I couldn't say no, so I agreed to explore our options.

Little did I know that all these numbers she was giving me were part of a program to get support for your child called "Early Intervention," which sounded to me like something you see on a scary reality TV show.

I thought, *Ugh, what have I done wrong as a parent that I need an intervention for my child?*

Early intervention is defined as a set of services that the government provides to children, from birth to three years old, with developmental delays or medical conditions. These are covered under Part C of the Individuals With Disabilities Education Act, to minimize the long-term cost of special education and encourage treatment in these critical early years. It has generally excellent results, with many delays resolving by the time a child enters preschool. Yet up to 90 percent of eligible children never receive these services.[5] In my case, I would never have known they existed if I waited to hear about it from Matias's pediatrician. Thank God for Mom.

EARLY INTERVENTION BARRIERS: TRUST

As a member of a middle-class family, I hadn't previously known what it felt like to qualify for government support or services. As we all know, society and the media often stigmatize those who receive them. I can only imagine this discomfort heightens if you already have reason to distrust the system, or you come from a community not treated with respect. I heard from a few parents that they felt evaluators were coming to their houses less to screen their children than to check up on their parenting skills and surroundings. According to the *Journal of Developmental and Behavioral Pediatrics*, black toddlers are up to five times less likely than white toddlers to receive early intervention services when they need them.[6]

So, once you agree to actually trust the system, you have to learn how to swallow your pride and bare your soul to complete strangers in order to qualify for assistance. The first step involves calling a hotline, leaving your number and enough of your heartbreaking story on a voice mail that will then live on in the unknown holding area of a large government system.

Hopefully, someone will be sympathetic enough to your needs and your story to call you back. As J. M. Barrie, the creator of Peter Pan, once said, "The world is made of faith, trust, and pixie dust." Here's hoping you get plenty of the dust in return for your faith and trust.

EARLY INTERVENTION BARRIERS: TIME AND EDUCATION

Yes! A call back—we did it! I was lucky enough to have my mother, a speech therapist, to educate me on the code words I needed to say in order to qualify Matias for services. "Make sure you emphasize the weakness in his muscle tone when making sounds. This is a qualifying characteristic," she'd advised me.

This call will be followed by multiple calls and emails back and forth to schedule yet *another* call, this time with a therapist, who will use your intake to see if you make it to the next round, where the prize is an all-expenses paid trip to your house for twelve weeks of appointments. Finally, you will bare your soul again, this time to the therapist, under pressure to say the right things intelligently and garner the services you need for your child. This long and arduous process is not for the faint of heart; you need lots of time, if not a PhD in education, to make it through.

WE QUALIFIED!

After all that effort, the services were mediocre at best. I liked the fact that they wanted to work within the child's "natural environment" when possible, as it was convenient for us. But something always seemed to go wrong on execution. They couldn't find parking, so the sessions were shortened. It also took them a long time to get into the meat of the session (due to his short attention span), and it left me wondering how much they could really accomplish within the forty-five-minute time frame that ended up being thirty minutes in reality. Overall, we saw some progress, but I'm not sure it was anything I couldn't have learned from a YouTube tutorial. This is not a critique of the professionals themselves—I just think the system needs to be built better to have more time to make it work.

WHAT'S NEXT?

If for some reason you want to continue after the allotted twelve weeks, good luck, as that requires another qualifying process. And if your child ages out, as ours did at this point, you must follow up with your school, as it is considered an educational issue for children three and above.

HELPFUL HINT

If your child qualifies for the twelve weeks of early intervention, you should follow up with their pre-K school, as it is their responsibility to continue to monitor and care for your child's educational needs. This approach typically buys you an early diagnosis and support from the state.

FROM EARLY INTERVENTION
TO BEGINNING EDUCATION

Now that you've completed early intervention, be prepared to hear your child is "now within normal range, so there is nothing to worry about," when you raise developmental issues with the school. This happened with us at Matias's first school when we brought up his speech development and the early intervention support he received, but they didn't feel it warranted support in pre-K. So we continued to lean on my mom, who built a custom program for Matias.

In at least a few states, according to the National Center for Learning Disabilities, educators appear to have identified specific learning disabilities very early. It is much more common for this diagnosis to come in third grade, when reading typically is a more visible and developmental concern. In the 2015–2016 school year, 8,252 children ages 3–5 were identified with SLD. Three-fourths of these children were in just four states: California, Iowa, New Jersey, and New York.[7] We were not so lucky in Jersey City, as early identification takes foresight and funds, and our school system has been severely underfunded below adequacy for years.

HELPFUL HINT: BEFORE STARTING SCHOOL

Here is a list of the things I wish I had known *before* Matias started school:

- I wish we had pushed more to understand our family history, in order to have more intense screening earlier.
- I wish we had explored how schools in Jersey City supported learning differences before committing to moving into the area.
- I wish we had understood the different school types and what resources they had for his needs.
- I wish I had been more open about my developmental fears to other moms before making school decisions.

HIS FIRST SCHOOL: A LOCAL PRIVATE SCHOOL

I was so looking forward to our first walk to school, only two blocks away. Now two and a half, Matias was enrolled at a private, nondenominational school offering quality instruction and small class sizes. Matias thrived there. We worried a bit about his ability to keep up, but since the goal was more socialization than anything else, we were not too concerned. There were lots of rules—a bit strict for our tastes—but he loved it. He became fast friends with Aidan, who had a smile that shone for days, and is still the sportiest kid Matias has ever known. Aidan's mom was the connector of the neighborhood, and I could not have made it through the year without her, especially since I was pregnant with our second child. Every Monday, she would say in her strong Jersey accent, "Micki, remember this week is Taco Tuesday, Wednesday there is a show at noon, Thursday you need to turn in these forms, and Friday after school there is a playdate at the park near school. Got it? I'll send you an email with the details."

During playdates, Matias mirrored Aidan's behavior, and quickly gained physical and expressive skills. Their friendship is still going strong six years later, despite the boys being in different schools. They have always accepted and loved each other's strengths and weaknesses, just like they did in the early days. We are so grateful this family is still in our lives.

When we checked in with the school periodically, asking about any developmental delays, they told us Matias was fine and they saw nothing to worry about. So we believed them. But the school's emphasis on rules was not what we wanted for Matias in those early years. I thought back to my own childhood and remembered how much I thrived at a Montessori school, so at the end of the year, we moved to one, where Matias would be encouraged to use his imagination and explore.

KEEP ON PROGRESSING

As a child who had flourished in the Montessori setting myself, I wanted to pass down this experience to Matias. I had fond memories of it encouraging creative thinking through independent areas of exploration. My husband likes to joke about how it did not teach me how to push in a chair, but it taught me how to build one.

We also liked the idea of Matias continuing to learn from older kids—and teach the younger ones—in a mixed environment. Also, the content of the lessons seemed relevant, socially conscious, and aligned with our values.

We reviewed a few of the Montessori options in Jersey City and ended up applying to one downtown. In retrospect, the interview process, which involved saying all the right things to prove we fit into the cohort of like-minded thinkers they were looking for, was laughable. But at the time, we were so excited. The school felt like a family, with friends who worked there and people we knew from the local community.

SHINY AND BRIGHT

Matias went to the Montessori school for three years and loved every minute. After all, what was not to love? The children were greeted every morning with Beatles songs being strummed on a guitar, for a group sing-along. Parents cooked foods related to their family origins to teach about world history, or read books to the class when they had free time. We got daily pictures and updates about what our child did that day. The visiting specialists were world-class language experts, professional musicians, and artists with work respresented in galleries.

But most important, Matias was truly happy.

Unfortunately, the wonderful Montessori experience I had as a child didn't hold up to how I experienced it as a mother. Once we scratched below the surface, once we got a good look behind the curtain, it was becoming increasingly clear that the school wasn't really painting in all shades of the rainbow. Instead, they were only using the colors they had resources for. And the dyslexia shade wasn't one of them.

* * *

I remember our first parent-teacher conference. Fede and I had wanted to talk to Matias's teachers as colleagues, so we were all on the same playing field and could speak with candor. My husband had said, "Look, we are not the parents who care about grade marks and success. We simply want you to be honest and tell us what's working with him and what's not. We want to have open communication with you, not only in these types of formal meetings."

"Of course," they'd reassured us. "We'll always shoot straight and tell you what's going on."

But in reality, these lines of communication did not run both ways. During pickups, we would constantly ask his teachers how it was going. We always got a kind smile and some fun anecdote about Matias, but nothing deeper. We couldn't figure it out. Was everything really fine, or was there something they didn't want to tell us?

Finally, at the next parent-teacher conference in the following marking period six months later, my husband dropped the niceties and said, "This is ridiculous. We see kids passing Matias on the basic alphabet and foundational work. We see him weak in writing. What's going on here?" The teachers suddenly looked frightened, as his macho Argentine accent came through full force.

I could tell by the look on their faces they wanted to come clean and tell us the truth. How could they not want to help my sweet, amazing child to grow? Finally, they started to tell us a few of their concerns, such as him needing support with reading and that instructions needed to be repeated multiple times. But they reiterated the Montessori philosophy of a range of milestones, a variety of ages in class, and the emphasis on allowing children time to ponder and progress as they see fit, rather than pressuring them to do more than they were ready for. Fede pushed back, saying, "I have dyslexia, and it's really clear to me that my son is struggling to learn." They stuck to the script and instead gave Matias some time once a week with a reading specialist, who also reported back to us with vigor that she saw no problems at this time.

By now, my mom and my husband were done with the excuses, and we requested that the reading specialist do the Comprehensive Test of Phonological Processing (CTOPP), so we could have some real data to assess. When the results came back, it was clear that my son was nowhere near the nationwide range of kindergarten ability, for a public or private school. This was the turning point for me. I was no longer going to let the school skirt the issue.

* * *

Why did we need to push so hard to have a real conversation about my son's abilities at a progressive private school? Years later, other parents and administrators would tell me that it seemed to them they had a strict (off the record, of course) policy of "don't ask, don't tell" when it came to any behavioral or learning issues with the children. The thinking was, we don't have the resources to address it, so don't call it out; wait and see if it goes away.

In my subsequent research, I also found out a lot more about how nonspecialized private schools really work.

THE PARADOX OF PRIVATE SCHOOLS

Private schools exist to increase the amount of choice and control you have in your child's education. During the application process, they generally try to determine whether your values, beliefs, income, and your child's disposition are a good match for their culture and structure. The goal here is to produce a cohort of unified thinkers along these qualifying criteria. They might align by type of education belief, religious point of view, or mindset you want to instill in your child. They may give special consideration to the children of alumni, donors, or other "friends of the school."

The problem with nonspecialized private schools is that those who learn differently are not considered part of the qualifying criteria. The resources needed for support are not calculated into the budget, and in most cases, there is no larger power (such as the board of education) to subsidize them. Since enrollment is voluntary, it is perfectly within the rights of a private school to say, "I'm so sorry, Mrs. Boas, we cannot meet the needs of your child. We suggest you enroll him in a school that is better equipped, with a format to meet his needs."

KEY POINTS: PRIVATE SCHOOL FUNDING FOR SPECIAL EDUCATION

- Evaluations for children in private school are supposed to be funded by public schools via the federal Child Find law, which states that schools are required to locate, identify, and evaluate all children with disabilities up to twenty-one years of age. However, because private schools aren't subjected to the same levels of oversight, and given the time it takes to coordinate district resources, many sceenings and evaluations are never conducted.
- If a child is deemed eligible, an individualized service plan (ISP) can be implemented in an effort to provide the child "equitable services" to his peers, according to the Individuals with Disabilities Education Act. ISPs are paid for by public funds, and therefore in high demand.

- Private schools are not required to implement an individualized education plan (IEP) from another school.
- Parents do not have the same procedural safeguards as in public schools, because private schools do not need to follow IDEA laws that dictate free and appropriate education.

WE WERE LEFT HOLDING THE BAG

After the CTOPP reading test showed some serious reason for concern, we asked for more testing. There was a private floor built in the Montessori school for occupational therapy, speech therapy, reading support, and more. But here's the catch: You could only access these resources by paying privately for them, as they did not take health insurance. So in addition to paying tuition for the school, we were also responsible for paying the cost of supportive services.

After reviewing the results from the speech, OT, and PT evaluations, we realized Matias needed significant resources to help him thrive and catch up. So we begrudgingly went ahead and paid for all the therapies recommended, simply due to the convenience and comfort Matias had with the school. We continued for almost six months, and learned a lot from the staff, eventually continuing the support at home.

But I was disheartened by the whole experience. Who knew that such a welcoming place would think so narrowly when it came to different learning profiles? I found it ironic that the very openness and tolerance that drew me to the school seemed to go out the window when faced with true neurodiversity.

A CALL THAT CHANGED IT ALL

As the Montessori fees began piling up, we decided midway through the year to enroll Matias in the lottery for the charter schools in our area. The last week of that school year, we got a call from a charter school saying that they had a spot open up on the waiting list for us to enroll him into the kindergarten class, and we had twenty-four hours to decide if we wanted to take it.

We didn't know much about the school except that it was nearby, and we knew a few kids who went there. We dropped everything and headed over for a visit. We were pleasantly greeted by the salt-and-pepper-haired principal, who already knew a lot about us. She referenced our shared heritage, and showed us other children in the school who also had these roots in common. At first glance it looked like a caring place, with a similarly progressive approach as Montessori, and the teachers seemed lovely. At this meeting we spoke about Matias's learning struggles and the progressive educational environment he was coming from, and we shared our concerns regarding the academic difference in formats, but we were assured that "he would catch up."

We decided that the charter school made a lot of sense due to the price, proximity, and progressive environment. So he said goodbye to his friends and teachers at Montessori on a Thursday, and started the charter school on Monday. Over the weekend I reached out to a few parents I knew there and tried to introduce Matias to a few kids before his first day. He walked into school like a champ, and made new friends immediately.

The spot had opened up two weeks before the end of the school year, which is not uncommon, as parents make their choices for the following year. At the end of week one, I checked in with his teacher, who was nice but tough. I asked how he was doing, and she said okay, but she thought he was behind. She asked if we could speak again the following week, to evaluate whether it was simply first week jitters, summer brain, or something else. I agreed, but waited impatiently.

Finally, she told me the news I didn't want to hear—that Matias was extremely behind. His writing was of concern, he could not work independently, he had a hard time focusing, and his reading was definitely not anywhere near a first-grade level. She also mentioned that she did not think he should pass to the next grade but should repeat kindergarten in order to catch up with the Common Core State Standards.

I wanted to scream, "Are you serious?" But for my son's sake, I smiled patiently and took notes. Trying to control my emotions, I begged them not to hold him back, as it would crush his self-esteem and remove him from the friends he had just made. I believe it's the responsibility of the education system to adjust to different types of learners. Yet now I know that one-third of all students with a learning disability have repeated a grade.[8]

HELPFUL HINT

If your school is pushing for your child to be retained a year, ask to see the documented results of his/her levels of proficiency and consult the state laws for alternatives, such as participating in a summer program. According to research from *Sociology of Education*, repeating a grade increases the rate of dropping out, and has negative effects on socialization.[9]

My husband wanted to hold him back and let him catch up. I selfishly thought of how that would be one more year of schooling he'd need to go through, decreasing the space between him and his brother, and one more year we would need to plan into our future. I didn't want him to feel self-conscious in an already new school environment. Fede felt I had ignored his opinion. It was a huge strain on our relationship. Finally, the charter school agreed to let him move forward to first grade. After all, they had inherited the learning differences and weren't sure what to make of them yet, so they gave us the benefit of the doubt. I was thrilled. Fede was apprehensive, at best.

A NEW START

As the first day of school neared, we were invited to meet the teachers. Matias's new teacher was very sweet. He liked her and felt comfortable. As I wanted to stay close to the academic situation, I eagerly volunteered to be the class parent. This was not my usual MO, but my son's future was at stake, after all.

One day after school, I stopped in to have a fully transparent conversation with "Mrs. B," his classroom teacher, about our concerns. She agreed to be honest with us, and shared some struggles Matias was having, albeit in a casual manner. She quickly became our ally for the first half of the year.

For Matias, it was a daily struggle to keep up with the class. He didn't want to go to school; he did everything he could to avoid reading in front of the class; and he felt like he had to wait too long to get the help he needed. He was in a class of twenty-three kids, with one teacher and one assistant; he wasn't learning the key topics in class, which made homework a nightmare. He began to dislike my rigor around getting it done, and deflected to Papi, whose brain worked more like his. Of course, passing the homework struggle to my husband also meant that I could keep my head in the sand a bit longer.

THE MOMENT OF TRUTH

One of my favorite mom moments comes at the end of every night, when I tuck my boys in and hear about their days. They call it "the talk." My talks with Matias were not about the academic issues of school, but the emotional components. He was making friends, playing soccer, so those elements seemed intact.

However, that all changed one night when he told me, "Mama, today my teacher gave me a nickname, the Statue of Liberty, because I always have my hand up. I told her I keep my hand up so that she'll know I'm still here, and she hasn't gotten to me." Suddenly, I saw red. Nobody, let alone a teacher, will talk to my child that way and make him feel less than in front of his peers. I knew something needed to change. Now.

A few days later, at our first parent-teacher conference, we had another frank conversation about everything. We discussed that he needed more help than she could give, and that it was unacceptable to call him the Statue of Liberty. She told us the other kids had made up that name for him, but it was unclear why she could not control the use of it in the classroom. Fede's patience was wearing thin, so he asked her directly, "Do you think there is something wrong that needs to be assessed?" She said yes. The look of "I told you so" he shot me was impossible to avoid.

She recommended that we meet with the child study team (CST), a group of professionals spanning several disciplines, including speech, OT, and PT, who would conduct a full evaluation of his strengths and weaknesses. According to the National Center for Learning Disabilities Report "Identifying Struggling Students," when educators recommended to parents that their children be evaluated for special education services, the parents only followed through 56% of the time. But this would not be the case with us. I believe this fear most parents have is spawned by not understanding or wanting to accept the unknown that lies ahead.

Mrs. B helped us write the request for testing and provided supporting evidence from the classroom. We are grateful that we started the conversation early, so that three months into school we could begin the process of getting Matias the proper support.

THE PAPERWORK PROCEEDS:
SEARCHING FOR AN OFFICIAL DIAGNOSIS

This is the moment where the invisible red tape really begins to kick in. By law, the school has sixty days to complete the evaluation from the day you request it. They also have an opportunity to deny the request, but luckily, we didn't have to deal with that.

Imagine the effort and cost it takes to gather all the outside vendors needed—a psychologist, a social worker, a speech/language therapist—as a charter school does not have these roles on staff. Then let's talk about what is required on your end, as a parent. You must schedule calls, confirm calls, and reschedule calls for the whole team whenever someone's calendar changes. Then you must tell the whole team, on separate calls, the same information of his birth, delays, and family history. (Imagine if you could have this basic information shared digitally.) The point of this duplicative process seems to be to see how much time you can take away from work, and how good your storytelling skills are.

Estimated time spent on intake from CST: 40 hours (5 days)

* * *

Now the assessments could officially begin. We explained to Matias that he'd be undergoing some testing to figure out how his brain worked best, and he was okay with that. However, I was not told exactly when the assessment would happen, so I couldn't prepare him. For a child who thrives on rules and schedules, this was anxiety-inducing.

Estimated time spent on assessment: 60 days

THE BIG REVEAL

In January we returned from winter break to find a shiny new individualized education program (IEP) in my email. While the report did address the issues we knew about, such as his focus and reading stuggles, and gave an official diagnosis with a DSM-V code that we agreed with, it didn't scope out a plan of support we felt was comprehensive and could address his needs.

An IEP is a legal document that defines the educational goals for your child, and the planned support, services, and accommodations to help him get there. This document must be honored for three years, and can be updated and discussed as the child progresses or needs more support. Therefore, it is important that it covers what your child needs right from the start.

From the time I received the email until the date of the IEP meeting, I was up many late nights searching on Google for the details of what happens at the meeting so I could be prepared for what was to come. I looked up the recommendations for dyslexia and ADHD.

A RECAP OF IEP FINDINGS (IN LAYMAN'S TERMS)

- Matias is reading way below grade level.
- Matias struggles to put his thoughts on paper.
- Matias has trouble with fine motor skills and writing.
- Matias needs constant attention and individualized support.
- Matias is in constant motion, which impacts his work.
- Matias thrives at math and science when text is read to him; otherwise he struggles reading the context.

Actual Diagnosis

Instructional implications from his evaluation suggest that Matias displays a specific learning disability based on his basic reading weakness, which is characterized as dyslexia. Based on his writing weakness, he will experience difficulty learning to recognize words by their letter pattern, resulting in poor sight word recognition and spelling. To help him learn to recognize and spell words, several strategies will help. These include systematic practice with a controlled amount of new information, modeling, immediate feedback, and multisensory instruction.

A month before he turned seven, we finally got the official stamp of 315.02, the diagnostic code for dyslexia, which meant it was time to put on my advocate shoes and dig in.

Estimated time spent on IEP: 90 days

DIAGNOSIS VS. DEFICIENT SUPPORTS

After reading the diagnosis, which I had already understood, the CST described the planned support for my son:

- 1x week Orton-Gillingham support for 30 minutes
- 1x a day reading support group 45 minutes
- 1x a week OT individual 30 minutes
- 1x a week OT group 30 minutes

Let me put the gravity of his needs in context, so you can understand why we were shocked at what we believed to be an inadequate support recommendation. The school had spent almost three-fourths of the year defining what his struggles were, but little time defining the support they would provide him. At the end of first grade, children should be reading near the high end of the Fountas & Pinnell (F&P) range at level J and understand fifty sight words. However, Matias was only reading at the high end for *kindergarten* (F&P level D), and could not retain ten sight words. The class should be able to follow two- to three-step instructions and complete lengthy projects that focus their attention. He was nowhere near these milestones.

The research states that in order to help struggling readers, you need a systematic and multisensory approach to learning visual materials. This was their solution during the forty hours in a school week— *a whole thirty minutes* of the systematic approach he needed to learn how to read in the most important time of his life?

Can you imagine if you had a vision problem, and you were told you could only put on glasses once a week? Imagine if you were in a wheelchair, and they didn't provide the ramp to access the door. Those who have language-based learning disabilities are typically not "seen," as the use of spoken and written language is not in plain view. Thus, proper support cannot be provided as easily, or measured in terms of the effects it's having on the student's outcome.

The school was also offering group reading support for forty-five minutes a day—extra time to do the same work the kids were doing in class. But logic suggests that extra time with four other kids in the class who had a range of behavioral and other learning issues would not teach him the fundamentals. He constantly complained that he could not concentrate in general education class because it was loud and rambunctious. And to create further chaos, he was returned to the general education classroom at an asynchronous time in the middle of the lesson, completely lost.

He also needed related services for OT to help him control the pencil. His writing was illegible, and they gave him thirty minutes in a forty-hour week to help him with this critical and complicated skill.

He also received group OT once a week for thirty minutes, in whatever space was available. I saw this support being provided in the hallways, stairwells, and other public spaces. Imagine being a kid who is struggling, and trying to keep your self-esteem up, only to be paraded around the school for all to see, to receive your services. Not to mention doing sit-ups on the dirty floors.

LOOKING FOR A "SIGN" OF APPROVAL

It is perfectly within your legal rights not to sign the IEP. In most states the school cannot proceed unless you approve the plan. You can also approve some parts and ask for changes on others. But after devoting so much time just to understanding the process, who has the will and determination to also research alternative solutions to the recommended changes? Here's an example of the results of time as a barrier: in Massachusetts, on average, only five percent of parents reject the IEP proposed for their children—who knows what else they're going to get?[10]

My motherly instincts told me this wasn't enough. I needed more time to negotiate with the school. I also needed to learn more about Matias's rights.

THE FACADE OF FAPE

I started by reaching out for second opinions from private professionals in speech, OT, psychology, education, and law, and they all confirmed my suspicion that what was being proposed for Matias would not work. This is when I officially lost faith in the school.

So if what they were delivering was not enough, what was within my rights, under special education laws, to ask for? I soon learned about four letters that would dictate the next four years of my life—an important law known as FAPE.

It stands for "free appropriate public education," which every qualified child has a right to under the the Individuals with Disabilities Education Act. It is a very complex law with many technical terms, and many schools use this opacity to get away with providing something that seems substantial, but is not. While I'm not a lawyer (but would love to play one on TV), here is how it breaks down in everyday terms. FAPE states that the program must meet the child's unique needs, provide access to the general education curriculum, and meet state grade-level standards. Who knew that a law written more than forty-seven years ago would still be standing in the way of helping my child today?

WHAT IS "APPROPRIATE"?

What exactly does "appropriate" mean in reference to the education of your child?

For many parents, this is the crux of the fight against FAPE. "Appropriate" is such a subjective term that it was bound to be challenged in court, because as a parent, you feel that what is appropriate is the best quality of education that the schools your taxes pay for can provide. In fact, in 1982, the U.S. Supreme Court stepped in to define the subjective terms in FAPE in the case of the *Board of Education of the Hendrick Hudson Central School District v. Rowley*, which involved a deaf student who was a good lip reader and was doing well in school. However, when her parents asked for an interpreter to help her reach her full learning potential, she was denied this support service.

The U.S. Supreme Court was on the side of the school, saying the law requires schools to provide a "basic floor of opportunity." It doesn't require them to "maximize" a child's potential.

In an appeal, the reference was used that ". . . schools provide the educational equivalent of a serviceable Chevrolet to every [qualified] student. . . . [Schools are] not required to provide a Cadillac."[11]

Can you imagine sitting in court and being told that your child's future is no more important than a serviceable set of tires?

The highest court in the nation said that we should be grateful to our public institutions for giving us a basic floor, after a year of paperwork, consultation, and expenses. I hope you have a good plan, because you are sending your most precious cargo on a very bumpy ride.

QUESTION: WHAT'S APPROPRIATE?

A friend, who had already gone through the fight requesting more support, gave me some wise advice. She said, "The only way you can move the needle for your son is to question what's appropriate, and why the school feels it meets his needs." In the words of Albert Einstein, who was also dyslexic, "The important thing is not to stop questioning." Just because the public school system tells you that something is right doesn't mean that it is. Unsurprisingly, confidence in our public schools was at its lowest point at 2014, when only about one in four U.S. adults felt public schools were meeting our children's needs.[12]

My two main questions for Matias's child study team (CST) focused on how informed the instructor and the curriculum would be.

Question: How Informed Is the Instructor?

In order for the Orton-Gillingham (OG) multisensory learning system to work, it needs to happen over a sustained amount of time, by a properly trained instructor, with consistency that continues back in the classroom.

I questioned the principal about the training that his OG teacher had received. I found out she had the "basic floor" as well—only about thirty hours of training. This limited time frame allows for minimal, surface-level knowledge, but not a full understanding of the practice.

I thought there must be a way to fix the holes in the floor. I presented a range of ideas, with hope and heart, to the principal. Her answers always started and ended with budget. She could not provide more training for Matias's OG teacher because this would require bringing in a substitute teacher for the rest of the class. I suggested using Matias's highly trained private OG tutor to train or replace his teacher on his IEP. The principal answered that bringing in outside resources was a liability, and when she'd tried it before, the people were late, costing her double. (By the way, according to the Made By Dyslexia research, 98 percent of teachers agree that they need more training in how to identify and support dyslexia.[13])

Question: How Informed Is the Instruction?

I asked that the school use an instructional program that is structured, systematic, sequential, repetitive, and phonologically based. The key to helping dyslexic brains learn is to have a reasonable rate of intensity or duration, so that the material is able to stick.

I found two main issues with the instruction recommended by the school. It was not able to teach Matias the foundational skills for reading in the time allotted. It was also not providing materials that allowed him to access the general education curriculum.

For extra reading support, they provided forty-five minutes of group instruction daily. The group consisted of six kids with various behavioral and learning issues. He constantly complained that the kids were so loud he could not even hear what the teacher was saying. And this teacher was not using Orton-Gillingham; she was simply reviewing, at a slower pace, what happened in the general education classroom. I knew this wouldn't work for Matias, so what good were these forty-five minutes?

It didn't seem like my son's school was viewing reading as a necessity. So I asked why the Orton-Gillingham methodology could not be used in this setting, for a reasonable rate of consistency. I was told that not everyone in the group could benefit from such a system. But in reality, the research shows that all learners benefit from this program. In another court case, *Evans v. The Board of Education of the Rhinebeck Central School District*, the U.S. District Court for the Southern District of New York ruled that "an integrated, multisensory, sequential method is a necessity, rather than an optimum situation."[14]

I thought that they would take the foundational decoding skills from Orton-Gillingham and apply them to science, math, and other subjects so he could take in the content successfully. But there were no modifications at all. No buddies assigned, no checklists to guide, no fewer words on the page, no tech to assist. Nothing.

When I dug into the status of each modification stated in the IEP and how it was being implemented, the administration simply evaded the answer, saying they had made the modifications. I asked to see proof that they were using materials dictated in the IEP goals. I was tired of hearing empty promises and lip service, and I never saw the proof I was asking for.

ANSWER: THE BUDGET DICTATES WHAT'S APPROPRIATE

In the end, it all came down to money. I believe in my heart that this school wanted to give him more, but they simply couldn't due to the way the budget stacked up, for him and many others.

Let's start with the obvious: It costs twice as much to educate a child with special needs as opposed to one without.[15] So how does this differential of funding get met?

As I noted in the introduction, Part B of IDEA states that Congress is authorized to contribute up to 40 percent of the "excess cost" of education for those with special needs, to assist the state and local districts with compliance. This means that 60 percent of the special education costs are paid for with state dollars, and then the local districts are asked to use this small amount to implement programs on an already strapped budget.

However, there is nowhere near 40 percent of excess costs being contributed by the federal government to the states.[16] In my beautiful Garden State of New Jersey, we are receiving $366 million out of the full funding estimate is $1.115 billion—a funding gap of more than $740 million for FY 2019–2020. This leaves districts a huge amount to pick up when they are already struggling.[17] Through my work with Jersey City Together, a local action group where I am a member of their education team, I know firsthand that the Jersey City school system is currently experiencing a budget shortfall of $125 million. How can they hold up a roof for special education under these dire circumstances?

Regrettably, I have seen few proactive models in the education system so far. In my case, charter school admission operates on a lottery system, they must accept whomever is on the list (in theory) and then take on a triage process for those admitted with needs beyond the average student. Imagine if you were to buy a house sight unseen, then you are told when you walk in that it needs a new roof, electrical system, and pipes. If you were on a very limited budget, you would figure out a way to move in and fix only the "essentials," like the roof. Water and lights are nice to have, but not essential. This is what happens to one in five children with learning differences that come up against the reactionary budgets of school systems.

The principal of Matias's school told me they relied solely on a matching grant from a local foundation to make up for their budget shortfall. They even publicized it as a reason to attend the spring gala. Every dollar raised on a glass of wine or an expensive vacation at a silent auction was matched by this foundation. So if the gala was rocking, with no clouds in sight, then my son could get services next year. But if the patrons were feeling fickle with their wallets, then my son's services were in jeopardy. To me this was infuriating, insane, and insulting. What happens if these donors walk away? What is the alternative to close the gap? And most important, what happens in schools that aren't able to fundraise within their communities?

With all the wealth being built in my quickly gentrifying city, I couldn't believe we didn't value our kids enough to do better.

ASSEMBLING MY INVESTIGATIVE TEAM

Now that I understood the law, and funding, it made sense to me why the schools believed what they were offering in his IEP was appropriate, but I needed to explore whether the program they had proposed would move the needle. I feel privileged that I had the money, time, and knowledge to do so. Whenever I felt myself flailing, I'd look at the pain in my son's eyes, and find the strength to soldier on.

I began to share the IEP with experts who knew Matias and had provided private therapy to him over the years. His speech, OT, and reading support specialists all agreed that it was not enough to "maximize my child's potential." In order to push for a more appropriate program, I'd need to gather evidence to support my request—a goal best achieved by putting the IEP in action and watching the progress in real time. I asked for a few clarifications on the IEP, then signed it.

HELPFUL HINT

Listen to your gut when something is off, and bring in people who know more than you do about the special education system.

OUR PARENTAL ASSESSMENT OF IEP GOALS

As parents assessing the appropriateness of our child's education, here's what we're up against with our (mostly) untrained eyes.

GOALS FROM MY SON'S ACTUAL IEP

- Given a series of spoken words containing three phonemes, Matias will identify initial, medial, and final phonemes in each spoken word.
- By the end of his IEP he will do this 80 percent of the time as measured by weekly probes and assessments, the anecdotal records and checklists, and by teacher-devised tests or worksheets.

Huh? You need a PhD in education in order to translate this! How do I know if this is something my son can do in the thirty minutes of support they are giving him? Is it challenging enough? Can it be effectively measured by an untrained teacher? On what planet do general or even special education teachers have time to do this accurately?

It's a scary feeling to know that you are signing off on such lofty goals for your child without any real sense of whether he will reach them.

FAMILY FIRST RESOURCES: THE MISSION EXPLORATION

I was lucky that my mom was trained in a related field, so she understood such documents. She's also a really good researcher, and can collect evidence like a pro. She explained everything to me and Fede; as a family we determined it would not be enough, and we should start considering plan B. So I put her on the case to find a specialized school or summer program that could be an alternative to our current situation. I'm not sure how people without such skilled resources navigate the school discovery process.

Not content to simply deliver her recommendations in a spreadsheet from Florida, Mom flew up to New Jersey in the middle of winter to tour the schools with Fede while I worked. Luckily, I trusted their decisions completely.

They were supposed to see five schools in five days. Mom had chosen them based on cost, driving distance, focus on language-based learning differences, and summer programs. She also spent a lot of time reading reviews. The tour began for them in sleet, navigating the unknown highways while I juggled babysitters for my other child.

Each school gave a pitch for their campus: how great the teachers were, their technology solutions, class size, social dynamics, etcetera. I tagged along to one of the schools and instantly fell in love. But the reality of giving it to him wouldn't be so easy. How could we thoughtfully sort through a relative sea of sameness? We spent many late nights debating it.

Luckily, a nor'easter hit, and my mom was snowed in for three more days, so we had lots of time to overanalyze. As the snow cleared, the sun shone a spotlight on what we needed to do next to get into any of the schools, or even summer programs, we had visited. We needed a lawyer. Why, you ask? Lawyers help you assess the merits of your child's IEP and negotiate with the school for more. They can also recommend out-of-district schools and connect you to admissions offices for a streamlined process, if you decide to go that route.

THE EXTENDED TEAM: SUBJECT-MATTER EXPERTS

Thank goodness we were financially stable and had the resources to bring in experts. The cup didn't runneth over, but we could drink. However, I understand this is not an option for everyone and I am not recommending this extended team as a must. I am simply telling my own story, in my own circumstances.

FIRST UP: THE COMPLICATED SEARCH FOR LAWYERS

A director of admissions at the school I was crushing on recommended a lawyer that had helped many of her students get placement there and had a good reputation in the community. So we called him to set up an initial consult.

In most situations, you call a lawyer when there is a problem or to prevent a problem from happening. When it comes to private placement for a special education school, you need a lawyer to help you frame the case of why the current school is not meeting FAPE. The private schools don't really want to open their doors to see paradise, if you can't pay to get in. You must have a lawyer to present the favorable chances of you winning the lawsuit against the current school to be considered for a tour. If you want to pay privately and not be reimbursed by the school, you can bypass these steps.

For context, the average cost of a consult in my part of the country is $700 for around two hours of legal consultation. One hour to review your documentation, and one hour to meet with you in person. We also met with another lawyer in New York City, who was recommended by a friend, before realizing the two states are governed by different laws regarding special education, and she therefore couldn't help us. So we were out $1,400 on consults alone. However, she did recommend some interesting schools that we visited and applied to in NYC.

Unlike other professions, where you can showcase your portfolio of work, special education lawyers can't really make their cases public—who they represented, and what the outcomes were. You can only go by their credentials, word of mouth, and gut instinct.

Our first lawyer stated that he understood the charter school system, knew our district well, had many cases there, had written many academic papers on dyslexic thinking, and was dyslexic himself. All these factors were compelling for us, and we signed a retainer with his firm.

He gave us a lot to read, which made me realize that even I didn't know everything about dyslexia (yet). He recommended that we document every interaction with the school via email, and keep good records of how the IEP was being implemented. He also said that, in order to prove that what they were proposing was not appropriate, we needed to bring in a neuropsychologist, who would provide additional testing and, ideally, testify on our behalf.

MY ALLY WAS ALLY MCBEAL

I'm not a lawyer, but I swear I was in another life. I've always been fascinated by legal dramas and the process of gathering evidence. So since our real lawyer told us what to document, I made sure to detail every infraction, every mistake, every conversation via email, pictures, and what's more, I went straight to the source: Matias. It broke my heart as our goodnight "talks" became a detailed inquiry about his day at this mediocre school. I tried to keep the shock off my face and listen with empathy to what my little guy was going through.

Fede thought I was off my rocker with my records and files and quotes that the lawyer was asking me to keep. He questioned what this would ever accomplish. For me, it was my way of controlling a situation that felt out of my control. My manic documentation was the only thing keeping me from going mad while we waited for the slow turn of the bureaucratic wheels.

NEUROPSYCHOLOGY JOINS THE TEAM

Our lawyer had a team of experts at his disposal, and that's how we met our neuropsychologist. She was probably the most thorough of the whole team. For those of you who have not heard of the medical specialty, they basically dig into the *why* behind the *what*. They conduct psychological and psychoeducational testing to understand the relationship between behavioral, cognitive, and functional deficits, and the underlying brain functions. This requires around eight hours of testing, and around eight hours to score the testing and write a detailed report of conclusions and diagnosis.

I was amazed at how detailed this process was, and the barriers to access that most people would encounter in trying to retain a neuropsychologist. The main barrier is insurance companies, who distinguish between "medical necessity" (their responsibility) and "educational issues" (the school's responsibility). If you can show, via a script from your pediatrician, that there is suspicion about brain damage or a neurological issue, this part of the testing will be covered as medical necessity. However, testing to determine learning disabilities is not covered by the insurance company or the school. Talk about red tape for our one in five.

I tried to fight the insurance company with Current Procedural Terminology (CPT) codes, hours of phone calls, and a list of alternate testing solutions, but finally I realized that *no* neuropsychologist would take our insurance because reimbursement is very low despite all the time it takes to test and write the report. Also, we would not get the results in time to include them in our investigative report, which we needed to present in June. Therefore, as a family, we decided that we needed to invest around $3,200 for this member of the team. And though our insurer promised we would get reimbursed as part of our "out of network" benefits, it never happened.

Fighting for coverage was only the first hurdle in the neuropsychology process. We had five sessions that were seventy minutes away from our house, which meant we needed to take Matias out of school and make sure his brain was primed with snacks. We had to add another session because one day he was off and they could not make it through. One more day off work, another seventy minutes in the car, another school absence. I asked, after every session, what she was seeing. She gave no answers except that the case was complicated, not a straight diagnosis. This left an even bigger pit in my stomach.

Finally, after a month, the waiting process began. It took two months from the end of testing until the report was in our hands. I couldn't understand why it would take so long. Do the test, score it, write your thoughts. But it was more complicated than that; an art, not simply a science. All I could do was have faith.

DELIVERING THE NEUROPSYCHOLOGY REPORT: ANSWERS AT LAST

Fede and I drove out to the neuropsychologist's office one last time, to listen to the results. I was still in evidence-gathering mode, and I guess I missed some key points. My husband looked like he had seen a ghost. I didn't understand why he looked so grave. It wasn't until the car ride home that he shared with me the things I had missed. Apparently, in addition to dyslexia, Matias will struggle with executive functioning and attention issues all his life.

I remember taking my foot off the gas and pausing to think about the long road ahead for my sweet boy. I thought about all the struggles he would have to overcome in a society that is not so forgiving. I thought about how we, as parents, could make sure that he got everything he needed to succeed. I panicked, thinking about how we would provide all of this as two freelancers living in New Jersey. I thought about how we would share the updates with Matias. I thought about how we could share all this new information with the school, in hopes they would finally come around.

PREPARING TO PRESENT OUR EVIDENCE

We sent the report from the neuropsychologist to the CST, so they would have time to read and process the results before our meeting. I also let them know that I had hired a lawyer as part of the process, and that's when the tone changed to adversarial. I was no longer simply an educated mom who had done lots of research, but the head of an official team with legal power behind it. All I'd hoped it would say was: I'm serious, stop the BS, and bring your best offer to the table.

My lawyer also asked the Jersey City Public Schools to send a representative from their offices to attend our meeting so that we did not need to present our evidence twice. If for some reason the charter school could not provide the resources needed, we wanted JCPS to be able to weigh in on the options they could offer. But this was naive on the part of my lawyer, "who knew charters and the district," as they refused to attend. I was floored.

THE CHARTER DISTRICT VS. THE PUBLIC SCHOOL DISTRICT

I thought that the charter schools were supported and funded by the public school system of Jersey City. I understood they got less money from the school district because they played by a different set of rules, but I had no idea there were such distinct lines in the sand when it came to who was responsible for my child's education. We trusted our lawyer with his experience, as he stated he knew about these lines of distinction, but he never explained the BIG point that would be critical to our success.

Here is what I was told via email a week before the meeting from the special education coordinator at Matias's school:

Mrs. Boas,

Having a representative from the JCPS [Jersey City Public Schools] would not be appropriate at our meeting, as the meeting is not for the JC school system.

The public school representative said he isn't qualified to make placement choices. It will be up to the home school CST to interpret the IEP and determine the type of environment that will meet Matias's needs best.

These setbacks are more about procedure, and in that way, the representatives' hands are tied. This is the way that JC handles this situation.

After reading this, I thought, here was just another case of passing the buck on responsibility for educating my kid. Most charter schools like mine are managed as their own fiefdoms and organized as a separate local education agency (LEA), answering to their own school board, who make the decisions on what is appropriate and what is not. If legal action is taken against charter schools, they are managed by a separate governing body called the Office for Civil Rights, which is a federal agency that will funnel your complaint to the state division.

Wow, talk about a big disconnect. I thought funding from public schools funneled to charter schools, and that they both looked out for all kids no matter what designation they were a part of. This is not the case at all, as charter schools thrive on being independent from the district and have less oversight, whereas special education is highly regulated and requires state and federal oversight. Charter schools often "counsel out" students with disabilities because they don't have the resources to support them. For example, New York charter schools receive on average 20 percent less state funding per pupil.[18] One study shows that one-fourth of the charter schools surveyed reported having advised parents that the school was not a good fit for their disabled children.[19] This is why most students with disabilities end up in the public school system, which has a broader scale of support, administration, services, and resources to provide more than the charter school can.

WHAT I WISH I HAD KNOWN ABOUT CHARTER SCHOOLS BEFORE SENDING MY SON TO ONE

- The mindset and independence is appealing, but you must weigh this against the minimal support for the one in five.
- They are working with less money to serve all needs.
- The tale of two districts is detrimental when you have a problem, as you must take your complaints to the state, and that's a whole other level of bureaucracy.
- Special education oversight and excellence in charter schools is lacking. Supervision is typically run by community members on a board who might have another set of objectives than yours.
- There are more financial resources in public schools for children who learn differently.

THE SHOWDOWN: IEP MEETING #2 (MAY)

More Support Needed

My lawyer was up first, presenting all the key facts from his research and from the neuropsychology report. I was feeling pretty confident. For the first time, I felt I had someone on my side who had my child's best interest at heart and knew how he could thrive.

Here is what we asked for:

1. Reading intervention that was defined by the type of program, instructor, and frequency.

2. Reading intervention that helped develop expressive writing skills.

3. An integrated, consistent, and predictable school day.

4. To the extent possible, teachers should be selected for a bottom-up teaching style. It is expected that Matias will be more comfortable learning all the parts before the whole and should not be expected to generalize concepts to unfamiliar circumstances without having learned all the elements upon which the concept is based.

5. Matias should be assigned a facilitator, one person that knows him sufficiently to be able to advise other staff as to what each needs to know in order to interact appropriately with him.

6. Metacognition support and graphic organizers.

7. Regular communication between the home and school, as it is critical for effective carryover.

I presented the problems that I saw in how they were implementing the IEP, and how it was making Matias feel. He had constant headaches from the intense workload. He didn't like being lost in transition between his general education classes and pull-out support. The times were not synchronized, so he felt as if he wasn't good enough in this difficult environment.

We also presented our Orton-Gillingham instructor's vision of what was needed, to show how the structured literacy instructor was falling short. (Of course we did it in a kind way.) Dawn Dennis, our tutor, was such a blessing from the beginning. She is a highly skilled learning specialist in the Regional Center for Learning Disabilities at Fairleigh Dickinson University and an adjunct professor teaching multisensory reading courses at the graduate level.

The reaction from the charter school was varied. The psychologist literally fell asleep, and the principal wore a complacent smile that I read as "thanks for the information; you'll be hearing from my lawyer."

I walked out of the meeting feeling I had given Matias the best shot I possibly could. Now the ball was in the school's court.

THEIR REPLY TO OUR REQUEST

After all this effort they agreed to give Matias thirty more minutes of the reading system he needs. To clarify, going into second grade, he would have one hour of reading support out of the forty hours in a school week. I should be jumping for joy, right?

He also got a bump in writing support, which was good, but with a music teacher who was only lightly trained in special education. Without a strong OT presence, our evaluation suggested, his fine-motor skills still wouldn't be up to "writing without tears."

They offered daily check-ins with the staff, but Matias was supposed to ask for it when he needed it. Ha! They also said that they had a digital system to manage IEPs, which would allow all the teachers that worked with Matias to check in daily and see what had changed and to stay updated. Again, with twenty kids in every class, what teacher or specialist is going to check in daily on what my precious little boy needs?

In this adversarial relationship, where the school holds all the power, these modifications seemed like lip service, not something that would provide the basic floor the law required. I'd have to keep digging.

THE SUMMER OF SEARCHING

To recap: Last summer I was celebrating that Matias was passing to first grade, and trying to close the gap with Mrs. Dawn Dennis. This summer I was celebrating that there was a name and diagnosis behind his struggle, and some mediocre support and services he could take advantage of as he kicked off second grade.

This fight was tiring, it was expensive, it was time-consuming. I had to ask myself, was it worth it?

Would a few more rounds of requests really move the needle? What outcome was I hoping for? (That last one was an actual question from Fede, as we discussed the topic for the umpteenth time.)

I truly believed it was my right, as a member of the community, to have the school system provide what my child had a right to by law. I was determined to prove that the school's attempts to skirt me were unacceptable. Alas, this was not a view my husband shared. He was tired of seeing the lawyers' bills come in the mail and hearing about the latest plot to take down "the unequal system." He wanted to call it off and send Matias to a school for language-based learning differences, where he would thrive. "Why would we send him back to a school that had clearly stated they were not going to budge?" he'd asked. What was more important—proving I was right, or getting Matias into the right environment?

My husband has lived through the pain of dyslexia firsthand, so of course I was very sensitive to his concerns. But I had begun questioning my lawyer after the district debacle and the neuropsychologist he'd recommended, because there was no clear path or outcome set forth. It didn't seem like the school cared to budge, so who was going to help me keep pushing the argument? This ambiguity of outcomes led me to seek yet another second opinion. My child's education was at stake. It was worth talking to a few more folks.

TEAM OF EXPERTS, TAKE TWO

I began to think about how I would seek targeted information on the most effective support for my child. Coincidentally, while having lunch with a friend, she said I should meet her friend Jena Cordova. So we set up a call, and my mind was blown. She was a badass mom who worked for a special education lawyer in Manhattan and had advocated for her own children there. I learned so much about how things worked across the river. It sounded like New York did not have as adversarial a relationship with special education parents as Jersey City did. They seemed more willing to place a child in the right environment without much of a fight.

Jena gave me a renewed sense of hope that my thoughts for a second opinion were warranted and that my team had not gathered all the data or presented a clear vision in the right way. She recommended to me her trusted resources, and fast-tracked me to them before the summer ended. Poor Matias had to go into the city again and do a few more tests and talk to a few more people; I'm sure he felt like a guinea pig at this point. These tests showed that the current program was not working, and he was not progressing. Why couldn't my neuropsych show this?

I interviewed a few more lawyers, and chose a new one. The discrepancy model, still used in thirty-nine states, is defined as the difference between IQ and performance. My son has a high IQ and was not performing far enough behind to form a compelling discrepancy. Our new lawyer assessed the merits of our case and told me the same thing as our first lawyer: Due to the discrepancy model, Matias was not far enough behind to be considered a good candidate for out-of-district placement. She suggested we place him in the public school district, let him fail miserably, and show how the support they were providing would not meet his needs. Again, not what I wanted to hear, as putting my sensitive child into a larger, louder student body seemed like a recipe for disaster. Not to mention that the lawyer's theory would mean that my son's self-esteem would suffer due to all the changes. This sacrifice was not something we were willing to accept as a strategy because damaging your child's self esteem is irreversible. Fede literally said, "Over my dead body."

We called in another expert from the lawyer's team to find an alternative route, an educational consultant, who said that the public school system should have the resources to support him, so the fight for private placement would be futile. I was not satisfied with this advice. I wanted someone innovative who could read between the lines, and she was not it. So it was goodbye to lawyer number three.

Enter lawyer number four, who came recommended by the private language-based learning difficulties school we wanted Matias to attend. We really liked him, and he ended up staying with us for the long haul. In essence, he said the same thing as the others—that we didn't have a strong case—but he saw other ways to potentially make it work. Exactly what I wanted to hear.

We had a hard decision to make: enroll Matias in the school we wanted, and pay privately; keep him in the charter school and let them fail; or enroll in the public school and serve them a ten-day notice letting the school know we would be removing him upon entering. All of these strategies were risky. We tried to figure out which would cause the least amount of damage to Matias and provide a healthy start to second grade.

Toward the end of the summer I checked in with the charter school and had a candid conversation about what we had discovered in our new neuropsych testing, to see if there was anything more they could do. Basically, they encouraged me to withdraw Matias's placement and instead enroll him in a public school, where they had more resources to help him.

I was appalled, again, but something told me that if I stuck with the charter, where Matias was at least comfortable, they might slip up with a procedural violation of FAPE—and I could get close to my dreams of a summer without strife.

SCHOOL'S BACK IN SESSION—SECOND GRADE

Matias was excited to go back to the charter school and see his friends. I was a nervous wreck. My only comfort was our backup plan.

In the first two months, his OG teacher only provided a few days of service. She had hurt her foot and could not make it to school to teach. There was no backup specialist. There were no extra funds from the gala. So my son lost out.

This is what they call a "procedural failure to provide FAPE." They promised to make it up, and that the gap in services would not affect the overall quality of the IEP. (Remember, my son only gets one hour of reading support a week, and now for eight weeks he had had nothing.)

They also did not put into place any of the modifications they had agreed to, such as graphic organizers and daily meetings. The writing teacher forgot to show up many times. It was a complete mess.

So we sent them a ten-day notice, which highlighted the deficiencies and showed that we were serious about discussing how to fix it—or we would place him in a better environment that we would expect them to pay for. They did not want to work it out. They stated that what they were providing was enough, and they would not be paying for the Craig School in Mountain Lakes. The message, essentially, was see you in court.

WELCOME TO PARADISE

Exceeded Expectations

The Craig School came recommended by *all* of our experts. The toughest part of the search had been finding a school that specialized in educating younger children of Matias's age. Early intervention through private pay is not a route many parents take. Most kids come into schools like Craig around the fifth grade, when the discrepancy model really kicks in, and their schools can no longer ignore their needs. The

Craig School had a proven record with kids in second grade, led by a super-smart lower-school director, so it became the obvious choice. Not to mention the beautiful scenery was a perk; driving up to lake views is not too bad.

Paying for Paradise

The main question, of course, was how we were going to pay for the land of mountain lakes and dreams. I was a freelance strategist and my husband a freelance photographer. Our income was never stable, but we mostly made it work. Throw in the cost of a college education every year for our seven-year-old, though, and the math gets fuzzy.

However, we believed that giving him the proper foundation for reading in the first place would have better results than remediating bad habits. So it was an investment in his future—earlier than we had expected—but it set our financial goals in a different direction. I took a full-time job to make sure our income was stable, and Fede booked a few more gigs and hustled.

There were other sacrifices attached to paradise too. The commute to Mountain Lakes from Jersey City is an hour in the morning, and forty-five minutes in the evening. It made no sense to do this back and forth every day, so Fede decided to get a coworking space in the middle of a suburban strip mall, near the school.

As I mentioned, Fede is a gregarious, passionate person who is full of energy and life. This place was not. But he enjoyed the quiet, the banter with the receptionist, and the reliable coffee machine. I visited a few times, and it reminded me that I'm a city girl.

The other sacrifices included paying for aftercare for my younger son, who would need to wait at school until Fede made it home from his commute to pick him up. We needed to upgrade our car with snow tires and fix the brakes, and we put some serious miles on it in year one. In subsequent years we found people to carpool with, and that lightened the load.

Yes—spoiler alert—this was going to be a multi-year commitment. Which made our day in court that much more important.

Enjoying Paradise

On a fine fall day in November, Matias entered the Craig School. He was greeted by a sweet girl named Ev. She was the only other person in second grade, so she was happy to have a friend in tow. She showed him the locker she had personalized for him, introduced him to all her favorite teachers, and taught him the schedule.

He came home glowing on the first day, talking about how great the teachers were and how great of a welcome he had received. This was the first time on this journey that I was able to breathe a sigh of relief. That night, we had a beautiful conversation that lasted for hours. Our family finally began to sleep well.

He started the first two hours of each day with a highly skilled Orton-Gillingham teacher, Mrs. Schilling, who is dyslexic herself. She crafted each lesson around his interests, his progress, and abilities. Then he worked with the language arts teacher, Mrs. Wallace, who headed the department and graduated from the best school in the state for special education. To this day Matias still cries when he sees her, remembering their time together.

All the other subjects were built for how his brain learned, too. They learned science by planting and composting in the garden with Mr. Furlong. For history, his teacher would roll out a large map onto the floor and help them with visual-spatial skills to understand where each country was by standing inside the map. Math was Matias's jam, and there was a system in place that brought context to the equations, which was a plus.

Did I mention there was swimming on Fridays, a reward program called badger points, and a fishing club?

Like I said, pure paradise. I wish everyone could experience it.

COURT'S IN SESSION

Pre-Court Prep

With a sigh of relief, I took a break, enjoyed the holidays, and prepared myself for the final showdown in court.

I couldn't sleep the night before, because I stayed up studying some good TV lawyers. Ha. I was so nervous about what would unfold. I arrived in Newark at nine a.m. and went through the metal screener before heading up to the seventh floor to meet my lawyer in person for the first time.

We chatted, and I found out he had Midwestern roots like my family, so I felt at home with him. I also met his badass partner, who tried to calm me down with her knowledge of Jersey City cases.

Nobody really explained what was about to happen, but for those of you who haven't been to court, here is a quick summary. In due process cases you have a right to an impartial hearing officer and to present evidence and witnesses. This trained and impartial hearing officer acts as a judge and makes the final decisions in the case. In my situation, most of the conversations happened behind closed doors, and when we agreed on the verdict we all met in a traditional court setting to sign the paperwork and other formalities.

It started to get uncomfortable for me when I saw the school's team come in, lawyered up and smug. I couldn't look the principal in the eye. The due process was getting started; their team and my team had multiple exchanges about the facts and situation surrounding the case, in closed quarters without me present to see the antics unfold live. Then my lawyer came out of the discussions and walked my way with a hard-to-read face. It looked indifferent, which to me was not a positive sign of progress.

When he shared the monetary amount they were offering, it seemed ridiculously low. After all the time, money, and effort I put in, I thought the first offer presented would be more substantial, reflecting their concern over not providing what my son needed. To put it into perspective, their offer was so low it would not even cover a month of Matias's private tuition. I took a deep breath after coming out of my shock and awe and asked my lawyer to go back to the negotiating table with the school's lawyers and put together an offer that reflected our grave concerns.

My lawyer stated the events that happened at the negotiation table which I was not allowed at. He stated the facts that the school did not provide the services dictated for my son for three months, which was a procedural violation, nor did they put in the modifications that were agreed upon in the IEP, a legal document. However, while this legal argument compelled twice the original offer from opposing counsel, it didn't even come close to meeting the financial requirements needed to support my son.

The reason they gave for their subpar offer was based on the founding principles of the charter school. They believed that they were treating me with the respect just like they would any other member of the community. Therefore they would not negotiate any further with their offer. To me, this was a logical fallacy. They were not treating my son equally, because his needs were not the same as others'; Matias's were greater. The school's rationale was a total power move of dominance, in my mind, reflecting their lack of support and tolerance for the one in five. When schools behave like this, it showcases the root causes of education inequality.

This, for me, was one of the hardest moments of the journey so far. It felt so disingenuous. The documentation, the experts, all the proof I had put forward came down to a seemingly moral line they drew in the sand that seemed arbitrary at best.

I asked my lawyer what he thought of the offer, and whether they might budge any further. He told me he knew the opposing counsel well, and that this was the best we were going to get.

To Stay or Fold

We debated all the scenarios of accepting this offer. I wanted to stand firm and take the fight to the next level, to showcase the inequality and begin to change the system. My lawyer reminded me, however, that we had a "weak" case to begin with. Matias was not locking himself in the bathroom, refusing to go to school, or causing a ruckus, so there was no slam dunk.

He laid out for me all the costs, experts, and evidence we would need to bring to the next round. And then he said one more thing that stopped me in my tracks: "I wish that parents had the same legal protection that the school has." I asked him what that meant, and he shared a loophole that would ultimately cement my decision.

The school's legal protection was not as costly as mine for a simple reason. They had dual coverage, a school counsel and insurance coverage counsel. I didn't understand what this meant until my lawyer detailed the role and benefits of insurance coverage counsel. The insurance coverage counsel is a backup plan to provide additional legal support without paying an expensive school counsel's hourly fee, but simply paying a small deductible associated with their plan. This meant they had infinite legal coverage for a fraction of the fees I would incur. This education inequality sparked a business idea for me, but my adrenaline was pumping too much to think on it at the moment.

So after a long speech about the inequality and the unfortunate David versus Goliath situation we were in, at this point I had to fold for the sake of my family's future.

My lawyer saw the look of disappointment and disgust on my face. He offered up one final glimmer of hope, like innovative lawyers do. He said that I could ask to speak to the judge privately to hear her thoughts on the matter and her recommendations to a stressed-out mom that didn't want to give up on her kid or the failing system. I waited another two hours to see her, which seemed like an eternity.

My only comfort was hoping the school's legal bill ticked up a bit with every minute.

My Legal Brief with the Judge

Finally, I was up. The judge was very nice. I pleaded my case yet again, and inquired about the legal interpretation of the decision and any other opportunities I might consider. She told me that this was a "good" offer and that they were making efforts to meet his needs, which is more than most schools do. I asked her how it was legal that they could fail to provide services? Isn't that a procedural violation? She stated that they could make up the time, and had plans to fix the situation of the OG teacher (which they never shared with me). She also stated that Matias was not far enough behind (discrepancy) on any of the tests to show that the program in place was not appropriate or not working.

The judge also noted that charter schools were always strapped for resources, and I should use this year's progress at Craig as evidence to take to the public schools, to match the environment he can thrive in and pay for it with their bigger pockets. I told her they refused to show up to my meeting with charter early on, and she said to register him in our local school, and then they were obligated to listen.

I was super grateful for her advice and for her taking the time to walk me through the *why* of it all. It was good to hear, from an insider, how she believed justice could be served.

Let's Seal the Deal

The judge read out the agreement in front of witnesses, along with other formalities. I couldn't even look at the other side like they do in the movies, as I knew my rage would spillith over.

I signed the documents, thanked my lawyers for their time and efforts, and walked out the door. As I stood outside the courthouse, all

I wanted to do was cry, sob, and scream at the unfairness. If an educated woman with a big mouth and time on her hands couldn't win, who could? I swear I aged at least five years in those eighteen months. But worse, I felt like I had failed my son. How could I go home and tell him what happened?

My husband was smugly sweet. He said I had done my best, and to give myself a break. I think he knew all along how it would end.

* * *

A few days later, I got a call from my lawyer. I thought it was simply a call to "settle up your bill, please." But instead it was the call that allowed me to write this book. Their lawyer forgot to have me sign a non-disclosure agreement (NDA), which would mean that I could talk about what happened regarding our case. In most settlements, an NDA is standard.

My lawyer informed me that I should be aware of this mishap, and that the school's lawyer had asked that I keep things confidential. I asked my lawyer if I was legally bound to stay quiet. He said no, it was simply passing it along as a courtesy.

While this was not cash in my pocket, or an apology, it was a ray of hope. I could use my actions and words to tell my story, in the hopes that it could change the behavior of the schools, give parents more information, or simply showcase the pure injustice within our broken education system for our children with dyslexia.

When the settlement check came in the mail I thought I would feel some comfort, as it was the first sign of reparation in this horrible experience. As I went to deposit the check into my account, hoping to fill up the hole from my legal bills, I realized there was a big amount missing from the amount we agreed upon. I called my lawyer to inquire. "Taxes," he said. I said, "Taxes to support a school that doesn't meet the needs of the one in five?" That's irony.

THE THIRD-GRADE TIRADE

For months I continued fuming over the injustice of the court case. The judge's words about using Matias's progress at the Craig School to show public schools with big pockets what kind of environment he needed to thrive replayed endlessly in my mind. I was also an anxious wreck about the years of private-school tuition bills ahead of us. How was it possible that public schools could so blatantly shirk their responsibility to children like mine?

I couldn't officially rest without being absolutely sure that I'd left no stone unturned in giving our son equal access to a quality public education, and so I decided to go to the Jersey City Public Schools (JCPS). Our district has more than twenty-seven thousand kids, as of 2020, and supposedly has a plethora of resources. Surely they'd be able to offer Matias the academic support he needed if I provided the blueprint.

When I broached the subject of checking out JCPS to my husband, he was adamant about laying down ground rules: (1) we had to set a finite budget for legal fees, (2) Matias would have limited exposure to this environment, and (3) we had to be clear with him about why we were even considering pulling him out of paradise.

The experiment was an epic fail. When I came to pick him up from an evaluation, all it took was one look at my son's fearful face, as we passed other special education students being screamed at to stand still in a crowded hallway, for me to know this school would never be the right fit. Meanwhile, the school created the most vaguely worded IEP document possible, saying they'd only offer Matias "high quality" support *after* he was enrolled and had spent time in their classrooms.

I was furious enough about this stonewalling to write a letter to my lawyer, asking if there was anything I could do with the IEP, this useless piece of procedural toilet paper. He basically said no, unless I wanted to put my son in that environment and call their bluff, then move toward legal action.

I had heard this approach from lawyer number three, and Fede's response was "over my dead body," and it was part of our ground rules for exploring third grade in a public school. However, I thought about it, I really did. But my lawyer reminded me there would be a time when I would find justice, but it couldn't come out of my red fog of fury.

So I poured myself a cocktail to mark the end of a seemingly endless, agonizing struggle of exploring all options. I allowed myself to feel a wave of temporary relief and I was exhausted, but at least Matias was happy and we could simply move forward.

Little did I know that I'd have another fierce educational battle to fight just a few years later on behalf of our second son, Oliver, despite knowing that 40 percent of all children who have siblings with dyslexia also have reading issues.[20] In the Epilogue, "One Last Fight: My Second Son's Story," I'll reveal how I used the knowledge I'd gained in my first fight for justice to cut through the invisible red tape and help my younger son to find the academic support he needed to learn and thrive.

First, though, I want to share the stories of other parents from around the country—many of them heartbreaking, all of them inspiring—who have struggled to educate their children with dyslexia. They offer a clear lens on the problems that children with dyslexia of all ages, backgrounds, and income levels face in accessing education in our country. These stories also offer some surprisingly easy, practical solutions you can use in your own battles, proving that parents are often the best educational advocates for their children—provided that we know how to hack the educational system.

SECTION III

THE OUTRAGEOUS HIGHLIGHTS REEL

INTRODUCTION

Most of us are optimists when we take those first exciting steps into our parenting journeys. We hope that our children will be healthy and happy, and that we'll be granted the patience, wisdom, and humor to guide them as they grow and succeed in school, make friends, find their passions, and leave us to pursue their own adventures. We expect that our partners on this journey—friends and families, and especially teachers—will be as concerned about our children as we are.

Then reality hits. No matter how much we love our children, or how hard we work to do our best to raise them, the one in five struggle more than others. And worse, we might discover that the people we trusted most to help us educate our children start falling down on the job. We're bewildered at first, then angry as we face outrageous obstacles in meeting the individual needs of our children so they can thrive.

As I began searching for answers during Matias's journey, I didn't realize how common these struggles were for so many parents. Seeing these common threads made me realize I had to share the experiences of others as well. In this section of the book, I've collected outrageous stories from parents around the country who, like me, are raising children with dyslexia, and fighting to give them the resources and opportunities they need to thrive. We all have to hack our way through the invisible red tape; if we're not vigilant in our advocacy, it can easily ensnare our kids.

Because education is administered at the state and local level, especially elementary education, I wanted to talk to parents from distinct geographic regions around the country to examine how dyslexia is recognized and addressed differently from place to place, and in different formats—public schools versus private schools and charters.

I also wanted to talk with families from different educational backgrounds, income levels, and careers to see how those factors affect outcomes. Ultimately, I decided to group their stories according to the most common hurdles we face as parents of children with dyslexia. Those hurdles include denial of the condition, early interventions gone wrong, faulty accommodations, poorly trained teachers, and lack of funding.

The sections are somewhat arbitrary, of course. Most of us have had experience with several of these pitfalls, if not all of them. However, when you finish reading, I hope you will feel less alone. Perhaps you will find a new way around a problem of your own, or maybe you'll hand this book to a neighbor and say, "See? This is what I'm facing. I could really use your support."

Most of all, I hope that you'll come away from this section understanding that we can only change things for our children if we all keep pushing for appropriate laws, thorough specialized teacher training, full funding, and effective practices. Our voices are louder together. Make yours heard.

DENIAL

"He's dyslexic, but not disabled enough."

A Cop Builds a Case for Her Son's Diagnosis

Emma was a police officer in the UK for sixteen years before moving to the U.S., meeting her husband, and becoming a stay-at-home mom. When her son, Logan, struggled early in school, she summoned her old investigative skills to find the cause of his struggles. In the process, she discovered that her husband, John, a successful entrepreneur with his own business, was also dyslexic.

Logan had been receiving speech therapy since kindergarten, but Emma was dismayed by how much trouble he was still having in first grade, while learning to read. She went to his teacher, described the problems she'd seen, and asked if there were things she or the teacher could do to help him. "I didn't know it then, but I was describing dyslexia to a T," Emma said.

The teacher assured her that she saw no red flags. Yet Logan's school performance continued to tank into second grade, and Emma dug harder for clues. That's when she made a stunning discovery: Every time her son had speech therapy, he was being pulled out of class during core subjects like language arts and mathematics. Was it any wonder he couldn't keep up?

Her next step was to meet with the school principal and ask if Logan could be pulled out of class during less critical times. "That's not possible," the principal said. "That's just not what we do."

Emma was furious. For the first time, she began to suspect that school officials weren't necessarily going to any great lengths to find strategies that might help Logan learn more effectively. What were the laws, she wondered, protecting her son's right to an education?

She knew the laws in the UK, but now she was determined to bone up on those in her adopted country, especially the laws governing special education. This took countless hours of research. "I was a police officer, so I was used to doing research on legislation, but it was still difficult," she said. "I can't imagine how people whose first language isn't English or people who work full-time could ever do it."

Finally, she found the answers she was looking for, called the superintendent's office, and questioned them intensely as to why Logan's school couldn't accommodate a change in time for speech therapy. Eventually someone from the district called back and said yes, it could be done.

But there was a catch: Emma would have to drive her son to school half an hour earlier. "I think they expected me to say no, I can't do that."

She called their bluff and said yes. This caused a domino effect: Now other children taking speech therapy with Logan were also required to come at that early hour. "I wasn't everyone's favorite mom at that point," admitted Emma, who saw this move by administrators as evidence that the school was using a one-size-fits-all model for struggling students due to a shortage of trained staff.

Soon after that, Emma and her husband decided to leave Florida and relocate to North Carolina, which would offer better weather and a more central location for her husband's growing business. Emma hoped the schools in North Carolina might do a better job giving Logan the services he needed too.

Logan was halfway through second grade by the time their family was settled into their new home. His IEP for speech therapy remained in place, and he did fine at first.

"Then I started noticing a real problem with reading comprehension," Emma said. "I'd ask him to read a passage and ask him questions about it, and it was clear he wasn't taking in any of the information."

Emma was puzzled and disheartened. With this additional help, why was her son still struggling in school when he seemed like such a bright kid? There had to be an answer. Clearly, the teachers were missing something.

One day, she was waiting in the school pickup line when she happened to listen to a podcast with Susan Barton, an international expert on dyslexia. "Barton went through all the red flags for dyslexia, and I nearly passed out laughing, because she described in detail exactly what Logan was going through."

She experienced a heavy sense of guilt and shame. How could she have missed all the clues for dyslexia not only as a mom, but as someone professionally trained to dig for clues?

By then, Logan had started third grade. Emma didn't know many people in their new neighborhood yet. She certainly hadn't met anyone with dyslexia—other than her husband, John, who was diagnosed casually as they were exploring Logan's struggles with reading.

Then she realized that part of the reason she might have missed the signs was because nobody talked about it in her circles. "I don't remember dyslexia ever coming up in conversation; nobody else discussed their kids getting special services. So many people have this expectation that their children have to be perfect, straight-A kids. They're ashamed if their kids need help. That seems sad to me. All I wanted was for Logan to feel secure in himself and be happy."

Who could she turn to for help in achieving this goal? Like most parents, Emma still clung to the hope that her child's teachers would be as concerned about his academic progress as she was. She fired off an email to Logan's speech therapist, asking about getting him tested for dyslexia. The reply shattered that hope: Logan's teacher and the school psychologist saw no need for additional testing. "They said he probably just needed repeated practice."

Emma felt very alone and very bleak about Logan's future. How could these people keep denying her instincts and expertise? How could they keep denying her son's need for more specific help? But she wasn't about to give up. She was going to *make* the school do the right thing.

According to the laws she'd researched, the next procedural step was for her to send a formal written request for additional academic testing. This, too, was denied. The administrators claimed "insufficient data to support an intervention" and said they wanted an opportunity to collect more data on Logan's academic performance.

Foolishly, Emma trusted them to begin that process. "I was still naive," she admitted.

Six months later, there had still been no additional testing or meetings organized by the school. Logan was more than halfway through third grade. With each passing week, he fell further behind academically. Even worse, Logan was desperately unhappy; he began saying he was sick to avoid going to school.

"It eventually got to the point where he had a huge meltdown and said he wanted to 'die' because he was so miserable," said Emma, who was gutted.

This was her big breaking point. Emma filed a formal complaint with the Department of Public Instruction and found a private psychologist. She and her husband paid out of pocket to have the necessary evaluation done rather than wait any longer. When the psychologist came back with a definitive diagnosis of dyslexia, Emma felt a mix of despair and euphoria.

When we told Logan, he was happy, pure and simple. "He literally did a fist punch in the air," Emma said. "His father is dyslexic but a successful businessman. That made Logan think, okay, I just need to learn differently, but I can still learn."

Newly confident, Emma brought the diagnosis to Logan's school and asked the psychologist to sit in on the meeting with the school's administrators. She was certain of a positive outcome. How could they keep denying the evidence, when she'd done the hard work of laying it in front of them?

Once again, however, the school's response was outrageous: "He has dyslexia, but he's not disabled enough to qualify for testing or special needs," they said.

Emma was stunned. "No matter how much information we brought them, they kept making us jump through higher and higher hoops."

More determined than ever to prove her case, Emma took Logan for a second evaluation, driving almost four hours to see education consultant Dr. Rebecca Felton, who serves as an adviser for the North Carolina educational curriculum. Dr. Felton confirmed the dyslexia diagnosis.

Going solo against the school was no longer an option. The next time Emma and her husband set up a school meeting, they brought an advocate with them to witness this circus. The advocate assured them that, if the school didn't give Logan accommodations, they'd be in a good position to petition for the district to pay for private-school placement.

The upshot? The school agreed to give Logan a Tier 2 intervention.[1] In this case, that meant Logan would receive twenty minutes of *Recipe for Reading*, an intervention program for struggling readers, *once a week* for five weeks.

This was beyond belief. Emma had spent hundreds of hours doing research and a thousand dollars or more to get her son tested. Yet the school was giving Logan a mere hundred minutes of extra help. "That's not even enough to move the needle," Emma said.

Despite verbal and written requests and two outside evaluations, the school still hadn't tested Logan, either. By now, the school principal was dodging Emma's calls. She hired an attorney, who advised Emma to file a complaint with the school district, this time demanding that the school pay for private education.

At the same time, Emma was diligently researching private schools for students with language-based learning disabilities and found one she liked. Unfortunately, that's when she made a tactical error. For parents to receive funding for private education when a school district fails them, they must show due diligence in examining all of the public school options available and prove that those options won't offer their child the services they need. Afraid Logan might lose his place at the private school that seemed so perfect for him, Emma put down a deposit before the school district agreed to fund private tuition. Her claim was denied, which caused the attorney to walk away.

Emma was furious, both at herself for having misinterpreted the law, and at the attorney, too. What kind of lawyer asks a client to file legal paperwork herself?

By now, she was ready to wash her hands of the public school system and the lawsuit. Her son's education meant more to her than proving this seemingly unwinnable case. She decided the best thing for her family was to simply walk away from the lawsuit, put Logan in private school, and pay for it themselves. She took a trip back home to the UK with Logan to recover from the whole ordeal, which had left her feeling like she had post-traumatic stress disorder.

She returned to a happy surprise: Her husband had filed all the necessary paperwork to fight the school district for financial compensation. John was firm in his conviction that the school should pay for their son's education. It wasn't about the money for him—although at that point, the total cost for private evaluations and attorney fees were astronomical—but about doing the right thing.

"Of course, if you add up how many hours I've spent researching special education laws and fighting for my child's right to an education," said Emma, "we'd be out hundreds of thousands of dollars if we paid a professional to do this work."

Ultimately, what matters most to Emma and John is that Logan is happy at his new school and learning to read. She added, "He looks like a different child." Still, they felt vindicated when both of the complaints they'd filed about the school district—one with the state Office for Civil Rights (OCR) and the other with the state—concurred that the school had violated Logan's rights by denying him the appropriate services.

As Emma soon found out, however, there were still plenty of obstacles for them to overcome. First of all, she discovered that she was only supposed to have filed a complaint with either the OCR or the state, not both. "In hindsight, I can't believe how lucky I was that both offices chose our complaint to investigate," she said, "and found the school in violation."

The OCR's budget has been slashed under the current administration, so the state of North Carolina's governing body of education, the Department of Instruction (DPI) took over the investigation, issuing "a whole list of the corrective actions that needed to be implemented by the school," Emma said.

Two years later after initially filing the complaints, she felt both happy to be proven right by the DPI and furious that only now was the school going to be held accountable for the missteps they'd made in Logan's education. "We were lucky that we'd been able to remove Logan and put him in a private school while we waited for the decision," she said, "but I feel so sad thinking about all of those kids struggling in school without the appropriate services because their parents don't have the resources or knowledge to pay out-of-pocket for a private placement.

"And here's where my story really begins," she added.

The school was ordered to reimburse the cash that Emma and John had paid for private academic evaluations. In addition, the people on his IEP team were ordered to undergo a "retraining" to review Logan's IEP. Then they were expected to sit down with Emma, John, and their attorney to come to an agreement on what backdated services the school would now provide for Logan to make up for the services he didn't receive after March 2018, when he was first found eligible.

Part of Emma wanted no part of this exercise, which she felt would probably be useless, while another part of her enjoyed the idea of "kind of sitting back and looking at them, and having them know that we haven't gone away, and that they were wrong and we were right."

What's more, this process led to an astonishing discovery that made her sick to her stomach. Emma had found an "amazing advocate" named Elizabeth, a speech pathologist whose husband was a retired principal, who reviewed all of Logan's test results and realized that only partial test results were presented from the speech evaluation, leading to an inaccurate assement for Logan being pulled from speech therapy. If they'd submitted the complete scores, Logan would have qualified to receive the services he should have been getting all along.

"We wouldn't have known that, if we hadn't had our expert, there to go back over the data with us," Emma said. This led to them filing another complaint with the OCR.

There was another road block with compensatory services provided for Logan, in that they wanted to give Logan the two years' worth of makeup services outside of school, at a rate of ninety minutes, five times a week. Emma recognized the impossibility of this immediately.

"Logan has extracurricular activities," she pointed out, explaining that hockey practices are after school and games are on weekends. "He couldn't possibly be expected to spend the whole day at school and then have ninety minutes of tutoring every day. So we're arguing right now with the DPI, the office that issues the corrective actions, to show them that what they're requesting isn't practical." Instead, Emma and John are suggesting that the school district provide their family with an equivalent sum of money they can spend on tutoring at times that are more doable for their family.

Here's another snarl in the invisible red tape that keeps children from having an equal education, Emma noted: In North Carolina, the DPI is both the office that issues the corrective actions and the office that sees that laws are implemented and districts are held accountable. "So, basically, the people who investigate the complaints against the districts are also the ones that are supposed to see that districts issue compensatory services."

In addition, even though she had won intervention services for Logan, the services the school wanted to provide weren't appropriate. "They're offering the *Recipe for Reading* program again, which is totally inappropriate," she said.

Having to fight school districts for what their children need is frustrating for parents, Emma added, not just because it's difficult and exhausting, but because it's not a level playing field. It's a rich person's game; most people just don't have the resources, stamina, and information to play, and ultimately give up the fight.

Even Emma's own lawyer is trying to keep her from filing due process or getting in over her head, but she and her husband forge ahead both on principle and on behalf of other parents.

"Honestly, we're doing it out of a sense of justice," said Emma, who has joined a number of dyslexia advocacy groups and sees their numbers growing fast. "I don't want to be stupid with money or thought of as a crusader, but I keep thinking about all the schools that are letting kids down and not being held accountable. I have to walk the walk and talk the talk, because if I'm not willing to stand up and say this is wrong, what's the point of it all?"

Emma's Advice:

- Talk about your child's issues openly with family, friends, and people in your community. Sharing your struggle can help everyone.
- Research your legal options and bring in outside experts to help you fight for your child's right to an education.

"He can't be dyslexic because he has autism."

A Marketing Executive Makes the Case for Rebranding Her Son's Diagnosis

Christopher is eight years old and "in a happy place right now," said his mom, Kimberly, a marketing executive and mother of four who lives in a middle-class suburb of Houston. "He'll tell you he can't read, but he's confident that he's smart."

Kimberly and her husband, an executive who recognized his own dyslexia through Kimberly's work with their son, hope that Christopher will continue this way in his public school, but they're not always optimistic.

"Things haven't clicked for him yet," said Kimberly, who has logged and documented more than two hundred hours just in the past six months researching dyslexia, the special education laws, and the services available. Every step has been a battle, largely because Christopher was diagnosed early on with autism, and the school district refused to acknowledge that he had dyslexia, too.

"At this point, it's really clear that the district is either lying or incompetent," Kimberly said. "I've made every effort to give them the opportunity to do the right thing here, but they have consistently stonewalled me."

Kimberly first knew something was off with Christopher because he missed social cues, but she was confident she could get him the resources he needed through the school district. After all, they lived in a community many people choose explicitly for the fine schools, and their two older children hadn't had any issues. When Christopher experienced reading difficulties in kindergarten and was held back, "We thought, well, he's kind of a daydreamer," she said. "We honestly thought the school was taking care of it."

When a school district evaluation showed that Christopher had autism, the school crafted an educational plan geared to address that disorder. Kimberly didn't disagree with their diagnosis, despite the fact that Christopher is a verbal kid who developed normally, plays imaginatively, and seeks out friendships.

However, when Kimberly saw the school's IEP for her son, she didn't see anything that would address his reading issues. She questioned his ARD team (admission, review, and dismissal—the team that prepares the IEP) about it, pointing out that the reading program they planned to use wouldn't address Christopher's particular needs for systematic, explicit training.

"A child with autism can typically decode without any problem, but they struggle with comprehension," Kimberly noted. "It was clear that Christopher couldn't decode words."

The ARD team's response? "I was told that Christopher can't be dyslexic, because he has strengths in auditory processing and long-term memory."

Kimberly came out of the meeting determined to rebrand her son's diagnosis as autism *and* dyslexia. She thought that with her marketing background, she could frame the story in a compelling way to affect the outcome. She paid for an IEE (independent educational evaluation) for Christopher—one conducted by a clinician on the district's approved list—and gave the report, which clearly diagnosed Christopher as dyslexic, to the ARD team.

The team refused to budge. "They told us they're not required to follow an outside evaluator's diagnosis of eligibility or recommendations. They're only required to consider it."

The only real factor preventing the team from acknowledging that Christopher was dyslexic was the school diagnostician saying, "In my professional judgment, his reading deficits are due to autism."

To complicate matters further, Kimberly was told that there was a difference between the district provider's diagnostic criteria and the diagnostic criteria for dyslexia, as stated by the Texas Education Agency (TEA), the state agency overseeing primary and secondary education. Meaning he had a medical diagnosis of dyslexia, but yet dyslexia couldn't be accepted for eligibility on his IEP.

According to the ARD team, Christopher didn't meet the TEA criteria.

Kimberly felt her frustration boiling over. "The only possible explanation I can come up with for the school to refuse the dyslexia diagnosis is that it would force them to allocate more resources and lose money, since the state mandates intensive instruction for dyslexia but doesn't fund it," she said.

In other words, a diagnosis of autism means the school district *receives* money from the federal government, but a dyslexia diagnosis earns less federal compensation.

This is a shame, since the interventions outlined in the Texas Dyslexia Handbook "are great, and the laws to back it up are really good too," said Kimberly, "but they don't actually get funding to fulfill the requirements."

Putting her marketing skills into overdrive, Kimberly made phone calls, starting with the district's autism coordinator and the state's dyslexia specialist, asking them how the IEP might look different if Christopher received services for both dyslexia and autism. Diving into the literature, she uncovered startling information: In 2004, the TEA capped special education spending. At that point, about 13 percent of students in Texas were receiving special education services; once the cap was set, schools were "dinged" if they funded services for more than eight percent of their students.[2] In 2018 the federal government intervened, saying the TEA cap was in violation of the law, and fined the agency $225 million.[3]

"It's horrifying," Kimberly said, "because there's this culture in Texas that's all about denying services to special education students. It's a lot like insurance companies, you know? They try to deny first, and only pay out to people who fight back. Can you imagine all the kids affected who were not served due to this cap? Absurd!"

Kimberly knew she needed backup. She joined a local chapter of the Texas Dyslexia Initiative and continued to educate herself, and tried to bring to light for other parents the issues she's experienced. "As much as I'm frustrated on my son's behalf, I'm much angrier on behalf of students whose parents don't know what's going on."

At their IEP meeting after first grade, Kimberly faced more hurdles: Christopher's team included only two reading goals—the same goals set for every student in the classroom. "That didn't even come close to closing the gap between where my son is and where he should be in second grade," said Kimberly.

She requested a second IEP meeting before second grade to express her concerns. Rather than fight the "autism versus dyslexia" brand name, this savvy marketer decided to put a laser focus on Christopher's reading ability, saying she wanted to add goals for fluency, comprehension, and spelling. "I just wanted to address methodology at that point, because no matter what's causing the specific deficits in reading, they needed to be addressed."

This meeting "was a very crowded room." In addition to ten school and district representatives, there were two district instructional program and curriculum officers, plus Kimberly, her husband, and an advocate. "We wanted to have a third party there as another voice that pipes up and asks them to explain things," Kimberly said, because at that point she could no longer trust herself to remain calm. "I strive to be logical and support my arguments with evidence as a marketing professional, but this was my son we were talking about, and these people could push my buttons."

At the meeting, the team agreed to add the reading goals Kimberly requested. But shortly thereafter, Kimberly ran smack up against another roadblock, despite all her detailed planning. The school wanted to use a certain multisensory, hands-on reading program that didn't meet the requirements of the Dyslexia Handbook. With the advocate's help, Kimberly and her husband pushed back, asking the team to use Reading By Design instead, since it's the dyslexia intervention program approved for the state of Texas.

Again, the ARD team balked. "We walked around the question for about an hour, and finally we just asked straight-out why we couldn't use the Reading By Design program for Christopher."

The ARD team leader said she wasn't sure why not, and went off to call the elementary intervention coordinator for the district. The answer seemed straightforward at first: "They said Christopher needed to be reading at the second-grade level before he could use Reading By Design."

At this point, they were two hours into the meeting. Everyone was tired, and they ultimately agreed that Christopher would receive thirty minutes a day of the multisensory program followed "to fidelity," Kimberly stipulated, "from lesson one straight through." Furthermore, as soon as Christopher met the prerequisite reading level, they would meet again and consider switching to Reading By Design.

It wasn't until Kimberly left the meeting and reviewed her notes about Reading By Design that she thought to look back at the district's parent informational brochure for the program. There, in black and white, it said the program was meant for grades K through 12.

Her mind reeled. She photographed a picture of the parent brochure with her cell phone and fired it off to her advocate, who immediately emailed it to the elementary intervention coordinator with that information highlighted, asking for an explanation.

They received a three-page email in return, basically saying that they had "no right to specify what methodology would be included in an IEP."

Of course, Kimberly didn't get to be where she is in her career by backing down from a challenge, and she wasn't going to start now. Instead, she called her district contact for the Reading By Design program and asked, "Please, can you clarify for me whether or not there are any prerequisites for doing this program?"

The short answer: No.

Kimberly sent this answer to the advocate, who forwarded it to the ARD team. She's waiting to see how the conversation plays out, but she has a complaint letter prepared and ready to go. The letter will be sent to both the school and the TEA.

"There's always a tension between advocating for change for all students who need it, and making sure Christopher gets what he needs," she admitted. "This can be a very long battle, and I don't want to delay getting the intervention Christopher should have right now. We're seriously considering sending him to a private school for children with learning differences."

They have already done some trial days at two such schools, and

Christopher really loved one of them. "I think it was a really perfect fit for him. If we were able to afford it, he'd probably be there already."

With four children, private-school tuition would put a significant financial burden on the family, so they're giving the IEP at the public school one more shot. "If I don't see sufficient progress in the first few months of school, or if I see any bullying because of his difficulties, then we'll find an alternative immediately," Kimberly told me.

For now, though, all they can do is wait.

Kimberly's Advice:

- Sign a consent form today to allow for school district evaluations, and get all of your requests for evaluations and reports in writing. Those will tell you about your child's strengths and weaknesses. Then you can decide what to do with that information.
- Get involved with your local dyslexia activist groups. We're not going to see changes at the school level for children until parents push for the implementation of appropriate laws and practices.

"You've got to stop paying to tutor your child."

A Maryland Mom Takes On the Broken School System
on Behalf of Black Children with Dyslexia

As a former high school teacher and school administrator with a master's degree, Destiny knows a lot about the public schools of Baltimore, Maryland, where she currently lives in a middle-class suburb. "I know things the average parent couldn't know," she said.

For instance, Destiny understands firsthand that there is a severe teacher shortage, especially in early childhood education, and that this shortfall sometimes leads public schools to place poorly qualified teachers in the classroom out of desperation. She also knows that those early years in school are probably the most profoundly important to a child's future academic and life success.

What's more, as an African American mother, Destiny paid close attention to the struggles of black children in Baltimore schools. She witnessed how too many of them never received the help they needed to succeed, or were misdiagnosed by the predominantly white teaching staff.

"There's a high level of fear among the black community, especially around black teenage boys," she said. "Look at the pipeline to prison system. You see so many more black men in jail than white men, and that's partly because they've failed at school. When a little black boy acts out in class because he's got some energy, he's diagnosed and medicated. A little white boy who does the same thing is just called rambunctious. I feared for my daughter."

So when it was time for her own daughter to start kindergarten, Destiny refused to let her go to the public school. Instead, she chose a Christian private school with small class sizes that allowed Kayla to receive "lots of one-on-one attention."

Despite this nurturing environment, Kayla had trouble learning to read. "She just wasn't catching on," said Destiny, a single mom who is currently director of workforce development at a nonprofit agency.

When that school closed, along with many other affordable private schools in the city, Destiny panicked. Her own neighborhood public school was severely overcrowded, with more than thirty students in each classroom, "and that wasn't going to cut it for my daughter."

At the very last minute, Destiny found a place for Kayla in a charter school nearby with a good reputation. "I cried when she got into that charter school," she said.

In many ways, this school was a great fit for Kayla, because it was project-based and had an integrated arts curriculum where academic lessons were enhanced by hands-on activities. By the end of first grade, however, Kayla's reading skills still lagged, and when the school suggested evaluating her for learning disabilities, Destiny readily agreed.

The test results showed that Kayla had a specific learning disability (SLD) in reading. Despite her academic background, Destiny had no idea what this meant, and said so at the school's team meeting, where they reviewed Kayla's test results and discussed putting her on an individualized education program.

"I kept saying, 'What is a specific learning disability? What does it mean?' and they all kept dancing around the diagnosis and doing what I call 'teacher talk,'" Destiny said.

At the very end of the meeting, the psychologist "slipped up" and said, "We know Kayla has dyslexia."

"Oh, she has dyslexia?" Destiny asked.

The other school officials and teachers at the table glared at the psychologist, who quickly backtracked, saying. "No, no, no, I didn't say that."

"I felt like they were hiding something," Destiny said dryly.

That night, she called her cousin, an attorney who had studied special education law. Her cousin advised Destiny to have Kayla evaluated independently, and suggested that she look into a Lindamood-Bell center in Maryland that offered reading instruction for children with dyslexia. Destiny arranged to attend one of the center's free webinars. The very next day, she was on the phone with them, asking if they could assess Kayla.

The center didn't do academic evaluations, the receptionist told her, only instruction. They offered an intensive summer program for eighteen thousand dollars.

Destiny was stunned by the price. She wasn't about to put Kayla in the program without an actual diagnosis. She started calling around, trying to make an appointment for a neuropsych evaluation, and was told that a private evaluation could run as much as $3,500 out of pocket. Altogether, Destiny was looking at twenty-two thousand dollars for the evaluation and the summer program. It was so disheartening that she broke down crying at work.

So she called a psychologist she knew personally and asked about evaluations. And she called the school principal, who also tried to calm Destiny down, assuring her that they would do whatever was necessary to give Kayla the instruction she needed, to address her reading challenges.

Still, Destiny was troubled. "I felt like I didn't really know what was going on with my daughter."

At last she found a psychologist willing to consult with her. During their conversation, the psychologist told Destiny that the best thing she could do for Kayla was inform herself about dyslexia so that she could be proactive about guiding the charter school to provide appropriate services. She suggested several books about dyslexia, and told Destiny to attend informational sessions at private schools for learning differences to see what reading instruction programs they used. That way, Destiny could ask the charter school to provide one of those for Kayla as well.

Most important, the psychologist directed Destiny to an advocacy group called Decoding Dyslexia.

"That group was a godsend for me," said Destiny.

She began attending their monthly meetings, where she found parents willing to help her come up with the specific services and language she needed to ask for on Kayla's IEP. "For instance, I could tell the school that, for Kayla to succeed in reading, she needed a structured literacy program."

Destiny also told the school that Kayla needed to be taught by a teacher trained in specific reading strategies for children with dyslexia. Right now, the way the IEP was written, "it sounded like any general education teacher could work with my baby, and I knew that wasn't true, because she wasn't progressing."

In response, the school trained one of their teachers in the Wilson

Reading System for dyslexia. Destiny was pleased to hear this. Then she asked what level of intervention Kayla was getting, and was told it was Tier 3.

By now, Destiny understood enough about special education to know this couldn't possibly true. Many schools help students catch up with their peers through RTI—response to intervention—support. The support is broken into three levels, or tiers. All students in a general education classroom are considered Tier 1, while those who aren't making progress receive Tier 2 learning support, like small group lessons a few times a week, often with a special education teacher. These extra small lessons are called "interventions."

Tier 3 consists of intensive interventions for children who still aren't progressing, despite special help. These children are considered at-risk students, and their interventions should include specialized instruction with trained teachers.

"I knew that was a lie, that they were giving Tier 3 support to Kayla," Destiny said. Just the day before, she'd called the Wilson training center and asked what level training the teacher had received, and she was told the teacher was not listed in their database, and therefore had not earned Tier 3 certification.

In fact, the school was hiding more than that. Later on, Destiny discovered that the district did, in fact, have a box to check that said dyslexia on the IEP form, but they were instructing the psychologist not to check that particular box.

Destiny also discovered that, in her daughter's class, there were students with diagnoses of emotional disability, autism, and ADHD. There was such a variety of learning disabilities in the general education classroom that "it put a lot of pressure on the general educators to provide services they weren't specifically trained to do." Kayla's teacher came right out with the truth one day, saying, "I don't know how to work with a child with dyslexia."

And, because Destiny was on the board, she knew that most of the school's budget went toward programming for students. She could also see that their special education population had doubled: the percentage of students on IEPs had gone from 7 percent to 13 percent, while the budget remained static. There simply weren't going to be enough resources to go around.

"I knew my daughter's school was struggling," she said, and the insufficient funding meant her struggles would continue.

Kayla remained there for second grade, but Destiny began looking at private-school options. "I knew my daughter wasn't going to get what she needed in a public charter school."

Meanwhile, she was taking Kayla twice a week for tutoring in the Orton-Gillingham (OG) method, another reading program geared toward children with dyslexia.

Slowly, Kayla's reading began to progress, so when the OG tutor went on maternity leave, Destiny began taking Kayla to the Lindamood-Bell center for special reading instruction. All of these tutoring hours were costly, about fifty-seven dollars per hour, for ten hours every week.

About this time, Kayla's father, who by now realized that his own school troubles were probably due to his own dyslexia, was diagnosed with cancer. He had to stop working, which meant Destiny began shouldering the burden of private tutoring alone. She went to an attorney to see if there was any way she might be able to get the school to pay for Kayla's reading instruction.

"Right away, he tells me to stop the tutoring," Destiny said.

She realizes now that the attorney was probably trying to develop a legal strategy to show that Kayla wasn't progressing in school and would therefore qualify for a district-funded private-school placement, "but I left the office in tears, telling him that I can't let my baby fail."

To make matters worse, the group rate of fifty-seven dollars per hour for tutoring shot up to $123 per hour for one-on-one instruction when several children dropped out of the Lindamood-Bell program where Kayla was enrolled. On top of that, Destiny was paying someone $150 each week to transport Kayla from school to tutoring.

"My credit cards were maxed out," Destiny said, "but I still wanted to apply for private schools."

By then, Destiny had become director of admissions at a school for language-based learning differences, so she knew that the emotional turmoil she felt about pulling Kayla out of the charter school—a place she loved—was normal. "I used to get all kinds of calls from parents asking about placement, and telling me they felt like they were going against their children's schools if they had to fight for their children."

Destiny felt torn too, but her decision to leave the charter school "wasn't personal." It was for her daughter.

She and Kayla visited three schools for children with dyslexia and applied to two of them. The school that accepted Kayla wasn't cheap—the tuition was more than thirty-five thousand dollars annually—but the school gave some financial aid, and at least it would eliminate the need for private tutoring.

Destiny was excited about finally finding a school that would directly address Kayla's dyslexia. Kayla's reading continued to progress, but it wasn't long before other challenges surfaced. The students at this particular school were mostly white. So were the teachers. Kayla was the only black child in the lower grades, and the only black teacher on staff was the athletic director. In addition, the children were wealthy and had already formed cliques. Kayla felt left out and miserable. Her only friend was a Jewish girl who also felt ostracized.

"She was having an awful experience," Destiny said. "My daughter had always loved school, and now she didn't want to go anymore. It broke my heart."

Kayla began asking Destiny why there weren't more black children and black teachers at the school. Although she was only eight years old, Kayla even suggested that people at the school "wanted to go back to when the white folks treated us bad."

Horrified, Destiny went to school administrators and asked if anything could be done to help Kayla adjust. She even suggested that the school give Kayla a mentor, perhaps one of the black students from the middle school, and was told that they'd look into that possibility.

Mostly, though, the head of the lower school was dismissive of her concerns. "He was pointing the blame at my daughter," Destiny said.

When nothing came of that conversation, Destiny went to the head of school to talk about her concerns, and once again suggested a mentor for Kayla. The head of school "acted like it was the first time I'd ever said anything like this. By now, I was getting a little frustrated."

Destiny happened to attend a gala not long after that. There, she met the head of another school for children with dyslexia. When he asked how her daughter was doing, Destiny "tried to be neutral," but told him that Kayla was having some trouble adjusting. "The environment is really new for her," Destiny said.

Right away, he said, "Oh, so she doesn't feel like she belongs there?"

Destiny was shocked by his candor, but impressed, too. She called Kayla's father to tell him what had happened, and he encouraged Destiny to see if she could get Kayla into that school instead. Destiny put in the application. Not long after that, she had a call from her own head of school, asking about a student Destiny had filmed during a speech and reminding her that it was against school policy to record the children. After Destiny assured him that the mother of that particular student had asked her to record the student so her dad could see it, the head of school let it go and asked Destiny how Kayla was doing.

"You know, she's still facing challenges," Destiny admitted.

"Okay," he said. "Have a nice weekend."

Destiny hung up the phone and sobbed with outrage. How could that man ask how Kayla was doing, and then, upon hearing that she was still struggling, tell Destiny to have a nice weekend?

That was her breaking point. When Kayla was accepted into the other school for fourth grade, Destiny enrolled her immediately. Kayla "is doing much better now," partly because the school is larger and there's more diversity among the students and the teachers.

Now, looking back on her experiences, Destiny realized that she was actually lucky despite her frustrations. "I knew that I was privileged," she told me with pity in her voice.

When Kayla first began struggling in school, Destiny explained, she had access to people with experience and expertise in special education, "and I had a credit card with a high enough maximum balance for me to pay for tutoring and an attorney's retainer. Yet I still couldn't do enough right for her."

That realization, coupled with her own school experiences, drove Destiny to start her own advocacy effort aimed at helping black families navigate the invisible red tape that keeps them from having their children identified as having dyslexia and receiving appropriate services. Today she's a popular public speaker who also wrote a book about her experiences.

"Ours is a population that has been traumatized by labels, so parents are less likely to ask for help. My aim is to get people talking and change that."

Destiny's Advice:

- Learn all you can about dyslexia.
- Educate yourself on special education law and your child's rights.
- Know your child's unique strengths, weaknesses, and interests.
- Find a community that will give you support.

"If he can read and write at a third-grade level, he'll be fine."

The Mother of a Biracial Child Fights for Equal Testing

As a foster kid and teen mom, Amber struggled with learning challenges all her life. When it came to dealing with her own son's school struggles, she nearly shut down completely because "I was so broken down by the system," said Amber, now a single mother of four who lives in subsidized housing outside Sacramento, California.

Between first and third grade, Amber tried and failed to get her son Ian special education services at school because he was struggling academically. Eventually she gave up and mostly shut Ian out, too, withdrawing from her son as a coping mechanism. "I didn't want to take out my anger about my experiences of the world on him," she said.

By third grade, Ian still couldn't read, and resisted going to school. Amber was terrified that if Ian didn't do better academically, he might follow in the footsteps of his dad, Leon, who is currently unemployed and homeless. His housing situation is a direct result of his inability to read; he was evicted after misunderstanding his lease contract and terms.

Amber met Leon in high school, and gave birth to their first child when she was only sixteen. The two never married, but they've had an on-again, off-again relationship and two more children together over the past fifteen years. Leon's own chaotic childhood in a neighborhood prone to gang violence came with enormous losses, including his brother who was murdered. Leon had learning disabilities and a spotty school attendance record. He eventually dropped out of school, dealt drugs, and served time in prison. Although Amber describes him as a "brilliant man" who can fix just about anything, he remains functionally illiterate and struggles to find and hold on to jobs.

By fourth grade, Ian still couldn't read or write, and Amber found herself praying for guidance. "I said, Lord, I don't know what I'm supposed to do about my son. I don't want my son to be like his dad. Can you help me, please?"

Help came in the form of paperwork from the school, saying they wanted to conduct an educational assessment on Ian to determine the nature of his learning disabilities and put him on an IEP (individual education plan). Amber was supposed to sign the paperwork and return it to the school to get things started.

When she turned the paperwork over, however, Amber found something odd stapled to the back: a note from the school informing her that, because of a California court case, *Larry P. v. Riles*, they couldn't give Ian an IQ test or the usual reading assessments. Instead, they'd give him alternative tests—because Leon, Ian's father, is black, and Amber had identified her child as black on his school forms.

"A big lightbulb went off," said Amber, who is white. She didn't understand why her son was going to be evaluated differently from other kids just because he was black. "I thought, why has my son been struggling, but they've been ignoring me when I've asked them for help? Is it because they knew they couldn't do anything for him, so they thought it was better to ignore a parent who couldn't even talk to her child because she was so mad at the system that's holding him back?"

And what the heck was the *Larry P.* case?

Amber went online to find out. The more she read about the case, the more outraged she became.

Basically, California is the only state where administering an IQ (intelligence quotient) test, or any other cognitive assessments that might include testing a student's IQ, to black students is explicitly banned. The ban is based on the 1979 *Larry P. v. Riles* court case, where a class of black students sued the California Department of Education.

Prior to that case, black children were being put in EMR (Educable Mentally Retarded) classes—a term once used to define children deemed educable only to a fifth-grade level—at an alarmingly high rate. The plaintiffs in the *Larry P.* case argued that this disproportionate ratio of black children in EMR classes was due to the standardized IQ test being culturally biased, and therefore unfair. They won, and California now requires educators to use less-biased, alternative means of testing black children for learning disabilities.

As Amber saw it, however, because of the *Larry P.* case, her own son would be denied the appropriate assessments, and therefore an equal education. In fact, the more she thought about it, she realized that Ian's father had also suffered because of the *Larry P.* ruling. Neither Leon nor Ian had ever been properly tested for dyslexia or other learning disabilities.

After reading the paperwork, "I hugged my son, and said this is about something bigger. This is about racism," Amber said.

Ian was bewildered. Although he's biracial, he resembles Amber, with dark blond hair, pale skin, and green eyes. He identifies as white.

"Mom, I don't understand," he said. "How is this about race? I don't get it."

"It's okay, baby," Amber said. "You don't have to understand. I'm just so glad to have a way to fight for you now."

Amber went straight to the school and said she wanted her son tested the same way all the kids who weren't black were tested. "The school said my son had an auditory processing issue, and that's why he couldn't read. I kept telling them that he had hearing loss—I'd had him tested by an audiologist—but that his hearing had nothing to do with his reading problems. I wanted him to have the right tests, but they refused."

She was furious. Amber knew that her son had 50 percent hearing loss in one ear, and by law, "You cannot have a child with hearing loss also have auditory processing issues on his IEP," because hearing loss is a health impairment, while auditory processing is considered a learning disability. She began asking other people for advice, even going on Facebook to air her grievances. Finally, someone suggested that she travel to Sacramento, nearly an hour away, and attend the special education advocacy board meeting for a predominantly black school.

"I was the only white person at the meeting, but I didn't care," she said. "I figured they'd probably know how to navigate the fact that he was being denied special education because of the *Larry P.* case."

The trip was a disappointment. This group told her that there was no way around *Larry P.*, and that she'd have to accept it. But Amber wasn't done fighting yet. At this point, "my son couldn't even write three sentences," she said.

Her next step was to pay for Ian to have an independent educational assessment at Sacramento State University. Because that testing center wasn't affiliated with any public school in California, they were able to do the assessments she wanted, including administering an IQ test and evaluating him for dyslexia, which the testing center confirmed.

Amber took the results to Ian's public school, but was told that the testing didn't matter. By law, they had to "consider" independent evaluations outside of the district, but didn't necessarily have to accept or act upon them.

"I even told the school that they didn't have to write the word 'dyslexia' on his IEP; they could just say he had a reading problem and give him the help he needed, but nope. They wouldn't even agree to that," she said.

Her requests were denied in fourth grade, and again in fifth grade. "It was the same scene. I kept getting shut down whenever I asked them to be very explicit on the agreement for what methods they were using to assess him and how they'd help him learn to read. They said they didn't have to give me that information."

Disgusted with the whole process, Amber stopped going to IEP meetings. "At this point, I didn't know how to file a due process claim yet."

Ian had been struggling for years in school due to self-esteem issues, and now he began falling apart emotionally, too, picking at his fingers until they bled. "He quit leaving his room," Amber said. "My son had no friends, and he'd pull his hair and hit his head, calling himself stupid. He had many tardies, too, because it wasn't easy to get him to school."

In sixth grade Ian would start at the public junior high school. Amber was worried about the transition, and wrote an email to his school, hoping this would be a new start for Ian. "I wrote to say, hey, I'm concerned, because my son is not ready to go to the junior high environment," she said, "because Ian was still reading at only a first- or second-grade level." She asked to be connected to the junior high's IEP resource staff.

"I knew that once kids hit junior high, there's no more reading instruction," she said. "Once the elementary school years are over, the staff are very biased and discriminatory toward kids who can't read."

In fact, the principal at Ian's elementary school had already pointed a finger at Amber, saying that the reason Ian couldn't read "is because you don't read to him." Even worse, the principal told her that, as long as Ian "can read and write at the third-grade level, he'll be fine. That blew me out of the water."

Ian, too, was routinely criticized by his teachers, several of whom said to him, "Stop being lazy. You're just not trying hard enough."

Amber gave up on the public schools completely when the junior high transition team refused to set up a meeting with her. Rather than be confrontational with school officials, she opted to let Ian complete fifth grade in his district, while searching for alternatives for sixth grade.

Within a few weeks, Amber thought she'd found the perfect solution: homeschooling Ian through a program provided by a local charter school. When she told the charter school that Ian had dyslexia, they seemed unfazed. "They said, 'yeah, we know how to deal with dyslexia,' and I was like, glory be to God." The charter school provided books, a laptop, and academic support so that Amber could instruct Ian at home.

Before the start of sixth grade, she gave the charter school the assessments that Sacramento State had done, showing that Ian was dyslexic, as well as Ian's public school records. That's when the other shoe dropped: The charter school, just like Ian's public elementary school and junior high, refused to accept the outside assessment or offer Ian specialized instruction for dyslexia.

"They told me that they had to go with the IEP from the old school." Amber couldn't believe it. Despite more than fifty pages from the Sacramento State evaluators showing that Ian had dyslexia based on their testing, "They were like, 'Well, we're just gonna go with the auditory processing.' They wouldn't even consider the test from the audiologist showing that Ian had hearing loss."

Not surprisingly, Ian kept failing academically, because the charter school demanded that he do 80 percent of the work assigned through their curriculum, but Ian wasn't capable of doing the assignments because he couldn't read or write at that level. That's when Amber finally consulted a lawyer, hoping he could find a way to get Ian retested and have the current IEP scrapped.

After a heated legal battle, "we won in some areas," said Amber, but lost when it came to arguing against the *Larry P.* ruling. "We weren't able to overrule the assessments that had been done, or to ask for any new ones, because they said the alternative assessments were as effective in identifying suspected disabilities."

It seemed that her son would be held back due to the lack of attaining an IQ score determined by the *Larry P.* ruling.

Throughout sixth grade, Ian was depressed and anxious. He was "noncompliant about doing homework," until Amber started doing more research on academic programs for children with dyslexia and found one that "allowed my son to work at a pace that was doable for him."

For instance, because reading was hard for Ian, she knew he wouldn't be able to read for four or five consecutive hours in different subjects. She decided to break up the material into smaller, more manageable chunks. "We'd still work for six hours a day, but for only two hours on, then two hours off," using an online program.

Amber also invested in learning technology, hooking the computer up to a big-screen TV so Ian could read larger print and follow it better. She made it easier by highlighting each word to help him track them. Between the science of reading curriculum and adaptive technology, Amber estimates that she probably spent a little over a thousand dollars—and countless hours of her own time.

The charter school, like Ian's other public school, "began lying about how I wasn't being compliant," Amber said, "because they were angry that we were doing our own thing." For instance, they said that Amber wasn't showing up to parent-teacher conferences and that she was being "educationally neglectful."

Amber had kept track of the meetings, even recording them, and was able to prove that they were lying in court. "It got really nasty," she admitted.

She continued fighting the school district with her lawyer's help. Meanwhile, within five months of Amber teaching him, Ian was able to jump up several grade levels in reading, putting him almost on par with his peers. The case eventually settled, with Amber agreeing that Ian would stay in the public school system if the district agreed to provide different assessments. Ian started seventh grade at the public school, and she's still awaiting the results of that new battery of tests.

Amber and her family were not the only ones in their district affected by the *Larry P.* ruling. In fact, she knows at least one mother who changed her biracial child's race to "white" on the school forms so that he would receive the appropriate educational evaluation.

"A lot of the schools make things really complicated and confusing, so you can't follow the law and you don't know what to do," she said. "A lot of parents don't even know they're being denied appropriate assessments."

Amber is currently taking advocacy courses, and hopes to help other parents navigate the process of having their children properly screened, identified, and served with the appropriate resources for an equal education.

Amber's Advice:

- If the school tests your child, research those tests and exactly what they measure.
- Attend workshops with other parents in the area of educational advocacy.

"There's no such thing as math dyslexia. I should know: I was a special ed teacher before becoming a principal."

A Feisty Grandmother Takes Control of Her Granddaughter's Education

It's not always easy being a grandparent. Ask Nancy, a college-educated, retired special education teacher and grandmother in San Jose, California, who's married to a retired aerospace engineer.

Nancy was thrilled when her daughter, Elizabeth, moved back into her house with her husband and newborn daughter, Denise, but it wasn't long before Nancy realized that her granddaughter was different from most babies.

For instance, Denise had trouble sleeping and was extremely sensitive to stimulation, especially to loud noises or light. "I was suspicious from the beginning that something wasn't right," Nancy said.

Elizabeth and her husband waved off Nancy's concerns. "I wasn't listened to," Nancy said. "My daughter didn't see anything wrong. It's very frustrating to be a grandmother and not have your kids take it seriously when you express your concerns. There's no way to get your grandchild help if the parents won't cooperate."

Nancy bided her time, spending as much time with Denise as possible, even after her daughter and family moved to their own apartment half an hour away. She could see that Elizabeth was struggling; Elizabeth worked full-time in tech, and her marriage was disintegrating as her husband's anger management issues spun out of control.

Occasionally, Nancy did "make a quiet comment" about Denise's progress—or rather, lack of progress—in preschool, suggesting that Denise might need extra help, but Elizabeth "always had some rationalization" to explain why Denise was doing fine.

"I don't think she had the energy or time to understand what was happening with my granddaughter," said Nancy. "Elizabeth was just trying to survive, and doing the best she could."

On Denise's third birthday, Nancy arrived at her daughter's apartment with a cake and presents, prepared to celebrate, and was horrified to find Elizabeth's husband scrubbing Denise's face so hard in the bathtub that her granddaughter's cheek was bright red and raw-looking. She sent her son-in-law out of the room and scooped up her granddaughter to comfort her.

"As time went on, things got worse," she said. "One day I looked at him and said, 'If you lay a hand on my granddaughter ever again, I'm going to kill you.'"

Nancy helped support Elizabeth emotionally and financially when she divorced him. By then, Denise was eight years old and in third grade, and her academic troubles were escalating, especially in math. Nancy knew this because she was the one who would often pick Denise up from school and take her for the weekends.

"Denise couldn't keep her desk organized the way her third-grade teacher demanded," Nancy said, "and it was clear to me that she had no grasp of numbers, even though I'd been working with her using pennies, flash cards, and everything else I could think of. She couldn't handle spelling, she had trouble reading, and her homework was taking all afternoon and evening."

Denise had no life other than school because, no matter how many challenges she faced, she was still determined to earn top marks. Her only respite came during flute lessons, which her grandmother paid for.

Nancy was fed up with her daughter's refusal to acknowledge Denise's school struggles. Without telling Elizabeth, Nancy brought Denise to a private testing center and paid for an academic evaluation.

It never occurred to her to get the testing done through the school, she added. "I'd seen what happened in my own school district with a friend who has three dyslexic boys. There were no programs available to help them."

Besides, she already knew all about dyslexia. Her own husband has it. He struggled with reading to the point where Nancy often had to drive if they were in a busy town or city because "he couldn't read the street signs fast enough."

From everything she'd read, "I figured Denise probably had a mild dyslexia when it came to reading, and math dyslexia, too, which I'd never heard of until I looked it up. There was even a special word that described her problems: 'dyscalculia.'"

The test results supported Nancy's observations. Nancy brought the results to Elizabeth, but Elizabeth refused to let her take Denise for the additional testing suggested by the private evaluator. Elizabeth did, however, agree to allow Nancy to attend a meeting with the principal of Denise's public elementary school.

Despite the testing, "Elizabeth and her husband still didn't see as much of a problem with Denise's learning as I did," Nancy said. "She and her husband both denied it. He still does, but that's okay because he's no longer around."

The principal, unfortunately, wasn't much more help than Elizabeth's husband. "She said there's no such thing as math dyslexia," Nancy fumed, "and that she knew that because she used to be a special ed teacher! Well, you can be sure I didn't interact with her very much after that."

Following that meeting, Denise was assigned to a special education teacher for an hour a day. Within a short time, however, Denise came back to her grandmother and mother and said, "I want out of that, because I get behind when I'm not in the regular classroom."

So Nancy went to Denise's teachers and arranged for her granddaughter's special accommodations directly. For instance, "We negotiated that she could keep a messy desk, as long as she kept the lid down on it."

Her teacher agreed that if Nancy worked with her on math concepts, then she would sign off that Denise could move to the next lesson. This gave Nancy a level of control in making sure she was on track and truly understood the concept and was not being passed up the chain as the easy way out. Denise also spent most lunch hours in the library, reading or studying, to keep her grades up.

By middle school, "Elizabeth finally woke up enough to get Denise put on an IEP," Nancy said, "but the school didn't use it very much."

Meanwhile, Nancy continued to diligently advocate for her granddaughter. "In junior high, I was the one who met with the teachers," she said. "The English teacher and I met every month to share any thoughts we had for helping her." She also continued picking Denise up and taking her to flute lessons, to ensure Denise had something she excelled at. "She competed in flute contests and did very well."

During Denise's last year of junior high, however, things changed again when Elizabeth remarried and moved to Oregon with her husband, an army veteran who suffered from dissociative identity disorder (multiple personality disorder). By then, Denise was old enough to speak up about her educational plan and what she needed to succeed in school, but things were still tough, given the turmoil at home.

After graduating from high school, Denise enrolled in a junior college in Oregon, "and everything fell apart again," said Nancy. "Denise needed rides either to the bus stop or all the way to her junior college, and she was always a few minutes late."

One day, Elizabeth "dumped Denise into the car with her second husband," who started railing at Denise about her tardiness. "He went on and on," Nancy said, until her granddaughter asked him to "please stop and be quiet."

At that point, Denise's stepfather kicked her out of the car. Denise called her grandmother in tears, and Nancy urged her to leave home and move back in with her, where Denise could walk to a good junior college only four blocks away from Nancy's home—provided Elizabeth gave her permission.

"I knew it was a toxic environment," Nancy said. "Denise had to get out."

Elizabeth apparently thought that was the right solution too, because a couple of days later, Denise called and said she'd be arriving in two weeks. She spent the next three years attending junior college near her grandmother's house.

Early on in her second year of junior college, when Denise was twenty years old, she went to her grandmother and said, "I don't understand. Why do I read so slowly?"

"When you read a paragraph, do you sometimes get to the end of it and decide it didn't make sense?" Nancy asked. "And then you go back and read the paragraph again, and find a word you read wrong that changes the meaning entirely?"

Denise nodded. "I do that all the time."

"Okay," Nancy said. "That's dyslexia."

With Nancy's financial and academic support, Denise was able to graduate from junior college. She went on to earn her bachelor's degree with honors from Sonoma State University and hopes to pursue a teaching career.

"My granddaughter is grateful that I'm always there for her," said Nancy, who wouldn't have it any other way.

Nancy's Advice:

- Become directly involved with your child's teachers.
- Be respectful of the school district, but continue to nicely request whatever your grandchild needs, and go after it.
- Support activities outside of school where your child or grandchild can excel, like music and sports.

THE UPS AND DOWNS OF EARLY INTERVENTION

"I don't know what's wrong with your child, but you'd better find out."

While a Suburban Mom Struggles to Understand How Her Son's OCD Complicates His Learning Difficulties, He's Suspended for Throwing Erasers

Melissa, a stay-at-home mom in suburban Atlanta, wrote a letter to her son Simon's school before the start of kindergarten, detailing her concerns about the speech and language problems he'd experienced in preschool. Simon's grandmother was dyslexic, and Melissa had a feeling her son was too.

Simon was placed with a teacher "who did not seem to care about the details of reading," said Melissa, who introduced herself to the kindergarten teacher at the start of the school year. "Simon had a lot of red flags for dyslexia, and I needed her to notice things too, and communicate with us."

Melissa did her best to watch over Simon's school progress by volunteering in the classroom's Parents Center each week. During Center time, the kindergarten class was broken into small groups so that students could move from one learning center to the next.

"Right out of the gate, I looked at my son and saw a child who was defeated," Melissa said. "He was unable to function in the classroom. While the other children were happy, my child would put his head down on the desk whenever he was given work that might involve identifying letters or reading words. I can't tell you how much it hurt me to see my bright, bubbly boy suffer in the classroom."

Simon's kindergarten teacher readily agreed that Simon wasn't catching on to things she was presenting in class and referred him to the school's early intervention program (EIP). Children in kindergarten were pulled out of the classroom regularly to participate in the EIP.

There was one big problem: Although Melissa didn't know this at the time, the EIP teacher "didn't have any specific training in any particular science of reading program, and it was kind of a catch-all for kids who weren't making progress." Simon was grouped with children experiencing everything from developmental delays to cognitive issues. There were no services specifically designed to address Simon's reading difficulties.

Once she discovered that, Melissa didn't bother waiting for the school to test Simon; she took him for a private evaluation. The results showed that Simon, now six years old, tested as "a profound dyslexic with multiple deficits, including OCD (obsessive-compulsive disorder)." With those results in hand, Melissa went to the school and asked for an IEP during the first week of first grade.

Was it the stress of coping with the chaotic kindergarten classroom, on top of his learning issues, that caused Simon to become anxious and develop OCD?

In first grade, Simon's learning issues were further complicated because his attention issues were attributed to ADHD (attention deficit hyperactivity disorder). Simon was put on a medication for ADHD that was "not helpful."

"I think the OCD was his way of taking control of a bad situation," Melissa said. "He was telling himself very negative messages and creating patterns to self-soothe."

The public school didn't seem to be doing anything to help Simon, so Melissa pulled him out in second grade and sent him to a private school for students with language-based learning difficulties in metro Atlanta. Through SB10, the Georgia Special Needs Scholarship Program, parents with children on IEPs may receive eight thousand dollars toward private-school placement. That sounds generous, but it fell far short of the thirty-five-thousand-dollar tuition bill Melissa's family had to pay for private placement.

Her blood still boils when she considers how unfair the scholarship program is. "The school district takes it for granted that parents with means will take their child out and put that child in a private school, and then the public schools don't have to deal with those families," Melissa noted. "But what happens to families that don't have the means to make up the shortfall for a private placement, or the knowledge to get the help their kids need?"

Simon's private-school placement soon proved to be a disaster. His teacher called Melissa almost every afternoon to report on the trouble she'd had with Simon that day. "It was like clockwork. Every afternoon about four, I would get a call with complaints about my child. The teacher would say he just wasn't 'getting it' or paying attention."

The gist of most of these conversations was that the teacher wanted Melissa to put Simon on medication for ADHD because of his misbehavior in the classroom. Previous attempts to do this had failed with Simon because the ADHD medications would heighten his anxiety and OCD.

Finally, the teacher wore Melissa down. She decided to give ADHD medication another shot. The day after starting his new medication, Simon was suspended for throwing erasers at his classmates.

The suspension was five days. When Melissa attempted to bring Simon back to his private school, he said, "I can't come back here."

They tried a reintegration day anyway, at the end of which the assistant head of school cornered Melissa in her office and said, "I don't know what's wrong with your child, but you need to find out."

"She was literally pointing a finger at me, even though I was crying," Melissa said. "She basically accused me of having a child who had something horribly wrong with him."

Melissa immediately enrolled Simon in his public school again. "We went right back into an IEP, so he could at least work with a small group teacher he adored."

Melissa next requested in writing that the school conduct a functional behavior analysis of Simon to see if they could puzzle out how Simon's OCD, ADHD, and learning issues were impacting him in the classroom. In other words, what was the primary problem? Was his anxiety causing him to exhibit OCD? Were his struggles to learn largely because of his attention issues or his dyslexia?

The school put her off, saying things like, "He was so good today, we couldn't collect data for the FBA." They were breaking the law, Melissa knew, not only because they refused to do the analysis, but because "it wasn't even supposed to be the teacher collecting data. It's supposed to be a specialist from the school district."

Simon continued struggling academically in third grade, where he was pulled out of the classroom for small group instruction in math and reading. Melissa was astounded to discover that this teacher "didn't even have a teaching certificate," and was clearly overloaded with too many children in her supposedly "small" group room.

Once again, the students Simon was grouped with in these remediation sessions suffered from multiple health impairments and learning issues; he was one of only two children in the group with language-based learning difficulties. "He was clearly not getting any help specifically with his reading. The teacher simply didn't know how to teach him at all."

Melissa began writing official complaints to the district and hired an advocate. She also continued her own research on special education, averaging around twenty and thirty hours a week between her reading, writing letters to the district, and doing paperwork to document her concerns.

At Simon's third-grade IEP meeting, she wrote a "parental concerns" letter saying that Simon clearly wasn't progressing toward his learning goals. She requested another evaluation. Finally, the school complied.

The results were devastating: "His IQ had dropped by forty percent," Melissa said. "School was literally making my child dumber."

School officials were clearly shirking their responsibility to teach Simon. Melissa and her husband couldn't afford a lawyer, since they'd already lost whatever they'd paid to the private school, and she knew it would take a lot of expensive attorney hours to bring a case against the school district.

All of this was taking a toll on their marriage. Melissa's husband had never been particularly interested in the details of their children's education. "That's very frustrating," she said. "I can't even have a conversation with my husband about what I'm working on. He goes to the office, and when he comes home he wants to focus on mowing the lawn and making sure the cars are running. I don't think he understands how much I know about what has gone wrong with our child."

The upshot? Simon remained at his public school through fifth grade. When it was time for the fifth-grade IEP meeting, Melissa wrote out "all of these new goals that were supposed to be meaningful, but the special education administrator laughed in my face. She thought they were impossible for Simon to achieve. Having her laugh at me like that was a real gut punch. It was so unprofessional of her. My child really needed help, and here was a way to help him. I felt disrespected and diminished."

Melissa's response was to join a dyslexia advocacy group and help create a handbook stipulating exactly how schools should be working with children diagnosed with dyslexia. "If schools provided objective data to parents about how their child's progress is being monitored, it would make it very clear that many students are fundamentally being passed through their education as illiterates. The interventions these children are receiving aren't effective."

That last meeting marked the end of Simon's public school journey. Melissa enrolled him in a different private school "that celebrates children who have learning differences."

Now in seventh grade, Simon went from failing school last year to receiving an award this year for "the most growth and progress" among all students at the school. He is also successfully managing his OCD through a combination of medication and therapy.

"It's like a veil has been lifted off our house," said Melissa. "Because Simon is happier, we all are."

"We're doing the best we can, and that's all we can do."

When the Public School Fails Her Kids,
a Former Elementary School Teacher Tries Homeschooling

After moving from Pennsylvania to Michigan for her husband's job, Grace pulled her kids out of their new elementary school after only four months.

"The services the school offered our kids were a joke," said Grace, the mother of four children, ages two to twelve. "The school was failing our kids."

Although Grace is only in her thirties, she knows a lot about educating children. She met her husband in college, where she earned a degree in elementary school education. As a fourth- and fifth-grade teacher in an urban school district, she learned firsthand that "you can't do it all as a teacher," especially in overcrowded, underfunded schools.

When their oldest son was diagnosed with autism, he stayed in his

Pennsylvania school and received services through the state. Grace opted to quit her job to better manage his care and therapy appointments. By then their second child, Audrey, was also struggling in school. The district paid for Audrey to have an educational evaluation by a psychologist. Her diagnosis: OHI, or "other health impairment," an umbrella term that covers any health condition that might impede learning, including asthma, attention disorders, chronic illnesses, and lead poisoning.

Grace looked the psychologist right in the eye and said, "My daughter's dyslexic, isn't she?"

"I have no doubt," he said.

"But that's not what you wrote down," she pointed out.

"I can't put that on my paper because I'm not a medical doctor," he said.

Grace had to work hard to hang on to her temper. "Then what are we doing here? I don't understand why you did the testing if it won't actually help my child. Why didn't they send us to see a doctor?"

"That would cost too much money," the psychologist said. "We can't do that."

Grace was furious, but decided to do her own research on the best methods for teaching her daughter to read, and asked for these special services during Audrey's IEP meeting. The Pennsylvania school agreed to provide the resources needed to help her learn.

Not long after that, however, Grace's husband, a pastor, was assigned to a new church in Michigan, about an hour north of Detroit. Grace assumed the IEP would transfer, and diligently brought a copy of that, plus copies of her children's school and health records when she went to register them at their new elementary school.

However, the new school in Michigan informed her that test results done out of state couldn't be accepted; her children would need to be reevaluated by the district's own specialists. This meant having new psych evaluations done on her two older children—a time-consuming process that meant months would go by before the school would even sit down and talk about what special education resources they could provide.

Once all of the forms were completed and Grace saw the services the Michigan school provided, she was in for another rude awakening: "The services this school offered were far worse than what we were receiving in Pennsylvania. It was a mess."

For instance, Audrey was pulled out of classes during core subjects for inadequate interventions. The general education teachers would leave the work that Audrey had missed on her desk, "expecting her to complete it on her own."

Grace knew that Audrey wasn't yet capable of completing assignments in spelling and reading fluency. Besides, she'd missed the lessons, so how could she be expected to even know what was going on?

When Grace complained to the school principal, "he'd feed you something to your face, and then do something different," she said. "Like, he'd say, 'I'm going to talk to the teachers about seeing if we can provide something different, or do the service differently,' or whatever, and then he would pat the team on the back and say 'good job' to each of us, but nothing changed. Audrey was literally coming home every day crying because she couldn't get her work done."

By late fall, Grace was fed up and lost her temper completely during Audrey's IEP meetings. She remembers one particular meeting where a teacher tried to get her to calm down, saying, "We need to speak kindly." But Grace had "flipped a switch. I was really angry."

The teacher continued to try and placate Grace, saying, "We're doing the best we can, and that's all we can do."

Grace glared at the school officials gathered in the room, then decided the teacher was right. These people didn't really care about her children, only the tax dollars they brought into the district and the district's graduation rates. She thought, too, about the high school kids who came to her husband's church who couldn't read or write, and knew she didn't want her children to turn out like that.

It was clear to Grace that she was going to have to pull her children out of school and teach them herself.

She began talking to friends who homeschooled their children, joined homeschooling Facebook groups, and did her own research online. Michigan has no reporting system for people who homeschool; all she had to do was write a letter to the school district stating her intent to teach her children at home.

Before the holidays were over, Grace had ordered the curriculum materials she needed to teach not only regular classroom lessons, but specialized reading instruction for Audrey. "It was kind of a piecemeal process," she admitted, "because I needed to fill in the gaps in their education."

It was also expensive, but she found a way around that by ordering used materials and then selling them when she was done. She estimates that she probably spent about four thousand dollars on her initial setup for homeschooling all her children. This year, she spent much less, no more than $2,500 on books and other curricular items for her three school-aged children, plus a few things for her preschooler. On the other hand, she saves money on things like school lunches, field trips, driving the kids to school, and expensive "must have" school supplies.

She knows some people who feel that the cost of homeschooling is a deterrent, "But I would argue that our overall costs are lower," Grace said.

The days have fallen into a good rhythm now. First thing in the morning, Grace's older children play with the younger ones while she works one-on-one with the Barton Reading and Spelling System curriculum— one geared toward teaching children who struggle with reading—for the first half hour of every day with Audrey. Then Grace rotates subject lessons with all the children, working with each in turn while the others are doing independent work. Her children have plenty of social interactions through their neighborhood friends and church groups, and she describes them as "very social."

"The best thing about homeschooling is that you can tailor the curriculum to your children's needs," she said. "Plus, we actually have the time and freedom to fit in the structured Barton system for Audrey." She noted that when Audrey was in a public school, she'd come home at four o'clock too tired to do any additional work on her reading.

She and Audrey fight occasionally over her reading instruction, especially when Audrey gets frustrated because she can't read better. "But we fight with sweetness," said Grace. "We just keep reminding her that it's in her best interests to read, because you have to read to do anything, even drive a car. If you can't read, you can't function as an adult."

In fact, that's Grace's main goal: "We want our children to function as adults." In addition to teaching them academic lessons, she's making sure that they all know how to cook, do laundry, and sew, so that they can care for themselves when they're living independently.

Her biggest complaint is that the public schools look only at graduation rates to see evidence of their success, and continue failing kids. "They think they're doing a good job, but they have no evidence of that."

Grace's Advice:

- If you're interested in homeschooling, there are plenty of resources online to get you started, as well as homeschooling groups on Facebook.
- Homeschooling is cheap to test out. You will see pretty quickly if it's working.
- You can tailor the curriculum to address your child's individual interests and educational needs.

FAULTY ACCOMMODATIONS

"If I bring in a tutor to help your kid read, then I need to allow coaches to come in for kids who aren't good at gymnastics."

Stubborn Minnesota Mom Executes a Plan to Put a Tutor in School

By the time her son Dave hit preschool, Suzie knew something was wrong. "I couldn't put my finger on the problem until first grade, when the teacher told me Dave looks like he's working, keeping his head down and acting busy so nobody would notice, but his work packets were a mess of jumbled letters."

The teacher's suggestion when she realized what Dave was doing? "We should hold him back."

Suzie, a former high school teacher, refused. "That's a knee-jerk reaction. I said no, we're not going to hold him back until we do some type of testing for a learning disability. Of course it would have been easier for the school to hold him back than to test him, but how would that get at the root of the problem? If they kept holding my son back until he learned to read and write, he probably would have stayed in first grade forever."

Suzie knew the school couldn't hold a student back without parent permission. She also knew she could circumvent the school and get Dave tested faster if she paid for it herself. The sooner the better, in her mind, because Dave was "already being punished for something he had no control over." For instance, if he couldn't finish his worksheets in time, Dave's teacher held him inside during recess.

"I had to pull that information out of Dave. You know, I'd ask how his day went, and he'd say, 'Oh, I didn't get to go to recess today because I had to stay in and do my work.'"

Suzie was livid. How could holding her son in from recess at such a young age possibly improve his ability to pay attention and do his work? But she kept a tight rein on her rage and focused on the big game ahead. Her first goal was to get documentation showing that her son needed to learn differently. Her best ally was Dave's pediatrician.

At the next doctor's appointment, Suzie expressed her concerns. The pediatrician was sympathetic and referred them to a diagnostic center half an hour away, for a private educational evaluation. The testing came back confirming the source of Dave's various struggles. In addition to dyslexia, Dave had ADHD, and he was also having trouble seeing to do his work because he needed glasses, too.

"It was such a relief to get answers," said Suzie "Most people don't know that they have a right to question things or get a second opinion."

Now that Suzie had a report, she could execute a plan for Dave's academic success. It was clear that the school was going to continue denyIng her son resources, so this no-nonsense, problem-solving mom doubled down on her mission to find them herself. After getting Dave a prescription for glasses, she gathered a list of tutors certified in the Orton-Gillingham (OG) approach, a program tailored to children with dyslexia, and one Suzie was familiar with from her own time as a teacher. She also took Dave back to the doctor to get a prescription that would address his ADHD and allow him to focus better.

But the school wouldn't provide a trained reading specialist for Dave. Suzie and her family live in a small town nearly an hour from Minneapolis, yet with a lot of determination and "by some miracle," she located an OG-certified tutor willing to drive half an hour to meet Suzie at the library during Dave's allocated school lunchtime.

Although she'd given up teaching to stay home once Dave's little sister was born, the time was still a major sacrifice on Suzie's part. She was not only dedicating five mornings a week to Dave's tutoring, but either paying for childcare for his little sister or bringing the toddler along in the car and entertaining her in the library during Dave's tutoring session. Then she had to bring Dave back to school and pray that traffic wouldn't make them late. If they were late, Dave would miss more key work and fall further behind; as it was, he was already missing recess and lunch with his friends.

Her decision to hire a tutor had a domino effect. Before long, half a dozen other parents whose children had dyslexia but weren't getting appropriate services through the school were also bringing their children for OG tutoring at the library. This was a hardship not only on the parents, but for the students, who had to miss lunch and recess. That's when Suzie went into problem-solving mode again and approached the principal to ask about having the tutor come into the school, making it clear that the parents would continue to pay for tutoring.

"She still said no," Suzie said.

The principal's reasoning went like this: "She told me that if we had a tutor come in because my son couldn't read very well, then she'd have to bring in a gymnastics coach if someone came to her and said their daughter couldn't do gymnastics very well."

Suzie didn't know whether to laugh or cry. She went to the superintendent and told her what the principal had said. "I was loaded for bear," she said. Ultimately, she received permission from the school district to bring the tutor to school—provided the parents paid for both the tutoring and a rental fee for the room being used, which would free the school from any possible legal liabilities associated with having a non-staff member work on-site.

Suzie wasn't completely satisfied with this solution, but she and the other parents were determined to get the tutor into the school, and ready to do whatever it took. "I wanted to offer them the path of least resistance because that meant faster help for my son."

"She can't be dyslexic because she is in a dual-language program."

Mom Hits a Wall Fighting Excuses around Two Languages as Cause for Reading Delays

Samantha's son, Christian, was in fourth grade when he came home in tears, saying he'd raised his hand when the teacher asked the class how to spell "cone."

"He spelled it with a *K*, and everybody laughed," said Samantha, a university professor in Chicago. "One of his friends said, 'Christian, did you drink the water in Flint, Michigan? You're so stupid, you must have lead poisoning.'"

This memory still rips her apart, because it was the first time Samantha realized, "Okay, I have to do something to help Christian learn how to read." It never occurred to her that Christian's school should be offering her son extra support.

"I didn't have anyone to talk to about learning disabilities," she said.

They also weren't aware of any family history that might explain the struggles Christian and his younger sister, Rosa, were having in school. That's because Samantha and her husband, also a professor, adopted both children from Guatemala when they were each six months old—Christian in 2005 and Rosa in 2007—and the children aren't related to one another by blood. Since they were adopted at such a young age, they had some exposure to Spanish, but English was the only language spoken in their home in the States. In school Christian followed an English-only path, while Rosa entered a dual-language program in kindergarten, where the emphasis was on Spanish.

"When you adopt kids, you have to learn who they are as they grow," said Samantha. "Our children are the complete opposite of my husband and me, and of each other, too. For instance, Christian is really gifted at sports. He's the fastest runner, and just made the high school soccer team. Rosa is gifted in singing and dancing. I have none of those skills."

Christian had exhibited some learning issues in his private, "very academic" kindergarten when the family lived in Wisconsin. There, the teacher strongly suggested that Samantha hire a tutor, but Samantha couldn't see the point of paying for both private school and a tutor, especially when the academic pressure at the school was so intense. "I felt like the public school setting might be better," she said.

At the same time, her intuition told her something was wrong. "There are these little things you notice as a parent, and you start to panic. That's my whole thing, really. I worried every day that something was wrong and I didn't know how to fix it, because I'm such a problem-solver."

Her only real goal with Christian was for him to be happy, she added. "He'd already had such a traumatic beginning in life in Guatemala."

Christian performed slightly better in public school, largely because his second-grade teacher worked closely to support him, but things fell apart again in third grade as the words got bigger and he was tested on reading comprehension. Samantha and her husband took both Christian and Rosa, who was exhibiting severe behavioral issues, for neuropsychological testing. "At that point, I didn't know anything about IEPs or 504 plans, or anything else."

The reports showed that Christian had separation anxiety and moderate dyslexia, which led to a 504 plan. "I was happy that the school agreed to give him some accommodations. It was only later that I realized they didn't list dyslexia as a disability."

Unfortunately, although Christian did begin receiving some support with a special education teacher as a result of the 504, "it wasn't even the right reading intervention."

Rosa, too, tested as having dyslexia, as well as having ADHD. She was put on medication for her attention issues, but her reading didn't improve. Samantha used the skills she'd developed as an academic researcher to ferret out other possible solutions and discovered a camp for dyslexic kids in Colorado. She and her husband both had the summer off, so they packed up the entire family, including the dog, and moved to Colorado, where they rented a house so the children could attend the camp. The camp helped both children read better, and did wonders for Christian's self-esteem.

When they returned in September, Christian began middle school in a "big school with lots of different teachers, and all kinds of problems." Samantha continued her research, and found a dyslexia center that offered the Orton-Gillingham reading program. "It sounded so great, but it was really expensive," she said.

They signed Christian up for the Institute despite the cost. It was a mistake. "By this time, our son was a teenager going through puberty and he really loved sports," said Samantha. "It was too hard for him to go to tutoring sessions after being at school all day and going to cross-country practice."

Christian's anxiety also made him shy in class. In seventh grade it became abundantly clear just how shy he was—and how little his teachers understood about him—when Christian failed a class and lost his sports eligibility. "Christian was devastated," Samantha said, "so I called the teacher to find out what was going on. When I asked if she'd tried to help Christian or ever talked to him about his grades, she said flippantly that she didn't know he spoke English."

This was six weeks into the school year, Samantha thought, "How could a teacher not know what language he speaks while engaging the classroom?" It felt as if she were making assumptions about his preferred language based on racial stereotypes, not on quality interactions. At the same time, his language arts teacher refused to accept the accommodation, under his 504 plan, that specified Christian's spelling shouldn't count against him on tests.

That was when Samantha hit the wall. "I had an emotional reaction at the next 504 meeting," she said. "I cried and got angry and demanded a school evaluation." Afterward, several people who'd been at the meeting suggested that Samantha run for a school board seat.

The school complied the results of Christian's school evaluation but they weren't what she'd hoped for: he tested "above average" and still didn't qualify for the school's IEP criteria. Newly infuriated, Samantha channeled her rage into advocacy work through Decoding Dyslexia Illinois, a grassroots movement organized by families concerned with limited access to educational interventions for language-based learning disabilities. She also started voicing her concerns about all of the ways in which the public schools were failing both Christian and Rosa, who was doing a dual-language program in Spanish and English.

"I was like an enraged mama tiger when I went to the state capitol to speak on behalf of Decoding Dyslexia," said Samantha.

She continued diligently researching dyslexia, devouring books on it, and pushing the public library to have the same books available as a resource for other parents—all while maintaining her full-time job. Christian's anxiety and self-esteem issues, though improving, were exacerbated occasionally by things like school physicals. Once, for example, he had a concussion screening that demanded he say the months of the year in order and then backward—something he couldn't do.

"He told me he failed the concussion test," Samantha said, "and he was really worried they wouldn't let him play sports."

Now that Christian is entering high school, many of his friends are taking AP classes, but he's afraid to take them because he thinks he'll be unable to cope with the work. The school still isn't giving him any sort of systematic reading program. Samantha believes this is a financial decision, and she's doing what she can to help support Christian academically.

"The academic bar was pretty low in middle school," she said. "Now I just don't know how hard to push him."

Sports continue to be one place where Christian finds inspiration. Recently he did a mini-triathalon in town and won his age group. In preparing for the event, Christian watched Ironman videos and found one where an athlete talked about his own dyslexia and the importance of working hard in school and finding a passion. Christian took the message to heart.

Rosa, who has Spanish emphasized in her dual-language program, is still struggling to read, Samantha said. "I try to help her look for patterns, but she gets so frustrated and anxious that she just starts skipping and adding words," said Samantha.

Because Rosa qualified for Medicaid, it covered the costs of occupational and visual therapy to address all of her disabilities, including dyslexia. She was put on an IEP in elementary school, after her neuropsych evaluation revealed health impairments and speech issues.

Despite the IEP, Samantha said the teachers continue to blame Rosa's reading issues on speaking two languages in the dual-language program and refused to test her or give her any special reading program. "One teacher actually said that Rosa can't be dyslexic because she's in a dual-language program," she said. "Whenever I said my daughter had dyslexia, they just kind of ignored me and said that dual-language learners are always behind in reading, and then catch up."

Even worse, Rosa's special education teacher said to her, "Your mom thinks you have dyslexia, but I know you don't."

Samantha took Rosa back for another independent evaluation. This time, the psychologist showed that she had dyscalculia, a learning disability in math, as well as dyslexia and ADHD. Despite this, the teachers continued their denials.

"They said she wasn't paying attention," Samantha said, "and asked if Rosa was taking medicine to deal with the ADHD." One teacher actually laughed about Rosa and said, "We never know who we're going to get from one day to the next with Rosa."

Samantha pushed back by hiring an advocate, who counseled her to demand to see copies of all of the testing the school had done. "She said she'd help me put it all into a binder, and that was the first step."

Next, Samantha brought the binder to her school district's assistant superintendent of special education and told him about all of the things the school needed to do to support her children, like training teachers in Orton-Gillingham. He promised to order it, but in the meantime, Samantha learned how to use the OG program and tutor Rosa herself.

"Parents think that once we get this beautiful, shiny new IEP, the red carpet is going to roll out for our kids," Samantha said, "but that's just not the case."

Samantha has decided her best avenue going forward is to "play nice." She's working with several teachers and the assistant superintendent to improve the ways in which dyslexia is addressed in the classroom, including special training, for which they can earn certification credits.

"I do understand the financial hurdles this district faces," she said, "but they have to do better than this. There are so many kids in our district who can't even afford food. How can they afford tutors?"

> Samantha's Advice:
>
> - Show love and tenacity when working on behalf of your children.
> - Look into starting a charter school in your school district that might offer better resources and support for dyslexia.
> - Become involved with your district's board of education and offer solutions as well as highlighting problems.
> - Make a website for your area, and ask other parents to contribute resources and solutions that have helped them address their children's reading issues.

"Your IEP is a bunch of bullshit. You can read just fine."

Even an Expert in the Special Education Trenches Failed to Beat the System

Hannah always dreamed of a career in teaching, and knew she'd become a special education teacher in her home state of Colorado because she loves the challenge of thinking outside the box. "You've got to always be on your toes and keep trying different things, to find something that works for kids with a variety of different learning capabilities," she said.

Sadly, Hannah's professional training in special education wasn't enough to help her beat the broken public school system when she was fighting for her youngest son, William.

William was a tougher kid than most. He was an overactive, impulsive toddler who fought with other children in preschool. As a school district insider, Hannah was able to have him evaluated early so that he could receive speech and language therapy, "but they couldn't do much with him because he was so hyper and couldn't focus," she was told.

It was clear to everyone that William had ADHD. In fact, the school told Hannah that her son "wasn't available for learning" because he was too hyper to sit still.

Hannah was conflicted. She didn't want to question William's teachers too hard or criticize them too often, since she was a professional working in the same district. What if pushing her personal agenda rattled the wrong cages and her job ended up on the line? She was trying to help many children besides her own son. Between the stress of her job and the ongoing frustration she felt for William, she often found herself coming home in tears.

She kept hoping his teachers would find strategies for his academic success. William was pushed up the grade ladder through kindergarten, first grade, and second grade. "Eventually, nobody would bother working with him," she said. "I felt like they could have tried harder, but his teachers called his condition a 'learned helplessness.' They felt like he was too difficult to teach, and just kind of gave up."

She finally worked up the courage to file an official dispute with the district, despite what it might do to her professional standing. "Basically, we were contending that the same goals were being repeated on William's IEP every year, and he was making no progress toward any of them."

A judge determined that Hannah's case had merit, and ordered the district to pony up money for a private education. Hannah found a private academy within the Denver city limits for children with learning disabilities and enrolled William there. Unfortunately, the district only had to pay about eight thousand dollars, the equivalent of their per-pupil operating revenue. "That didn't even make a dent in the private school's annual tuition," said Hannah, since tuition costs were more than thirty thousand dollars. "Still, William loved it there, so we struggled to make up the twenty-two-thousand-dollar gap in tuition." That required the family to make other sacrifices and live close to the bone.

Hannah's fears for her son's future reached a breaking point when she read a book called *The Short Bus: A Journey Beyond Normal* by Jonathan Mooney. "There's a scene in this book where the author is twelve years old and sitting on the floor of his garage, crying and contemplating suicide. I freaked out and wondered if I'd put my son in a bad environment, one that would lead him to see himself as abnormal. My son is very bright and articulate. He'll talk to people like an adult, and they can't understand why he can't read or write. What he has is an invisible disability."

This revelation about William's disability inspired Hannah to advocate even more passionately for her son. Since the ADHD presented as the main issue affecting William's ability to learn, they tried various medications. But these, too, proved problematic. "We went through the whole alphabet of drugs. Every one of them had different side effects, like leaving him horribly skinny or turning him into a zombie," she said. "But I knew he'd get into even more trouble in school if he didn't take them, so he did."

After two years, Hannah and her husband decided to put William back in a public middle school, "partly because we were broke, and partly because he was growing socially and emotionally."

Drawing on her own expertise in special education, Hannah tried to make sure that William received accommodations specified by his IEP, like being allowed extra time to take tests and copies of class notes, but he still was never given any formal reading instruction to address his learning differences in middle school. Even though she was now a special education administrator serving the entire school district, Hannah couldn't change the fact that her son's IEP was legally required to spotlight only ADHD or SLD (specific learning disability) for interventions, but not both.

Hannah knew the help William was receiving wasn't enough to help him succeed. When other kids said he was stupid, or teachers claimed he wasn't trying hard enough, William would hold it together in school, then come home and sob. Once, he slammed the door as he arrived at the house and howled, "'I just want to learn to read! Why can't anyone just teach me to read?'" Her heart broke for him.

Hannah began having nightmares, as her guilt and anxiety mounted. "I should have intervened with his teachers and fought harder for services sooner. I hated having this conflict between my career and helping my child. The guilt was absolutely killing me," she remembered.

Things improved a little in ninth and tenth grade, when William's English classes had a team-teaching approach, with one "regular" classroom teacher and another teacher skilled in offering special strategies for students who struggled with reading and writing.

In eleventh grade, however, his English class had only one teacher. When Hannah asked why, the response was that it was "too expensive" to provide team teaching. Even as an insider in the school district, she struggled to disprove this argument and failed.

William's one true love was football. He'd started playing when he was in elementary school, and by high school he was a star on the team. In eleventh grade, the coach—also his science teacher, and a man William had always looked up to and tried his hardest for on the field— called him out in front of the whole class. This time it wasn't to praise William as a star player, but to call him "lazy" for failing a test.

"Your IEP is a bunch of bullshit," the coach said. "You can read just fine."

William had suffered years of belittling comments from teachers and other students. "That was his big breaking point—suffering public humiliation from someone he trusted," Hannah said. "His attitude changed after that. He'd always been a handful, but he started getting into trouble at school and being suspended for stupid reasons. The school was clearly done with him."

Hannah was furious about the suspensions. At one point, William was kicked out of school for more than ten days. Hannah knew this was a clear violation of policy, yet her hands were tied.

Another time, she found out William had been suspended only when he told her; nobody at the school had bothered to call and inform her—another breach of school rules. "Nobody seemed to care about William or about the rules," she said, noting that, since the Columbine school shooting, Colorado schools were quick to remove angry kids from school when they perceived a risk, and her son stood over six feet tall and could be intimidating. "I found out when it was already done, and it was too late for me to do anything about it."

As a last-ditch effort to save William's academic record and his self-esteem, Hannah opted to enroll him in a district-run alternative school for his senior year, thinking the smaller classes would help him learn. "That wasn't one of my stellar decisions," she said. "He started getting into trouble constantly because he really felt like a bad kid now. Things got really ugly."

By October of his senior year, William was only able to read at a fifth-grade level, something that magnified Hannah's painful guilt still more. "How could I call myself an expert in special education, when my own professional training failed to help my child achieve more than very basic literacy skills? The out-of-the-box strategies I loved to use with other children when I went into this profession were completely lost on my own child."

The only positive note was that William had accumulated more than enough credits to graduate early, since the alternative school had given him extra reading classes and an additional set of electives. "He couldn't get out fast enough," Hannah said.

William hopes to become a firefighter or emergency medical technician, but he hasn't been able to pass the necessary exams because of his poor reading skills. His ongoing struggles to forge a future and a life of independence have caused him to be plagued by self-doubt.

"I failed him," Hannah said. "We all failed him, and it breaks my heart."

"She's too young to test."

An Art Historian Keeps Her Eye on the Prize:
Getting Individualized School Services for Her Daughter

Marie, a New York art historian, writer and curator, experienced one of her most exciting parenting moments when she saw her daughter, then eight, reading by herself. "Lily Anne was able to read without stopping, figuring out words she'd never seen before. That's when I knew she had broken through a wall."

This moment was a long time coming. Breaking through that wall required Marie to create an intricate road map for her child's success—a map that she was able to draw only after spending countless hours doing research. Since then, she has offered pro bono advice to more than two hundred families whose children have dyslexia, to help them develop road maps of their own.

"The schools seem to purposely make the process of getting your child diagnosed and receiving the right services opaque and obstructionist," Marie said. "There are no shortcuts to that. You have to keep your eye on the prize and advocate for your child."

For Marie, the prize was getting Lily Anne individualized educational interventions that would help her learn to read. "It wasn't an outlandish prize, but in the public school system, it can be tough to achieve. Schools often don't want to acknowledge dyslexia as a disability because it's difficult to remediate."

Even in the best-case scenarios, where schools do small group interventions with special education teachers, that small group often consists of children with distinct learning challenges—say, one with attention disorders, one who is cognitively impaired, and one who is dyslexic. "Now the teacher has to remediate children with three different disabilities. The children might not be at the same reading levels, and the teacher herself might be trained to address a completely different disability, like autism," she said. "How is she going to teach a child with dyslexia? It's too complicated, and to me that's unacceptable, because you're denying these children access to a free and appropriate education."

Although Marie holds a master's degree in art history and comes from a family of "educational privilege"—her father is a professor—she was "really ill-equipped" to recognize that her daughter had dyslexia. "That was one of the first hurdles I had to overcome, because we're severely undereducated about dyslexia as a society."

Her own education in understanding dyslexia began when her daughter was in kindergarten and couldn't acquire the basic pre-reading skills, despite being in an inclusive class with a special education teacher who worked hard to help her. "The whole-language approach just wasn't successful with Lily Anne," Marie said.

Despite this, the school said Lily Anne was "too young to be tested for any disabilities" and recommended that she be promoted, calling her performance "average."

Marie and her husband, who holds a fine arts degree and also struggled in school, rejected this idea. "We felt it didn't make sense for her to go forward without having any real literacy."

It was also troubling to see how depressed their daughter was. Not quite six years old, Lily Anne called herself "stupid" because she couldn't read like most of her classmates, despite being a highly motivated student who could pay attention in class and follow instructions, given the right support.

"She kind of fell on her face," Marie said, "and it was so sad to see how school broke her spirit."

They opted to pull her out of the district and put her in a progressive private school, where she repeated kindergarten and completed first and second grade. Her self-esteem blossomed, but her reading skills continued to lag.

"At the private alternative schools, they use different methodologies to teach," Marie said. Lily Anne's teachers used a multisensory approach to reading, but this didn't work for her. All her peers, meanwhile, were reading by now.

At that point, Marie enlisted the support of a tutor. "It wasn't fair for her to be going into second grade not knowing how to read, when everyone else was reading."

Through a combination of personal connections with teachers and good luck, Marie found the perfect tutor: a New York City special education teacher who was certified in explicit intervention strategies for children with dyslexia. At the start of the summer, Lily Anne could only read three sight words; within two weeks, she was reading books suitable for kindergarten and first grade.

At long last, Marie had found the outline for her road map. Now she just had to color in the details. "What the tutor did was show us how this kind of specialized teaching strategy made a difference," she explained. They continued working with the tutor after the start of the school year.

As time went by, it felt wrong for Marie to be paying for private school as well as tutoring. She began to explore what services might be available through her public school district. At the tutor's suggestion, Marie called a top legal firm for families whose children need special education. The attorney spent six hours on the phone with Marie—free of charge—and counseled her to pay for an IEE (independent educational evaluation), saying that would give her "clinical evidence" for her child's disability. They could then take that report to the school district, "and they'd have to design an IEP around that."

"The results of the evaluation opened up the skies for us," said Marie. "Lily Anne had moderate dyslexia, and the report specifically named her areas of weakness and gave us recommendations for educational interventions."

While Marie was happy to have Lily Anne's disability identified, she also felt completely stressed. "The burden was on me to learn the ins and outs of this disability if I was going to advocate for my daughter," she said. Her husband, though supportive, also felt traumatized by his own school experiences and overwhelmed by the complicated process of trying to help their daughter.

The problem, as Marie saw it, is that schools—private and public— "don't understand dyslexia, don't identify it, and don't train new teachers to remediate it. You're on your own."

So this art historian did what she does best: tapped into creative inspiration.

"I decided to learn everything about the disability I could as a layperson, so I asked a lot of questions and relied on a community of experts to answer them."

Those experts included the lawyer, other educational advocates, and the clinician who'd tested Lily Anne. Marie also talked to other parents who had children with dyslexia, read journal articles and books, and scoured free online resources for legal advice and teaching strategies designed specifically to address dyslexia, like the Orton-Gillingham reading program. In the first six months after her daughter's diagnosis, Marie devoted three full days a week to this research for well over six months—on top of her full-time job.

Most parents aren't prepared to navigate the invisible red tape that trips up their efforts to help their own children, Marie said. For instance, "It wasn't until I spoke with outside experts that I learned it's actually my right to ask for an educational evaluation from the school district, and then I had to learn the hard way that the evaluation didn't really qualify my child for anything."

Another hurdle is that schools tend to inform parents that a child is receiving "academic intervention services" and "making progress" without quantifying what that "progress" actually means. In addition, children can't qualify for special services unless the regular classroom teachers prove that they've "already tried to remediate the child, and that hasn't worked." School officials may also tell parents that a child qualifies as having a special learning disability—but that's a general term, and doesn't necessarily mean your child will get the best services for her particular diagnosis.

"Most parents don't realize there are so many steps to getting your child identified and classified. Even if they do manage to make it through those steps, they're often told the child isn't eligible for services. It's important to be informed at every single step," she explained. "There are no shortcuts to having your child become eligible for special education services. You have to be equipped to micromanage your child's IEP, goals, services, accommodations, and modifications." Once she realized how difficult the process was even for her—a woman with an advanced education and a stable financial situation—Marie became determined to help other parents find their way through the system.

Marie and her husband decided a public school would be better equipped to provide Lily Anne with special services once they had the evaluation done. They'd had an ISP—individualized service plan—done for the progressive school, and brought that and the IEE to the public school. "This provided a road map for what her disability was, as well as educational recommendations. These were put into her IEP along with goals specific to her areas of weakness. Then Marie and the school worked together to develop accommodations and modifications."

She was grateful the public school accepted the existing documentation. In the end, Marie said the IEE was "the real weapon," providing a focus for everyone to work together. "It's like we came in the side door, because we'd already had the testing done."

They got lucky again at the public school, because Lily Anne was paired with a special education teacher Marie described as "brilliant, compassionate, very smart, and trained." Even with a legal document like an ISP or IEE, Marie is aware that parents can't legally dictate the types of teachers or interventions the school assigns to your child.

"Who your child gets for a teacher is kind of a crap shoot," she said. "Every time my child enters a new grade, I have no guarantee that the person who's working with her will be trained to teach children with dyslexia."

Marie firmly believes that serving kids with dyslexia is a civil rights issue. "Not having a teacher specially trained in effective strategies for children with dyslexia "is like saying, 'I have a ramp, but guess what? The ramp isn't at the right angle for your child's wheelchair,'" she explained. "That results in misery for everyone: the child, the teacher, and the parents."

For now, Lily Anne has a "gold standard" of an IEP and teachers who are willing to work together to help her. Now in fifth grade, Marie says she's "really flying" through school.

Meanwhile, Marie makes it her mission to help other parents of children with dyslexia draw and color their own road maps, even through the blockades and detours thrown up by the schools. She doesn't charge people for her advocacy work because the people who helped her were so generous with their time and she wants to pay that back.

"I tell every parent that it's important for you to become informed about dyslexia to the best of your ability. This is an invisible disability that nobody understands well enough, and it's not served properly," she observed. "I'm constantly vigilant, and I expect to be like this until my daughter is done with college. No one else is going to fight as hard for your child as you will. Keep your eye on the prize."

Marie's Advice:

- Use trustworthy online resources like university websites, discussion groups, and dyslexia advocacy organizations to inform yourself about dyslexia.
- Understand the law as it relates to evaluations and special educational services based on your child's type of school.
- Keep your eyes on the prize: literacy for your child.

POOR TEACHER TRAINING

Being a teacher is one of the hardest jobs in the world, and I admire those who can do it. The purpose of this section is not to critique the teachers but the system that fails them. There are a variety of circumstances that contribute to the invisible red tape, such as the administrative lack of knowledge or funding to provide specialized training in their education preparation programs or on-the-job training in the science of reading.

"I don't know how to teach somebody with dyslexia."

"This mother runs as fast as she can to stay ahead of the system."

In his Oregon public elementary school, Stephen's problems with reading and writing became increasingly evident to his mom, Lindsay. Even when she pointed them out to his teachers, though, they continued to pass him. "His first-grade teacher kept saying, 'Nope, there's nothing wrong, he's doing great.'"

Then Stephen started second grade, and everything changed. His teacher, Caroline, noticed something was up in the first month of school, and alerted Lindsay that Stephen should probably be tested. Lindsay and her husband scraped together enough money to take Stephen to Oregon Health & Science University for testing. Lindsay watched the testing through a two-way mirror, her heart pounding as her little boy did his best to answer questions with a worried frown. It was all she could do not to jump through the mirror to help him.

The evaluation results showed that Stephen had reading, writing, and spelling difficulties. Lindsay's initial reaction was anger. "I knew something was wrong, but nobody would listen to me," Lindsay says. When she explained the report to Stephen, he decided to call himself "dyslexic" when he described the results to friends.

Lindsay has always done things by the book, so she still had trouble using the word "dyslexia," since it was never used in the independent evaluation. Still, she was determined to find Stephen help. Her next step was to personally deliver the report to the school, saying, "Here. I did it for you. No more stalling." She wanted results, and she wanted them immediately.

However, the school insisted on conducting their own separate tests first. She assumed they found the same results, because Stephen was soon pulled out of class regularly and sent to the school's Learning Resource Center for support. She was hopeful that things would soon turn around for him.

Her hopes spiraled downward as the months rolled by with little improvement in Stephen's reading ability. It wasn't until the following year, when Lindsay sat down at the next IEP meeting with a new principal, Stephen's teacher, and the teacher in the Learning Resource Center, that she realized the truth: The Learning Resource Center, where Stephen was supposedly being taught strategies to help him read, mostly served English as a Second Language (ESL) students. The interventions Stephen received weren't designed for a child with his particular language learning issues, but for students whose first language was not English.

"I don't know how to teach somebody with dyslexia," admitted the Learning Resource teacher.

Lindsay described it as a nightmare. "I mean, why were they pulling Stephen out of class, if he would actually get more help *in* the classroom?" she wondered. It was especially galling because this was a Title I school, with federal funding to train teachers in special education.

She asked that Stephen be pulled out of the Learning Resource Center and receive one-on-one help with reading specialists instead. By then he was in sixth grade, and Lindsay worried whether he'd lose his services the next year in middle school. Plus, with a rotating schedule of subjects and six different teachers a day, how would the school keep the teachers informed about Stephen's needs and accommodations?

Lindsay had always been an efficient person. Rather than confront the school and run into more bureaucratic roadblocks, she took matters into her own hands. Going forward, she decided she would inform the teachers herself about Stephen's needs. So, as Stephen started seventh grade, she emailed every one of his teachers and told them about his 504, clearly spelling out his accommodations. She continued sending these "cheat sheets" throughout Stephen's high school years, to stay ahead of the system.

This strategy worked. In eighth grade, the teacher actually came up to Stephen and asked if he needed help reading the assignment. "A lot of the teachers asked him what they could do to help him be successful. That really boosted his self-esteem."

Lindsay was glad to have the 504 in place whenever she had to push back against certain teachers. One stipulation among Stephen's accommodations was that he be allowed to sit at the front of the room, for instance, to make sure that he could see the board clearly. When a teacher tried to force Stephen to sit somewhere else, saying there were other students who needed to be at the front of the room, Lindsay said, "Sure, but I bet you don't have a legal agreement with them, do you?"

By high school, Lindsay had taught Stephen to advocate for himself. Once, when a teacher didn't give him written notes for a lecture—something his accommodations specified—Stephen went to the teacher and asked for them, saying, "Hey, you know I need a copy of those."

"I felt like the high school diploma was ours as well as Stephen's," Lindsay said, "because even when he was in college, if he got into a situation he couldn't handle, he'd contact me and we'd deal with it together. He's the only one of my three kids who earned a college degree, and I didn't earn my college degree until I was forty-five, so this was something really special to accomplish."

Lindsay added that her good friend Caroline, Stephen's second-grade teacher, had been the catalyst. "She was the one who told me that I needed to be the mama bear and stand up for my son, and I'm so glad she did," Lindsay said.

Lindsay's Advice:

- Once your child starts school, send a note ahead of time to introduce yourself and establish a friendly relationship. Adopt a teamwork approach.
- Whether your child has an IEP or 504, make sure you have written documentation to support everything your child needs in terms of accommodations, and share those with the teachers directly.

Sample Welcome Letter to Teachers—Back to School

Hello!

I wanted to introduce myself and tell you a little bit about a student you will have this term. My name is ___ and my son/daughter's name is ___, student ID# ___.

The reason I'm emailing you is that my student is on an IEP/504 plan with accommodations. I know that his/her counselor will be forwarding you a copy of this plan but it usually takes time to get it to you and by then valuable time may be lost. Therefore I've attached a copy of the plan for your convenience. He/she is aware of the accommodations and I'd like to request that you make these available as requested.

As you know, the IEP/504 plan is a legal agreement between the school district and my student, so I appreciate your assistance in advance.

If you have any questions or concerns, feel free to reply to this email or contact me at the phone number listed below.

Thanks, _____

"We're giving multisensory support with smelly markers."

A Skilled Social Worker's Desperate Search for Trained Teachers

Lori, a social worker who lives outside Omaha, Nebraska, described herself as a "painfully shy child" who found her voice when she had to stand up for others who were being mistreated, like school friends who were bullied. Lori always knew she would adopt children as another way of giving back to society, and she carried her courage and determination to serve others into her adult life as a social worker with kids who struggled to stay in school. Today she's a part-time advocate on behalf of children with special needs.

Her advocacy began on behalf of her adopted son, Peter, whose early school struggles led Lori to have him evaluated for special education services in first grade. Peter qualified for services under the general umbrella of "specific learning disability," and by second grade he was being pulled out of class for a reading program. In addition, Lori and her husband, a hearing-impaired special education teacher, paid for a private tutor and helped Peter in the evenings. By third grade, however, Peter was still floundering.

So was his teacher. "Her class was weighed down with kids who were getting pull-out services, and she had a student teacher," said Lori. "I think she was having trouble juggling it all."

The teacher began blaming Peter for not being able to keep up. "We got the whole 'lazy kid' thing," said Lori.

Lori began looking at different school options. When Peter told the teacher he might be switching schools, things went from bad to worse. Peter actually wrote the teacher's comment down on a Post-it note: "It doesn't matter if you change schools. You're still not good."

"It was heartbreaking," Lori said. "Really, incredibly painful. Peter took a hit to his self-esteem because of all the blame and shame."

Things were so toxic in that teacher's classroom that Lori pulled Peter out of third grade during winter break. The district offered a couple of different curriculum options; Lori chose a public school with Montessori elements, and Peter started there after the break.

It was a good change. "Peter loved the school's hands-on projects, and his teacher was really welcoming and awesome," said Lori.

Unfortunately, Peter's new school had a mixed class of fourth and fifth graders, and expectations changed at that level, with less access to hands-on materials. Peter began falling even further behind his classmates.

Lori's courage never flagged. She and her husband had been doing their own research. Although nobody had tested Peter and offered a diagnosis of dyslexia, they suspected that was the problem. They had learned about the Orton-Gillingham (OG) reading program, and at the next IEP meeting, they told the district facilitator that Peter needed it.

"The facilitator said they did have one of those programs," said Lori, who lives in a rural Nebraska town. "The school told me that he needed to show he was not thriving with one reading program before moving on to another one."

Lori was bewildered by this logic. It sounded as if they wanted to spend precious days of Stephen's education waiting for him to fail to propose another solution. He probably would, too, given that the reading program they chose had been designed not for students with learning disabilities, but for students who had "low exposure" to reading in the home—something Peter definitely didn't have.

"How long will it take before you decide the program fails?" Lori demanded.

"Six to eight weeks," the facilitator said.

Lori told the woman she'd put it on her calendar and would expect a meeting at that point.

It came as no surprise to Lori that the reading program the district chose didn't help Peter. They agreed to try the version of the OG reading program that the district had access to; unfortunately, the teacher wasn't adequately trained in that program and clearly didn't like it much. "They tried it for a couple of months," Lori said, "and then they wanted to switch back to the previous program."

That IEP meeting turned ugly fast, because Lori was determined to stand her ground. "When they said they were going to stop the OG program and revert back to the program that didn't work—we had documentation from them saying how it had failed—my husband and I both told them that was ridiculous."

The IEP team teachers said it wasn't up to parents to choose the reading program. "Only the members of the IEP team can make that call," they said.

Lori's temper caught fire. "I'm a social worker and my husband's a special ed teacher, yet they obviously saw themselves as the trained professionals and felt like they didn't have to listen to us as Peter's parents. I can't even think of the words for what I was feeling. I just knew I was tired of advocating nicely. That was when we really started to question everything they said they were doing to help Peter."

When she asked the IEP team leader to describe exactly what strategies they were employing to help Peter read, "the leader said she'd been looking on Pinterest for ideas," and offered to keep using "aspects" of the OG reading program in combination with the first reading program. They were also going to use a "multisensory" learning approach for Peter.

"Multisensory" was clearly an educational buzzword for this team, Lori discovered, because when she asked what they meant, they fumbled through an explanation. Finally the teacher said they were using "smelly markers" as a multisensory tool.

"You know, that's when everything crumbled for us," Lori said. "There was no consistency in their approach to teaching Peter. No fidelity, which research shows is the key to success. They were just mashing all these different things together in a sort of special education stew to get us off their backs."

The teachers also refused to put programming information in writing, Lori added, "because that gave them the flexibility to change the programming without the IEP team's input." She'd only find out the curriculum had changed for Peter when he brought different things to work on at home.

At the end of fourth grade, when it was time for Peter's re-evaluation through the school district, Lori requested a full evaluation by the speech pathologist. The results of the evaluation led Peter's IEP team to suggest adding LiPS (Lindamood Phoneme Sequencing), a program more intensive than traditional phonics programs, to his interventions.

Things got even more confrontational between Lori and the IEP team when she started asking them to explain their data and prove these strategies were effective. When the team suddenly couldn't find the right answers on the mood board they'd carefully crafted, "We just wanted it to end. They kept throwing more and more stuff at Peter and confusing the heck out of him, when all he needed was a simple reading program that would give him the strategy for breaking words down."

Lori's sister was homeschooling her children; when Lori told her about the latest showdown with Peter's IEP team, she asked why Lori didn't just teach Peter at home. "You're already doing it after school anyway," her sister pointed out.

Lori had been looking at private schools, but knew they were financially out of reach. Now she thought about what her sister had suggested, and decided to try it.

To prepare for homeschooling, they also paid for a more complete, independent evaluation for Peter. As they'd suspected, Peter has dyslexia. "Honestly, it was hugely emotional when the psychologist told us the results. She really made us feel heard, and turned the dyslexia diagnosis into something tangible, something that's on paper, so we can say 'this is what he has.' He can now take this diagnosis all the way through college and get the support he needs."

Lori and her husband homeschooled Peter during fifth grade. There were positive aspects to homeschooling, in that it allowed Peter to take frequent breaks and helped Lori "chunk the material into smaller, more digestible bits of information." Homeschooling also gave Peter opportunities to delve deeper into subjects that interested him. He made significant progress, but there were things, like science labs and sports, that he missed.

With middle school approaching, Peter had one more shot at a new start. That's when Lori and her husband did something drastic: They sold their house and moved to a different location a few miles away so Peter could start middle school "with the other newbies" in a district known for offering specific, individualized instruction, with fidelity, to students with learning disabilities.

She knew this not only because her husband had graduated from that district, but because Lori had become involved in the Nebraska Dyslexia Association and PTI (Parent Training and Information) Nebraska. "I knew this district was doing a lot of teacher training," Lori said. "The teachers and administrators stress that they want to partner with us, not work against us. That's the culture of this particular school district, and it makes all the difference. We were in a toxic school district and we had to get out. I just became really angry with paying taxes in a district that wasn't serving up to twenty percent of the kids, like Peter, who have dyslexia."

Lori's Advice:

- Fight for better teacher training on dyslexia and the science of reading.
- Join your local Parent Training Information and Dyslexia Association groups to get the information you need broken down into understandable language and get support from other parents, experts, and advocates.

"We're not trained to teach kids with dyslexia."

A Software Engineer Finds Bugs in the School System

Nicole's son, Richie, was returning to public school in his small northern Nevada city after spending a year in a private school for kids with learning disabilities. Richie and Nicole were both excited about this new start, but when Nicole, a software engineer, went to the "meet and greet" before the first day of school, she suffered a rude shock.

"I'd heard a lot of great things about the new special ed teacher, but when I introduced myself and asked how many kids were going to be in her class, she said, 'I don't know. I just got here.'" Nicole then asked if the woman was going to be Richie's case worker, and received the same rude response.

"Well, do you know what you'll be working on this year?" Nicole asked.

"I don't know anything," the woman repeated.

A few days later, the teacher called Nicole to introduce herself. "Clearly, she didn't remember me," said Nicole, who reminded the woman that Richie's IEP meeting was scheduled for the following week.

"Really?" the teacher said. "I don't know the process. I haven't done SPED in this state before, so I don't know how it works."

Nicole was taken aback—for one thing, no teacher should use "SPED" with parents, she thought—but she bravely forged ahead, trying to reprogram the conversation so it would run in a more positive direction. "Well, the school psychologist will send an evaluation for services, and I'd like to schedule a meeting with you so we can go over the results before the IEP meeting," she said.

"I don't know the process," the woman repeated. "I haven't done SPED in years."

Nicole hung up the phone and sat down in shock. Was there nobody in all of northern Nevada who was qualified to teach special education? Was this really the best her son's school had to offer?

Then again, she had been down this road before. Richie had struggled to learn to read, so he was put in a first-grade intervention program. His teacher had approached Nicole in a parking lot after school and said he suspected Richie had dyslexia. "I said, what? That can't possibly be it. With my rudimentary understanding of dyslexia, I thought it meant Richie would be writing words backward or something."

Nicole asked the first-grade teacher if she could get Richie screened for dyslexia through the school district. "Nope, sorry, we don't do that here. You have to do it independently," the teacher had said.

Next, she tried the school district. "No, we don't have anyone qualified to do that here," she was told.

"Well, who do I see to get my son evaluated?" she asked. "Can you give me a recommendation?"

They couldn't, or wouldn't, so Nicole surfed the web for answers. "I wasn't sure if I needed a psychologist or neurologist, a psychiatrist, or a pediatrician," she said. "I really didn't know what to do."

Still, she hoped things would get better. "I'm an expert in my field, and I expected the teachers to be experts in education," she said. "I trusted the school district to have resources to help my son, just like they'd have a nurse available if a kid has diabetes or gets hurt on the playground. I wanted someone to tell me that they knew exactly how to teach him."

But that never happened. Richie's academic struggles continued in second and third grade. Finally Nicole found a psychologist to evaluate him. When the psychologist confirmed the dyslexia diagnosis, "I said, great. He's already in special ed. Now that we have a diagnosis, the teachers can help him."

She told both Richie's general education teacher and his special education teacher about the report. "Their responses were exactly the same. They said, 'We're not trained for that. I'm sorry. I can put the report in his file if you want, but other than that, there's nothing we can really do.'"

And when it came to checking the box that said dyslexia on the IEP forms, the school told the teacher not to do it. She was told to check the box marked "specific learning disability" instead.

Richie was growing increasingly frustrated with his schoolwork. Homework assignments took three hours, even with his mother's help. Nicole began doing research on dyslexia, spending a dozen hours or more each week trying to educate herself about effective teaching strategies. "I didn't know if I was going to have to teach him, what my legal rights were, or whether there were other schools that would be better."

At one point, she discovered the Orton-Gillingham reading program and thought it sounded ideal for Richie. She called the school district to ask if any of the elementary schools offered it.

"They said no, but they did offer the Barton Reading and Spelling program, which used the OG approach to reading instruction. I said great, where?"

Nowhere, it turns out. School principals were required to purchase the Barton Reading program materials and see that their teachers were trained in using them. But not a single principal had done that.

By fourth grade, Richie was "miserable, incredibly stressed, and full of anxiety," she said. "He was getting pulled out of class for special education that wasn't effective, and when he'd go back to class, the teacher wouldn't explain what was going on, and he'd be lost. It was horrible. He'd bang his head on the table because he was so frustrated. They weren't doing anything to teach him how to read more effectively."

In addition, the teachers were completely ignoring or even violating Richie's IEP. One of the accommodations, for instance, was that Richie should have questions read to him on tests. When Nicole asked Richie if that had happened after he took a test one day, he said no.

"The teacher told me that if I had questions, I should ask a friend," Richie said.

"Did you?" Nicole asked.

"No. I'm not going to ask anybody. They're going to think I'm stupid if I do that," he said.

That was one of the many breaking points for Nicole. "I felt defeated. Angry. Deflated. And so sad for Richie."

She found a tiny private school also in the northern part of the state, about half an hour away, that accepted Richie for fifth grade. The school was run by two special ed teachers "who were fed up with the ridiculousness of the school system," she said.

These teachers used the Wilson Reading program with Richie. He thrived in the school, and Nicole thought the price tag, though steep— nearly $1100 a month—was well worth it to repair her son's self-esteem. After a year, though, Richie missed his friends and felt ready to try public school again. Nicole and her husband, who is a chemical engineer and researcher, had the money to pay private tuition, but it was still a sacrifice. The family agreed to have Richie move back to the public school in sixth grade and give it another try.

That's when Nicole met the special ed teacher at the meet and greet. Now she's afraid things will be exactly like they were before; recently, for instance, Richie came home from school "all excited," saying that English is his favorite class. When she asked why, he explained that the teacher had given them an assignment to write an essay of three to five paragraphs. One of his friends in the special ed class had only written one sentence. The other had written nothing more than his name.

"But I already wrote six paragraphs," Richie crowed. Once again, they were giving him work that was too easy, instead of challenging him.

Nicole has hired an advocate—one of the teachers from Richie's private school—to come with her to Richie's next IEP meeting, but Nicole was still pondering the idea of reprogramming Richie's education completely by moving him to another school with more resources and better-trained teachers.

"I think a lot of parents don't know what to do. They accept what the teachers say and don't question anything. I'm an anomaly here," she said. "A mother who works full-time and understands technology. We're at the high end of the education spectrum and the socioeconomic spectrum."

Despite this fact, even Nicole, an expert engineer, hasn't been able to debug the school system. "I'm worried that my son will turn back into that poor, stressed-out kid again if we stay here."

Nicole's Advice:

- Get an outside formal evaluation of your child as soon as you suspect there's a problem, and make the school check off all relevant boxes for learning disabilities in the IEP.
- Never go to IEP meetings alone. Hire an advocate, or, if you can't afford one, bring along a parent who is familiar with the school and the legislation protecting your child's right to an education.

"Your son has behavioral issues and needs a special school placement."

A Black Mom Discovers That Teachers Are Biased Against Her Son

Shandra and her son, a high school sophomore, "get up with the roosters" every weekday morning so that Shandra can drive Donald to a school bus pickup point an hour away from their home in rural Maryland. He then commutes another two hours by himself to his private school, while she goes on to her full-time job in health-care regulation.

Afternoons are just as long and complicated. Donald plays sports after school, so he doesn't arrive at the pickup point until early evening. Either his father or one of his grandparents picks him up and drives the last hour back to the house. His dad, a law enforcement official, switched to working night shifts to help out with driving, which means he and Shandra scarcely see each other, and Donald's grandparents retired from their own jobs so they could be more available.

These aren't the only sacrifices the family is making to support Donald's academic success. There's the financial hit, too: Donald's private school costs twenty-nine thousand dollars annually, leaving little money left over for extras like vacations.

"This whole thing has nearly destroyed our family," Shandra said.

By "this whole thing," she means the dragged-out battle she fought with Donald's public school to get him the academic support he needed after he was evaluated for reading issues and found to have dyslexia. "The school system failed us," she said, leaving them little choice but to leave the district and seek alternative educational solutions.

Donald is an only child who was born with a faulty heart. His academic problems may be linked to a congenital genetic heart defect (CHD), said Shandra, given that research studies show that children with CHD are much more likely to receive special education services than children born without defects.

"Every time he had to be put on a heart and lung machine, it essentially created a traumatic brain injury," she said. "We knew that would affect him academically at some point."

Donald's learning issues surfaced early, and Shandra was quick to spot them. Although neither side of the family has a history of dyslexia, her own family included a long line of teachers, and academic achievement has always been a prized family value.

Shandra brought Donald's learning issues to his teacher's attention at the start of kindergarten, but it took the school another six months to test him. Based on that evaluation, Donald was diagnosed with SLD (specific learning disabilities), and he began seeing resource teachers on a pull-out basis for extra help, while remaining in a general education classroom.

Things quickly slid downhill. By the time Donald was in second grade, funding issues had caused a reduction in staff. "Donald went from getting pull-out services three times a week to only once a week by second grade," Shandra said. "The reading specialist was shared among three schools." She knew this meant the teacher would be stretched thin, and couldn't know the students as well on an individual basis.

His teachers claimed that Donald was "making improvements," but he continued to fail the state's standardized tests. Meanwhile, teachers were complaining about Donald's classroom behavior, and pressed Shandra to see her pediatrician about medication for ADHD.

This infuriated her. "They were basically diagnosing my son with behavioral issues, and they weren't qualified to do that," she said.

Shandra gave ADHD medication a try despite her misgivings, but nothing changed. When Donald entered fifth grade, things fell apart completely. He was in a class of thirty-nine students who moved between two teachers, one for math and science, and the other for all other academic subjects. The science teacher was "something of an ally," who recognized that Donald "learned differently."

But the other teacher clearly had issues with Donald. She sent notes home about his behavior on a near-daily basis, and often sent Donald to the principal's office. Shandra sat in on countless IEP meetings to discuss the problems, and it became clear to her that "they didn't even know what dyslexia was, let alone have the staff to teach kids who had it."

School officials suggested that she send Donald to a different school in the area, one that specialized in children with behavior issues, but Shandra refused. As she saw it, this was the school's way of ridding itself of children who seemed to have serious behavioral issues without first evaluating them appropriately. "They didn't want to accept the reality that something else was going on. But I wasn't going to do that."

Especially not after visiting the alternative school, Shandra added, and seeing for herself that the students there were either out of control or "so heavily medicated that they were like zombies."

They were also predominantly black, like Donald.

That's when Shandra realized she was facing not only a school that was short on staff and resources, but also one that was culturally biased against black children. Donald was one of very few black children "in a mostly Caucasian school," she said, "and all of his teachers were Caucasian except one," the sympathetic science and math teacher, who was Asian American.

To put it bluntly, "there was a stigma in this particular school," Shandra said. "They believed that black kids were probably going to be failures, especially black boys."

Shandra also confronted a not-so-subtle racist attitude from school officials. "They'd be rude to me in meetings," she said. "They'd disrespect me, telling me I don't know what I'm talking about, or be mad because I'd bring someone in from the outside. I guess they thought I was stupid."

By this time, she had taken Donald for a private evaluation and knew that he was struggling in school in large part because he had dyslexia. She'd also joined an advocacy group for dyslexia to inform herself about the disability and how to help her son succeed in school, which by now Donald hated.

"His self-esteem was really low," she said.

Shandra even spoke to a lawyer about suing the school for not providing appropriate services, hoping to earn compensation to pay for moving Donald to a private school for children with learning disabilities. The attorney was honest enough to tell her that the chances of winning such a case were only fifty-fifty, "and that I'd be buying him a new car by the time we finished," with the money it would cost her in legal fees.

That's when Shandra gave up and jumped ship. She found a middle school for students with learning disabilities, and Donald immediately felt at home "with kids just like him" on his first visit. He did so well at the school that she and her family continued making sacrifices to pay for the private high school he attends now.

The events of the past few years have been "life-changing," Shandra acknowledged. Her family had to make the decision between leaving Donald in their local school district "and letting him struggle for the next seven years of school," or finding an alternative, albeit a costly one.

"We had to put aside a lot of things," she said, but they were able to make it work because of supportive friends and family members. And the sacrifices have been well worth it, she said, given that the prison system is filled with a disproportionate number of young black men who can't read, and she wasn't about to take the risk that Donald would become one of them.

One day, she hopes to see her son go to college, knowing that "he had parents who cared enough to make the necessary sacrifices to help him succeed in school—and in society."

Shandra's Advice:

- Knowledge is power. Be aware of any cultural or racial bias your child may be experiencing at school.
- There is no one-size-fits-all educational program for children. Find the one that best suits your child's unique learning needs.
- If you can't afford a specialized school placement, stay on top of your child's academics and keep an open line of communication between yourself, the principal, and your child's teachers.
- Before you sue a school for compensation, calculate what you might lose in legal fees, to determine whether you might be better off simply spending your money on a private placement.

"You can't drop out of my school a third time. That'll make my statistics look really bad."

A School Specialist Battles to Save Her Own Daughter from Suicide

Jackie, a learning disabilities specialist in a wealthy suburb of Washington State, was in the kitchen when her eleven-year-old daughter, Jennifer, came downstairs. "She wasn't crying or screaming, like she sometimes did when it was time to go to school. She just came down one step at a time, really slowly, and then sat on the bottom step with her head in her hands."

Jackie didn't have time for theatrics. She was going to be late for work. "Come on, Jennifer," she said. "Get your shoes on and grab your backpack."

Jennifer didn't move. She looked up at Jackie and said, "Mom, I can't go to school today."

"Yes, you can. You have to go to school today." Jackie's temper was rising. They'd been down this road too many times.

"No, Mom. I can't go to school today."

Jackie tapped a foot impatiently. "Why not?"

"Because I really suck at learning. I've tried, and I just can't learn. I can't, Mom."

At the note of desperation in Jennifer's voice, Jackie's own eyes filled with tears. She dropped her purse and went to sit on the bottom step with Jennifer, putting her arms around her. "You know what? You don't have to go."

"Really?"

"Really. You're not going to school today, and you're not going tomorrow, either. Let's just you and I do school at home, all right?" Jackie said. That very afternoon, she filed the necessary papers to homeschool her daughter.

This moment was a long time coming. Jackie worked in the same upper-middle-class school district where Jennifer was attending elementary school, yet she'd failed to find help for her own daughter.

The problems started early. Jennifer was a bright, articulate, social, artistic preschooler "who had an exuberance for learning," Jackie said, adding that Jennifer seemed especially gifted in math. This all made sense, given that Jackie was an art major in college, and her husband is a design engineer.

Then Jennifer's wonderful first-grade teacher went on maternity leave, Jackie said, "and we went from having a kid who was eager and excited about school, to having one who would wake up and cry and scream and yell and drag her feet about getting on the bus."

As the weeks passed, Jackie found that Jennifer was suddenly unpredictable—either quiet and complacent at the end of the day, or a "raging monster of a kid." She couldn't understand the change.

Because Jackie traveled from school to school in the district, working with different children, she occasionally walked past Jennifer's classroom. One day she was nearby when she heard a teacher yelling at a student. "Haven't your parents worked with you? Don't you know *anything*?" the teacher screamed.

Jackie was horrified, especially when she realized that the yelling was coming from her own daughter's classroom. She crept down the hallway. The classroom door was closed, but through the glass window she saw a scene that made her stomach clench with dread.

"This teacher was bent over with her hands on her hips, leaning over two little kids who looked absolutely terrified," she said. "Their little hands were clenched in fear." One of the kids was Jennifer.

The teacher went on and on, until finally she shouted, "Just get out of here and go outside!" Then she rushed the tearful kids out the door.

Jackie darted back around a corner so she wouldn't be seen. "I was shaking. I didn't know what to do. I'd just seen my child being verbally abused."

Next came a whispered encounter with the school secretary, who said, "Did you know that Jennifer's spending a lot of time in the front office?"

Jackie hadn't known this. "Why?" she'd asked.

"Well, the teacher sends her down often during class because Jennifer doesn't finish her work on time," the secretary said. "I try and work with her, and she always says that she doesn't want to go back to class."

Teachers frequently called Jennifer out in front of her peers, and even occasionally put her work on display as "what not to do." At home, Jennifer began having sleep problems and tantrums. Every night, homework became such a battle that Jackie gave up. Every morning, Jennifer screamed and cried, until the incident on the steps caused Jackie to file homeschooling papers.

They began homeschooling Jennifer at the end of fifth grade, and stuck it out through sixth grade, using a free online K–12 curriculum and materials provided by the state of Washington. By that point, Jackie had grown disillusioned enough with the school district to give up her job there, and was working as a preschool teacher part-time. This made it easier for her to work with Jennifer at home. "At first, we went after whatever she was most interested in, because I wasn't going to push anything academic at this point. I just needed this kid to refocus and get a better sense of who she was."

Jackie began doing online research and realized, with a shock, that Jennifer exhibited the signs of having dyslexia. How could nobody have caught this, or at least suspected it—including her—until now?

When Jackie contacted the teacher monitoring their progress in the online homeschooling program and explained her suspicions, the teacher told Jackie to go to the school district and ask for an evaluation. By then, Jennifer was completing sixth grade, but the experience of homeschooling was so difficult that the entire family agreed that returning to the public school for seventh grade would be better.

Before the start of seventh grade, Jackie went to a school counselor at the middle school and said, "You know, I think she has dyslexia. I'm really concerned about her transition this year. Maybe she should be tested."

The counselor suggested waiting to see how Jennifer did during the first couple of weeks in seventh grade before taking that step, explaining that Jennifer might need that time to transition back to public school.

Seventh grade was "literally the best year for her," Jackie added, with Jennifer passing all her classes and doing well socially. At the start of eighth grade, things imploded again, though Jackie didn't know it right away.

"Because I wasn't hearing from the school, I assumed things were still going well," said Jackie. Then she and her husband attended the annual parent-teacher conferences in November, where they had about ten minutes to speak to each of Jennifer's teachers, and one after the other asked, "Is something going on at home?"

"What do you mean?" Jackie demanded, taken aback by the question.

It turned out that Jennifer was struggling again. She wasn't doing class assignments or homework, and she was failing nearly every class. What's more, she was acting defiant with her teachers. "All I heard during those conferences were negative remarks."

Jackie and her husband called a meeting with Jennifer's team immediately. "That's when we kind of got an earful." Most of the comments had to do with Jennifer not paying attention or doing her work, and having a bad attitude.

Only Jennifer's language arts teacher seemed to like their daughter and enjoy teaching her. "Jennifer's such a bright child, and knows exactly what's going on," he said. "She's my 'go-to' in class because she can sit there and listen to the discussion about a passage we've just read, then summarize it for everyone."

"Wait," Jackie stopped him. "You're saying she's your 'go-to,' but she hasn't turned anything in all year?" She exchanged a glance with her husband. Something was definitely going on with Jennifer that nobody had figured out yet.

The truth was, they were starting to have problems with her at home as well. Jennifer was acting depressed or outright defying house rules. And so they pursued their own outside psych evaluation.

The evaluation showed that Jennifer had ADHD, but her attention issues weren't serious enough to warrant medication. They set her up with a psychologist for therapy. Jennifer also started working with the school counselor, who helped her organize and track homework assignments. However, the feedback from her teachers didn't improve. "They said she still wasn't getting it."

Jackie got a 504 from the school, which gave Jennifer some extra time on tests and projects, but didn't address reading issues, and Jennifer grew increasingly depressed as high school started, and once again began refusing to go to school. She wasn't sleeping; she started having panic attacks.

"We were seeing an explosion of mental health issues as she advanced into the higher grades," Jackie said. "I had no idea if this was because of learning disabilities, attention issues, or low self-esteem from the trauma she experienced in elementary school. I strongly believe that our education system is creating post-traumatic stress in our students with disabilities, because they experience such verbal and emotional abuse from certain teachers."

Basically, because Jennifer had been disciplined so often, been called stupid and lazy, had been sent to the principal's offices numerous times, and had had her work publicly ridiculed, Jackie believed Jennifer now suffered from post-traumatic stress disorder (PTSD), which explained the panic attacks and sleep issues. In addition, Jennifer had started associating with other kids at risk. Instead of hanging out with students who were excelling, she was now friends with other children who were creating challenges in the classroom.

"Kids with behavior problems get demonized by the teachers," Jackie said.

By sophomore year, Jennifer was severely depressed and missing between eighteen and twenty-three days of school each semester. If she did make it to school, Jackie would often receive a phone call from Jennifer, saying she was vomiting in the bathroom because of a panic attack. Jackie would call the school to let them know, and one of the counselors would have to go find her.

At that point, Jackie asked for something to be written into Jennifer's 504 plan stipulating that she could leave the room if a panic attack started during class. "Sometimes the teachers would acknowledge it, and sometimes they wouldn't."

At her wit's end, Jackie gave the school a written notice saying that Jennifer needed to be evaluated for a learning disability, "particularly dyslexia," and cited state laws saying the school district was responsible for evaluations. The school psychologist informed Jackie that they could test for learning disabilities at her request, "but they were pretty sure they weren't going to find any, because Jennifer's really smart and manipulative."

As she left the staff meeting, Jackie confided her worst fears about Jennifer's depression to the preschool director, who had become a friend. "I spilled my guts when she asked how I was doing, because I knew we were close to Jennifer taking her own life."

Those words were prescient. That night, she and her husband agreed to phone their local psych services department the next morning to see if they could move up Jennifer's counseling session, which was scheduled for later in the week. Then they went to bed, exhausted and wrung out.

About one o'clock in the morning, Jennifer woke Jackie, saying, "Mom, I can't stop throwing up."

"Well, don't do it in here," Jackie said. "Go to the bathroom."

She heard Jennifer being sick down the hall and went to her. "Something was wrong. She was shaking hard after vomiting. I thought she might have food poisoning."

When Jackie flipped on the light, she was horrified to see her daughter shaking so hard, it looked like Jennifer was having a seizure. Her eyes rolled back in her head and she collapsed to the floor.

"Oh my God," Jackie cried. "What's going on?"

Jennifer burst into tears. "Please don't get mad at me, Mom, but I took all of my antidepressants and I can't stop throwing up," Jennifer said.

Jackie felt time stop. By then, her husband had joined them in the bathroom. At last, Jackie found her voice and told her husband to call 911, as Jennifer started throwing up again. She sat on the floor with Jennifer until the ambulance arrived.

Because of the suicide attempt, Jennifer was admitted to a mental health facility. Jackie had no idea how to work on Jennifer's "educational stuff" with her hospitalized, so she asked the attendance person in the school district, who had become an ally through the years. "She said I should file a home hospital request so that I could get Jennifer one-on-one services, like tutoring."

There were only six weeks of school left, so the school district agreed to give Jennifer tutoring only for that amount of time. They still hadn't evaluated her for learning disabilities, and nobody seemed sympathetic about the suicide attempt, other than the attendance person.

"Honestly, this made us realize that it's a life-or-death matter, getting Jennifer well again, and our perspective totally shifted. We didn't care about her academics anymore." They found out that Jennifer passed math because the teacher knew how to connect and communicate with her.

Jennifer entered a community college program, since she had enough credits. However, things got even worse on the drive home, when Jennifer turned to her in the car and said, "Mom, I hope you're not mad at me, but I'm really not doing that great at the community college. The only class I'm doing well in now is creative writing, and that's because you're helping me."

Jackie was flabbergasted. "If that's true," she said carefully, trying to keep her voice steady, "then why don't you want to do the testing that your counselor recommended?"

"Because I just don't want to be in special ed," Jennifer said miserably.

At that point, Jackie laid it on the line, telling Jennifer that she definitely needed to be tested because she probably had dyslexia. "If you have a learning disability like dyslexia, there are strategies that we can use to teach you how to read better."

"Oh, I get it," Jennifer said, but Jackie wasn't sure she did.

Due to her previous traumas in school she dropped out of the community college program.

The next year was spent enrolling Jennifer in various private programs, only to see her drop out again. "The public school wasn't working with us at all at this point," said Jackie, who decided to file a complaint about their school district with the Office for Civil Rights about the district's blatant disregard of all legislation in place to give students with disabilities equal access to education. Again, luck was against her: She filed her complaint during the government shutdown of 2013.

During what would have been Jennifer's senior year, she was missing her friends desperately. She wanted one last chance to go to classes with them before everyone parted for college and jobs. Jackie went with her in January to sit down with the school principal and ask if Jennifer could attend school part-time, perhaps signing up just for art and music classes.

"He was like, 'Sure, we'd love to have you participate,' when he talked to Jennifer," said Jackie. Then the principal asked what Jennifer's plan was for the future. "Are you going to continue on at the alternative high school and graduate from the district?" he asked. "Or maybe finish your high school diploma through the community college?"

"Honestly, I don't know," Jennifer said. "I'm still struggling with depression, but I'm feeling better now, like I can concentrate and I'm in control of my anxiety. I just really want to be with my friends this last semester."

"Well, I can't have you dropping out a third time from the school district," the principal said. "It will make my statistics look really bad."

At that point, Jennifer stood up and walked out of the office. Jackie glared at the principal and said, "I can't believe you just said that." Then she and her husband walked out too.

Jennifer spiraled into an even deeper depression after that. A couple of times she said, "Mom, I don't feel safe. You need to take me to the hospital."

At long last, Jackie took Jennifer for independent educational testing and paid for it out of pocket. The results were clear: Jennifer had severe dyslexia and read at a third-grade level. She also had a form of dyscalculia. Although Jackie felt validated by the test results, she couldn't believe that it had taken them nearly eighteen years to get the correct diagnosis.

"It was actually a beautiful moment," she said, "because the person who did the evaluation also has dyslexia, and she had a doctorate. She told Jennifer about the many other people with dyslexia who have succeeded in life."

"That's amazing," Jennifer said. "You mean I'm really not stupid?"

"No," the psychologist said. "You're not stupid."

Just seeing that report changed Jennifer's sense of herself, Jackie said. "It opened up a path to a better situation, because Jennifer knew she was capable of learning."

Jennifer, who had been an elegant and determined figure skater throughout her childhood and teen years, decided to become a figure skating coach after she finished her high school degree. She lived on her own for a time, then moved back home to save money while she went through online mathematics courses offered by Khan Academy. "She wants to do a math placement test so she can get into precalculus," Jackie said, "and from there her plan is to become a computer programmer."

For the first time since she was four years old, Jennifer is excited to go back to school.

Jackie's Advice:

- Be on the lookout for sleep issues, depression, and anxiety in children with dyslexia. Because children with learning disabilities sometimes experience verbal and emotional abuse from teachers who misunderstand them as lazy or defiant, these children can develop post-traumatic stress disorder.
- Some children with dyslexia don't do well in regular school settings. Consider alternatives like online courses and one-on-one tutoring at private learning academies.

FUNDING ISSUES

"There's no funding to offer your daughter additional services."

A School Funding Problem Forces a Single Mom to Choose Tutoring
for Her Daughter Over Her Own Health

As a single mom and hourly hospital worker who struggles to make ends meet even in a small town in rural Iowa, Pam knows what it's like to work hard and live paycheck-to-paycheck. She raised two adopted special needs kids with her ex-husband before her youngest daughter, Tiffany, came along, so Pam also understands how to butt heads with a school system when your child needs special services. Yet even she was shocked by the lack of transparency in school funding.

Her latest fight began when Tiffany experienced problems in pre-school. Pam wanted to believe things would get better on their own. After all, Tiffany's teachers claimed that she was exhibiting "normal developmental delays." When Tiffany's academic progress stalled through first grade, however, Pam asked the school to test her.

"They told me she was too young," said Pam.

She didn't believe it. Pam kept pushing the school to test Tiffany and put her on an IEP, and that summer she took it upon herself to sign Tiffany up for a summer reading recovery program.

The school continued to balk about testing. The reading program did little to help Tiffany's skills. Pam's next move was to make an appointment with a specialist at the University of Iowa, four hours away, to have Tiffany evaluated. Even though the university offered a sliding-scale of fees to low-income families, this was still a costly endeavor. Every hour Pam missed work at the county hospital where she's a nurse's assistant meant another hour without pay.

Still, when Pam received the report, she believed the time was well spent. The evaluation showed that Tiffany had "severe" dyslexia and gave recommendations for accommodations. At least now Pam could take the report to school and finally get Tiffany the help she needed.

That's when she hit another bureaucratic roadblock. "The principal told me they couldn't offer my daughter additional services due to a lack of funding," said Pam. She felt helpless and infuriated. How could there be no money? She knew for a fact that the school gave athletes tutoring when they needed it. Plus, the high school had just paid for a brand-new football field.

"It made me so mad," she said. "Tiffany deserves help as much as any athlete."

From pushing the public schools to provide special services to her two older children, Pam knew that the schools were legally obligated to educate every child. There had to be a way to get Tiffany the interventions she needed to succeed. In search of advice and information, she struggled to get herself to a conference for parents of children with special needs in Iowa the next weekend, despite the financial burden of missing more work hours and funding her own transportation and conference fees. There, she was astounded to learn from a legislator that *schools were supposed to receive money to help establish programs for kids who were struggling to read.*

"I thought about our school's brand-new football field, and put two and two together," said Pam.

She went straight back to the principal and conveyed the information she learned at the convention. "I wanted to know where this money went to," said Pam. "I was told that those figures were not available at that time, which led me to believe they were covering something up."

It's never easy to be a single mom and fight your battles alone, but Pam refused to give up. Enraged by the lack of transparency, she reminded the principal that she'd had an outside evaluation done and now had an official diagnosis of dyslexia for her daughter. Tiffany needed special services to help her read and learn, and the school was legally obligated to provide those services.

"Well, I don't believe it," the principal said. "And we don't have to accept an outside diagnosis here, you know."

Pam dug in her heels. "I warned the principal that my next phone call would be to an attorney at the Department of Education, and that heads were going to roll if he didn't give my daughter the help she deserved."

The principal didn't believe she'd do it, and dared her to pick up the phone. Pam followed through.

Forty-eight hours later, the principal called back, this time to request a meeting to discuss support for her daughter.

"Can we bring some other people?" Pam asked.

This single mom had learned that backup can be essential when you're going up against a Goliath of a school system. At the conference, she'd met with other parents fighting similar battles. She showed up at that school meeting with a representative from the Iowa Education Association and another parent from a dyslexia activist group.

Having this support gave Pam the confidence to spell out exactly what her daughter needed and what she expected the school to do. "Otherwise, you'll have to give us open enrollment to another district that will provide Tiffany with the help she needs," Pam told them.

School officials "kind of hemmed and hawed, and said they'd do research on Pinterest to see what they could do for Tiffany," said Pam, whose response was bewilderment, then outrage. She could only guess they were suggesting Pinterest because it would be a cheap way to find creative reading materials. Eventually, the school tried to put together an intervention strategy, creating a messy folder of outdated, low-priced materials from the State of Iowa, copy-and-pasted into worksheets and reading materials.

What they did helped a bit, but by third grade, Tiffany was still only reading on a first-grade level. "She needed more in-depth, intense help on a consistent basis."

Pam spent more hours doing research, attending school meetings, helping Tiffany at home, and fighting for school services. This meant more missed work, less money, and higher stress. As Pam's income, already modest, continued to plummet, she wrote a post on Facebook saying how frustrated she was with the process of trying to help Tiffany.

To her amazement, a tutor from Minnesota contacted her. After exchanging a few emails, the tutor, who was trained in the well-regarded Barton Reading program for dyslexia, offered to do online tutoring with Tiffany. Pam agreed to try this approach, and was amazed by her daughter's rapid progress with the help of regular Skype tutoring sessions.

Unfortunately, the tutoring wasn't free, and Pam had to make sacrifices to pay for it. She was taking medication for a heart condition; at one point, she convinced her doctor to find a cheaper generic medication so that she could keep paying for her daughter's tutoring sessions.

"Not long after that, I was rushed to the hospital with a heart attack," she said.

She couldn't bear the idea of dying and leaving her little girl motherless. Something had to give. After diligently examining all the local public schools, she found one that specifically provided services to children with learning disabilities. This district could offer Tiffany small classes and special education teachers trained in the Wilson Reading System, another reading program that uses the Orton-Gillingham Approach to instruction.

Pam went back out onto the field and convinced the school district to grant them open enrollment privileges, which would allow Tiffany to attend that particular school even though it was in a different part of town.

It was a tough game, but this determined single mom finally outplayed her opponents. Tiffany is now in seventh grade in that district, and reading at a fifth-grade level.

"She has really flourished here," said Pam. "The struggle was worth it."

PAM'S ADVICE:

- Ask for transparency of funding. It's your right as a taxpayer to know how your district budgets its money.
- Explore other public schools in your district, as well as other districts in your area, and determine which public schools offer the best services for your child. Then petition for open enrollment.
- Connect online with other parents, associations, and experts for more resources.

"We don't say the word 'dyslexia' here."

One Hands-On Mom Discovers That Her Son's Charter School Educates Only the Chosen Few

The minute Cheryl stepped onto the campus of the new charter school near her suburban Arizona neighborhood, she set her sights on getting her son Brian admitted. Brian was then in a university-run preschool, where he'd been tested and found, at four years old, to have the vocabulary of a ten-year-old.

"We knew Brian was bright," said Cheryl, a small business owner whose husband works in infrastructure systems. Since Brian showed such early academic promise, she wanted to choose a school that would challenge him and help Brian reach his full potential.

With its gorgeous campus, the charter school seemed like the perfect mix of innovative and challenging curricula, said Cheryl. "I walked through an eighth-grade classroom where the kids were reading Shakespeare and debating about the morality of the Constitution, and I wanted my child to have the ability to reason and discuss heady subjects like that."

She and her husband submitted an application for Brian. When they didn't get in first or second year, they enrolled Brian in a local public school for kindergarten and rolled over their charter school application "to give it a priority status."

Meanwhile, she began noticing that Brian reversed certain letters when he was writing and seemed to have difficulty reading aloud. Cheryl brought up her concerns with his public school kindergarten teacher, who dismissed these things as "normal." Despite the fact that the teacher saw no "red flag" issues, Cheryl remained concerned enough to work with Brian over the summer. That's when she began noticing some other problems, too, like the fact that her son had difficulty understanding basic math concepts, such as increments of time and money.

She was thrilled when Brian was accepted to the charter school the following year for first grade, believing it was the sort of environment where her son's talents would be nurtured and he'd get the support he needed for his learning challenges. She eagerly shared her concerns about Brian's academic issues with his first-grade teacher, certain she'd have an ally.

However, that first parent-teacher conference was a disappointment, she said. "My husband and I walked in and sat down, and the teacher said only about three sentences."

And all of those sentences were positive statements about Brian as a student. Then the teacher stood up, "letting us know the conference was done, and asking if we had any questions as she shook our hands and walked us to the door. That was all the feedback we got."

Cheryl knew from volunteering in her son's classroom that the first-grade children were supposed to have three recess periods daily. One day, Brian mentioned that he wasn't able to go out for recess most days, "because he couldn't complete his copy work assignments that were being put on the board," Cheryl said.

Cheryl was horrified that this was happening without her knowledge. She contacted the teacher and emphasized the importance of recess for Brian as a way of helping him focus in the classroom. The teacher assured her that things were fine, and said that Brian was getting his recess time, explaining that he just had to "finish up some work when he's a little behind on it" before going outside.

Meanwhile, things were going downhill fast with Brian's homework. Rather than taking the expected one hour a night, Brian would take three or four hours to do his spelling and writing assignments—and then only when Cheryl walked him through them. Finally, Cheryl went to his teacher and said she wanted to have Brian tested for dyslexia.

"Oh, we can't say that word," the teacher said with a pained look on her face. "*You* can say it, but we can't say that word."

Cheryl stared at her, bewildered. "I didn't even know how to react." Her initial thought was that perhaps there were state or federal regulations prohibiting teachers "from using verbiage like that." She also had the strange sensation that the teacher was trying to help her in some way, even though she was clearly uncomfortable discussing the topic.

It certainly didn't occur to her that, since the charter school received public funds, she had a legal right to ask the school to test Brian. Besides, Cheryl knew that the school had funding issues. For instance, when Brian was first admitted to the school, Cheryl and her husband had been met with pressure from the school's head of "giving." Along with the enrollment forms they signed for Brian, they were given a form indicating that they could contribute money to the school at the suggested rate of $125 each month or with an upfront contribution of $1500 by check or credit card "as a tax donation."

This seemed very odd to Cheryl. If this was a public school, why was she being pressured to give them money? Besides, as she told the school official, she wanted to wait six months and see if the school would be a "good fit" for Brian before signing the donation form. The giving officer agreed, and followed up with her exactly six months later to ensure that she made good on her word. By now she'd been to enough school meetings and assemblies where school officials reminded parents to "please, please donate" that she was beginning to realize charter schools were more like private schools when it came to funding—relying on donations from alumni and parents to grow their endowments.

This made sense to her. She'd done some research and discovered that charter schools receive less government funding than public schools. "It's not like when you go to a public school, where the state pays a certain amount for teachers' salaries," she noted. "At a charter school, they have to pull from different areas to close the gap in funding."

Cheryl concluded that the school—despite its luxurious facilities and its promise of a "classical education"—probably didn't have the trained teachers or resources to help children with dyslexia. "I think [his teacher] was trying to tell me that if I pushed the fact that my child had dyslexia, we wouldn't be welcome at the school anymore."

Cheryl's concerns for Brian's academic progress drove her to take him for an outside, independent evaluation during first grade, an evaluation that she paid for out of pocket. The testing confirmed not only that Brian had dyslexia, but dyscalculia, a brain-related condition that makes it difficult to learn basic arithmetic, and dysgraphia, a learning disability that affects handwriting and other fine motor skills.

When she took the test results to Brian's teacher, asking if she knew anything about these learning disabilities, the teacher "literally turned and walked away from me, saying, 'No, no, I've never heard of anything like that,' ending the conversation right there."

Thinking the teacher must have been just too busy, Cheryl offered to send her information on these disabilities, and followed through.

A few weeks later, the teacher approached her while Cheryl was volunteering in Brian's classroom, and asked, "Hey, how do you think your son is doing?"

"He seems like he's doing okay," Cheryl said, taken aback. "Is there something that I need to know?"

"Well," the teacher said, "I was testing him today, and we had to pull him out and take him into another room."

"Oh, okay," Cheryl said. "Why? What happened?"

"Well, he just sat there and he wasn't writing anything," the teacher said, "and then he raised his hand and said he couldn't understand the questions and wanted us to read them to him." This was for a multiple-choice test; once the assistant teacher had read the questions to Brian, he could answer everything correctly, but he seemed to have difficulty with reading and comprehending them on his own. The teacher suggested that Cheryl talk to Brian's pediatrician about "a processing issue."

Cheryl thanked her and immediately contacted her pediatrician. When she discovered what a nightmare the medical insurance was to navigate, she decided to take Brian for yet another independent evaluation, this time with a neuropsychologist who could test for processing issues, ADHD, and dyslexia. It was already March, nearly the end of Brian's first year at the charter school. At no point did the teacher suggest that the school could, or should, do the testing.

Brian completed a second round of testing during the summer between first and second grade. This evaluation confirmed that Brian had dyslexia, dysgraphia, and dyscalculia. Cheryl requested a meeting at the charter school before the start of second grade. "I wanted to have a conversation with them about Brian's needs before there were more issues."

She was told the meeting would happen "right away." In the meantime, she sent the test results ahead to the school to keep them in the loop.

The meeting finally took place two days before school began. There, she met Brian's second-grade teacher, who seemed "very supportive" and said "we will find ways to make him successful this year." Cheryl reminded her to talk with Brian's first-grade teacher about the accommodations she'd given Brian during the prior academic year, and walked out of the meeting feeling relieved. "It seemed very positive," she said. "I was thinking that everything's going to be good."

Not long after that, however, she got a message from the new second-grade teacher, saying that Brian's first-grade teacher, who had since been moved to the high school, had not, in fact, documented any of the special accommodations she'd put into place for Brian. Nor had she provided the second-grade teacher with any of Brian's test results or other information about his special needs.

Cheryl was floored by this gap in communication, but she quickly provided what the teacher needed herself.

A few days later, Cheryl happened to stop by the school and saw Brian's first-grade teacher in the hallway. Cheryl greeted her warmly, even trying to hug her, but Brian's teacher ducked out the door. "I've never had anyone run away from me so fast."

Later, Cheryl discovered that the real reason Brian's first-grade teacher was in that building was because the vice principal had called her in to reprimand her for speaking with Cheryl about Brian's special needs. Seeing the tension between the administration and the teacher made Cheryl realize how far they'd go to deny Brian any services at all. She knew she'd have to fight for her son, and hired an educational advocate so she would be more informed and feel less alone.

When Brian's second-grade teacher informed Cheryl that they were going to do an "in-class assessment" of Brian, Cheryl's advocate pulled her aside and said, "They're not doing the formal assessment you asked them to do. This isn't a formal evaluation, and you're entitled to one within a reasonable amount of time by law."

Cheryl called another meeting, where the vice principal apologized for the teacher's conduct, saying "that was not acceptable," and asked Cheryl and her husband to sign the paperwork to do the evaluation. Meanwhile, Brian was given certain modifications and accommodations, like being able to take a break from writing when he was tired, and having red, yellow, and green "stress cards" that he could hold up whenever he felt unable to continue working.

By then, Brian was beginning to feel bullied by his teachers, who continued to place undue expectations on him, especially when it came to writing instruction. Brian became extremely anxious, to the point where he developed symptoms of OCD (obsessive compulsive disorder), like "having to flush the toilet twenty times in a row, and other fun manifestations. We'd never experienced things like that before," Cheryl said, adding that Brian also resisted going to school, saying that he was sick to his stomach, and began self-harming by hitting his own head.

On the day Brian was scheduled to have an evaluation done at school, he was in such a vulnerable emotional state that Cheryl drove him to the school and asked to reschedule the assessment. "He wasn't in the space to cope with it," she said.

The teacher did the assessment anyway. At one point, Brian was asked to write a long letter to his parents that day, and during this writing assessment, he was surrounded by the special ed teacher, the school psychologist, and the teacher's aide. Brian picked up a pencil and started trying to copy what was on the board.

Partway through the test, he broke down and held up his red stress card, representing the highest level of concern, saying, "No, no, no," when he was told he had to keep writing. Brian began to cry as the teachers sat there, and finally begged them to get the nurse to call Cheryl.

When Cheryl picked up the phone, Brian was sobbing, saying, "They made me write the whole thing and they wouldn't help me, and I'm so frustrated and so overwhelmed." Cheryl drove to the school right away. She never made him return, and it took over a month with a psychologist to patch up Brian's broken self-esteem.

"It seems to me that the mission of charter schools isn't to educate all children," Cheryl said. "Their mission is to select children that they want to, and can, educate."

She ignored the threatening phone calls from the school, saying she had to bring Brian back, and instead began investigating private schools. Eventually she hit on the perfect fit for Brian: Prenda, a network of more than eighty free and low-cost microschools, where children meet in small groups and collaborate on core academics and self-paced, creative learning projects with a specially-trained Prenda guide. (See the "Solutions" section of this book for a more thorough description.)

While the Prenda microschool model wasn't specifically designed for children with dyslexia, Cheryl calls it "dyslexia-friendly," because it's a visual curriculum, and the learning takes place with small groups. "Most important," she said, "this is a school model that's not about breaking your children," but about helping them discover and build on their own strengths.

"So many children with dyslexia have found Prenda helpful, that they've started partnering with dyslexia experts to make their curriculum even more dyslexia-friendly," Cheryl said. "It's amazing."

> ### Cheryl's Advice:
>
> If your child has dyslexia, be wary of charter schools. Most won't fund special education because they can pick and choose who to educate. You'll get much better special education services in the public school system.

"We will cause your family undue financial harm if you don't pull your request for another assessment."

A California Mom Blows the Lid Off a Funding Conspiracy

As a shy, quiet child growing up with dyslexia herself, Julie never thought she would become an activist, investigating how her school district stonewalled parents whose children needed special services. Then her son Nick hit sixth grade.

"His anxiety was so bad by then that he ended up with terrible OCD, and literally felt like he might die because everything around him was toxic," said Julie, the mother of three children, who works out of her California home as a computer programmer, and is married to a first responder.

Nick's anxiety had been mushrooming through the years, largely due to "having teachers who didn't understand his struggles and made him cry every day," Julie said. "They were harassing him so bad, he'd come home and roll up into a ball, saying, 'Mommy, I can't do this anymore.'"

Given her own struggles—Julie's own mother is dyslexic, and she herself didn't really learn to read until she was thirty years old—Julie's heart felt like it was shattering. She remembered all too well the shame that came from teachers telling her that she was dumb.

"I knew I wasn't stupid," she said. "I just couldn't do things the way they wanted me to."

Julie recognized signs of her son's dyslexia early on—or thought she did. She asked his public elementary school to test him in third grade. They refused. She asked again in fourth grade. Again, the school refused, even though Nick was struggling to read and write.

"I just thought, oh well, I guess there's nothing they can do because he's not bad enough," Julie said.

Then Nick's fifth-grade teacher wrote to Julie, telling her that Nick should be on a 504 plan—a blueprint, basically, for accommodations. That teacher also documented the various intervention services Nick had been receiving that year.

Meanwhile, Julie had finally convinced the school that they should do an educational assessment. The report had come back saying the results showed Nick didn't qualify for special services. "They said he was just 'slow,'" Julie said.

"Well, 'slow' doesn't happen independently," Julie told them. Then she asked about additional educational assessments, and was asked what sorts of assessments, specifically, she wanted them to do.

"I said, wait, what do you mean? You're the experts!" Julie said. "Then I told them that I wanted Nick tested for dyslexia, and they said they didn't do that."

Next, she asked for an educational psychologist to conduct an IEE (independent educational evaluation). The school complied, and also did a speech and language assessment. When Julie asked about Nick's scores at the next meeting, she was told that the school couldn't give her any, because Nick had not been given an age-inappropriate test.

"But your son is doing great," they said.

At that point, Julie hit the roof. "You did the wrong assessment," she said. "How can you tell me my son is doing great? He can't even read or write! You need to do another speech and language assessment."

That's when the director of special education called Julie into her office and said, "You need to pull your request for the speech and language assessment."

"Why?" Julie demanded.

"We will cause your family undue financial harm if you don't pull your request," the director said.

Julie's jaw nearly hit the floor. "How can you say that? You gave him the wrong test, and you say you can't give me any results. You need to do it again."

"You need to pull your request," the director repeated, "or we'll hire attorneys and take you to due process."

Only later, much later, did Julie uncover the truth: The district had a practice of intimidating and suing parents to make them go away, rather than granting children with special needs the basic literacy services they deserved.

After speaking to many, many parents whose experiences in the school district were similar to her own, Julie realized that this particular school district was "emotionally invested in not providing services for students."

In fact, shortly after that meeting, the school district had sent out a letter to teachers forbidding them to document and share by email any services children were receiving. Nick's teacher had gotten into trouble for doing it, Julie suspected. "The teachers had to play by the rules or they'd lose their jobs, so the teachers became very quiet."

She had one friend with a dyslexic child taken to due process, Julie added, "and the teachers lied under oath and said they never thought her child had any issues."

Meanwhile, Nick entered sixth grade. Although functionally illiterate, he received mostly As on his tests and papers, "when he should have been receiving D minuses," Julie said. "They were inflating his grades and telling me he was doing great, and I'd say, yeah, but he can't read or write."

The district did take Julie and her husband to due process. Before going to court, the school district required mediation sessions. Julie brought in all of the documentation from Nick's teacher, as well as his recent papers and exams. When the district's attorney asked what they were hoping to achieve, Julie tried to make a case for her son deserving more opportunities to reach his full potential.

The attorney stared at her and smiled. "You know, your son is faking it. Anyway, we need more janitors. Look, what do you really want from this meeting?"

"I want you to help my child," Julie said, and shoved one of Nick's homework papers over to the district's representatives seated across the table from her. "Here. My son got a hundred percent on this paper. He's dyslexic and has auditory processing issues. He also struggles with anxiety and attention issues. I want you to read what he wrote right here on the first line. If you can tell us what this says, we'll walk away."

Her opponents stared at the paper. Then they stared at each other. Even his sixth-grade teacher couldn't read what Nick had written. In fact, at eleven years old, Nick's reading and writing skills were dismal. He was still only able to decode at a first-grade level.

"Fine," Julie said coolly. "Take us to due process. We'll have our son tell his side of the story. Let's go to trial."

They spent the next two days in mediation. On the third day, the judge came in and said, "Yeah, I keep telling them they ought to do the right thing, but I don't know if this is going to work."

At that point, Julie's husband kicked his chair back and stood up. At over six feet tall and with his fireman's strong build, he was an intimidating presence. "You tell them that we're leaving and we're ready to go to f*@king court," he told the judge.

"Hold on a second," the judge said, and left the room.

Miraculously, minutes later, she returned and said, "Okay, we're going to settle."

With the settlement money, Julie and her husband put Nick in a private school that offered one-on-one instruction, where he was fortunate to get a skilled teacher who also taught remedial English at the junior college. They also used the settlement money to pay for many hours of intensive, specialized Lindamood-Bell reading instruction for Nick, and Julie bought him assistive technology and trained him on it.

By the time Nick finished eighth grade, he could read at a third-grade level and write a six-page essay. Meanwhile, Julie kept thinking about the horrible process they'd gone through. Even though she'd walked away with a settlement, she was still furious. That's when her life as an activist truly began. She started digging for information, anything she could find about how the school district funded or denied special services, "and I became very, very vocal" at PTA and school board meetings.

"I became that crazy parent who the teachers ignored," she said. Still, she kept pleading with everyone to talk about basic literacy. As she saw it, this wasn't a special ed issue, so much as an issue around the basic rights of all children.

Then one day she met another parent, a woman who was "extremely active" in the PTA. Her daughter was only in first grade, and struggling to learn how to read.

"Your daughter's probably dyslexic," Julie told her. The woman "looked at me like I was crazy and walked away."

Still, Julie couldn't drop the idea of helping other parents in her situation. She started a monthly support group for parents of children with dyslexia, and a Facebook page where parents could share information and resources. She also posted information about how she'd received a settlement.

A few months later, the same woman approached Julie again and said, "You know, I think my daughter's dyslexic." She, too, proceeded to undertake various steps to have her daughter receive testing and services through the school, only to end up fighting the district in court.

The woman won her case with Julie's help. From then on, the two women became friends and co-advocates, scouring everything they could find for information on school district funding and special services, and sharing whatever they found with the growing number of parents who were meeting with them and following them on social media.

One day they stumbled across an article in their local paper showing how the district had spent more than six million dollars on children receiving special education services. When they began combing through the school board notes and agendas, however, they discovered that this money wasn't actually being used to offer programs and services. Rather, part of the account was set aside to pay settlement fees for parents leaving the district, and another considerable pot of money was reserved for a special superintendent's consortium: money to be spent on school district attorneys fighting parents in court, so the district wouldn't have to pay for special education services.

Julie continues to share findings like these with parents, and the community of parents now asking questions about the school's policies toward offering special education services is growing fast. Recently, the school district approved a large settlement for another family, and to date, four children with dyslexia in their district have been placed in a private school that offers specialized reading instruction.

This year, Julie's son is a senior in the public high school he opted to attend so that he could play baseball and "be a normal kid," because there weren't any high schools with programs serving students with dyslexia. When Julie met with the high school's special education director to complain about her son still being functionally illiterate without assistive technology, he told her it was not the school's job to fix her child.

"I know it's not your job to fix my child," Julie shot back, "but it's your job to help remediate his deficits and allow him to live up to his potential."

If she could turn back the clock, Julie wishes she could have had her son's learning differences identified in preschool, so that he could have worked on sounds, blending, and rhyming in kindergarten rather than struggling to write sentences when he didn't have the capacity to do so.

But the past is past, and Julie continues her advocacy work, informing parents and referring those who can't afford private attorney fees to a local group of lawyers willing to take cases pro bono. She also attends every school board meeting and speaks up. "I say, listen, this is a general education problem, not a special education issue. These kids would never be in special education if you provided them with appropriate literacy programs."

Not much has changed. The district continues to be every bit as emotionally invested in fighting parents as parents are in helping their children.

Still, Julie hopes that, one day, there will be enough parent voices asking for the district to do the right thing that they can no longer be ignored.

Julie's Advice:

- Parents must understand what "benchmarks" really mean, because schools and teachers often say a child is fine and "reading at benchmark," or "just below benchmark," knowing that most parents won't know what that means in terms of actual reading skills and comprehension.
- All teachers need to be educated about learning differences and how to identify them.
- Track the money spoken about in public board of education meetings.

SECTION IV

SAVVY SOLUTIONS TO PERSISTENT PROBLEMS

WHERE DO WE GO FROM HERE?

Fighting the opaque, obstructionist school system has left me feeling exhausted, outraged, beaten down, angry, and sometimes all of the above at times. But in spite of it all, I know I'm lucky.

Why? Because I've had the resources to pull my kid out of harm's way. My own mother is a speech pathologist. I have a supportive husband and friends. I have time, money, and a professional career that has taught me how to take a bold, provocative approach to solving problems creatively.

I wrote this book because true educational equality doesn't exist for those who learn differently. My goal isn't only to help parents like me, but also to speak on behalf of parents who face even greater challenges because they lack emotional support, knowledge, or resources.

To everyone reading this book, know this: *I am on your side*, and I invite you to join the dyslexia fight club. No matter where you are on this journey with your child, or what your obstacles may be, you belong, we need you. Keep your eyes on the prize, and you will be surprised by the partners you'll find along the way. Remember that your child can not only succeed in school, but become an enthusiastic, curious learner who will explore—and pursue dreams.

LET'S REVIEW THE FACTS!

After interviewing hundreds of researchers, educational experts, attorneys, and parents, I have uncovered the three key root causes of the dyslexia crisis: underfunding, delayed early intervention support, and the lack of specialized training for teachers and administrators.

The crux of the problem is that public education relies on public funding, and 20 percent of school-aged children are not getting the resources they need. Because dyslexia is typically invisible, two-thirds of children with learning disabilities are not diagnosed at all, much less given access to the resources they need to thrive. And finally, if they are diagnosed, they are typically put in the care of teachers who lack specialized training in the science of reading.

In this section of the book, I'll drill down on why each of these problems exists. Then I'll offer simple, pragmatic steps you can take toward solving these problems that were pulled together from my experience and what I learned from listening to other parents' stories, and interviewing legal, medical, and educational experts.

My hope is that these solutions will have a profound impact not only on your own child's future, but on generations of children to come. Together, we will continue identifying the cracks in our nation's broken educational system and illuminate the path forward for all families of the one in five.

LET'S TALK MONEY FIRST: FUNDING PROBLEMS

"We don't have the money for that" is a common refrain from school administrators, whether we're requesting early intervention, teacher training, or structured literacy programs for our children. We hear it so often that many of us give up and cover the shortfall ourselves, if the financial resources are available. It is illegal for schools to deny resources for accommodations and services due to budget issues. However, instead of dealing with more bureaucracy, we pay for private testing, private tutoring, or, as a last resort, private schools, spending thousands of dollars most of us don't have or didn't plan for.

And all because the federal government isn't doing its damn job.

How the Federal Government Is Like a Deadbeat Dad

When it comes to taking care of children with special needs, the federal government is acting like a deadbeat dad.

Here's why. Back in the 1970s, when IDEA was put into place to ensure the American promise of a free appropriate public education for all children, Congress estimated that it would cost twice as much to educate every student with disabilities as it does to educate general education students. (In other words, if it costs six hundred dollars per year to teach a neurotypical kid to read, it will cost twelve hundred dollars to teach mine.)

The law authorizes the federal government to give only 40 percent of that excess cost to states. But guess what? Even back in 1975, Congress never funded IDEA for the full amount that was authorized when the law was signed.

In other words, states were left to fill in the funding gap.

Since then, we have made some progress in how to educate children who learn differently, but not nearly enough. There is a trickle-down effect to underfunding; most states currently see between 9 and 14 percent of their costs covered by the federal government, significantly less than that promised 40 percent. In my own city, Jersey City, the public schools were operating with a general budget deficit of $125 million at the start of the school year in 2019.

Bottom line: Many schools are already in the red, and that's just the tip of a very nasty iceberg.

Underfunding hurts everyone, because it means smaller staff, fewer resources, and fewer student services of all kinds. School districts are having their school budgets slashed, just as their needs are increasing. In addition to serving more special needs students each year, general education classrooms in many states are bursting. Smaller classes with no more than eighteen students per teacher in grades K–3 had the greatest academic achievement, but we know that class sizes across the U.S. are often larger than this ideal.[1]

The dollar is being asked to educate more kids per class. This dollar is being asked to feed the hungry for the 21 percent of America's children who live below the poverty line.[2] This dollar is being asked to help students who are learning English as a second language and students with mental health struggles as a result of divorce, parental addiction, or neighborhood violence. How much can a dollar stretch to meet all these equally important needs?

The number of special education students served under IDEA has increased by 25 percent in the past twenty years, yet the IDEA program was only funded at 14.6 percent of the 40 percent promised to cover additional costs.[3] Today, about three out of every four students with disabilities are spending at least part of their school days in general education classrooms.[4] Nearly every general education classroom in the country now includes students with disabilities, and school districts are legally responsible for figuring out how to pay for the services these kids need.

How are they supposed to do it?

They can't. Year after year, our country is failing our children.

The Trickle-Down Effect:
What Happens When a Deadbeat Dad Can't Pay?

To simplify: public school budgets fall into two categories, general operations and federal grants. The operating budget has dollars given to your district based on state funding formulas and local tax revenues.

This budget also includes items such as transportation, salaries, and capital improvements.

Federal and grant dollars are given to your state based on the number of free and reduced lunch students, ESL students, and number of special education students they serve. Then, the money travels from the state to local education agencies (LEA)—and that's how it gets tricky. That involves multiple funding sources and student count metrics. For most of this section, I will focus on funding sources.

Many agree that "the current system for funding special education is failing," as researcher Tammy Kolbe of the University of Vermont wrote in her June 2019 report for the National Education Policy Center (NEPC).[5] One of the biggest problems is that it's nearly impossible to estimate the current costs of special education.

She points out that federal policies and laws compel state and local education agencies to provide special education to students with disabilities, but then leave the states to develop their own implementation plans—without having enough money. The states essentially rob Peter to pay Paul, cutting funds from certain worthwhile programs, like music or art, to pay for legally mandated special education services. In the end, all children suffer, as school districts slide deeper and deeper into the red.

"In fact, the existing policy landscape reflects a hodgepodge of fifty distinct state funding policies," she says. "Each of which places different limits on state funding obligations and imposes different requirements for localities wanting to access state funding."

For instance, Wyoming reimburses districts for nearly 100 percent of their special education spending. Others, like Arkansas, fund only a portion of services to the most costly children, like those who need residential placement. California's block grant formula covers about 31 percent of special education costs, while Vermont reimburses almost double.

New Jersey uses a "census-based" funding model to determine how much special education money to spend. Under this system, the state assumes that each district has the same percentage of students who require special education, then applies an additional weight or dollar amount for those students. (Eight states currently use a census-based system.)

In my view, New Jersey should be using the more common multiple student weights system. This model assigns a different weight or dollar amount to each student based on certain factors. The weights can be assigned based on severity of disability (e.g., mild, moderate, or severe); on specific disability (e.g., visually impaired students receive X amount and students with autism receive Y amount); or on the resources that the student receives (e.g., students who are educated in a resource room receive X amount; students who have an aide for part of the day receive Y amount).

As of this writing, eighteen states apply either a single weight or multiple weights to some base-per-pupil funding amount, but there's no clear rationale for how those weights are determined. Seven states also use "resource-based allocation ratios," which means teacher-staff-to-student ratios. These can be generalized across disabilities and student placements, or they may be specific to student need.

And finally, seven states use a flat-weight system that gives the same amount for every student on an IEP or, alternatively, according to a disability type. Like pupil weights, these amounts differ among states: New Hampshire school districts receive an additional $1,956.09 per student with an IEP, while Ohio defines six categories of special education services and assigns each of those a specific dollar amount. *Arizona gets a miserly ten dollars extra per year for each specific language disability student.* Needless to say, outcomes there are especially dire.

Confused Yet? That's Okay. Most People Are.

Local school districts are legally obligated to pay for special education costs not covered by federal or state dollars. That means that each locality must raise additional revenue for these services. This is usually done by cutting other areas of the school budget or by raising taxes.

For example, for every dollar I pay in taxes in Jersey City, 24 cents goes to education according to the 2018 data. Those parents who can, leave Jersey City and seek out districts that value education more and buy into schools with higher property taxes. In the suburb of Cresskill, New Jersey, 58 cents of every dollar goes to education.[6] However, with all the wealth in Jersey City, it's not a matter of a high tax base, but about how we value education and our kids. It's especially dire for those with special needs who critically rely on the funds for services.

Naturally, both of those things raise the ire of taxpayers, and politicians never want to confront these issues, especially during the campaign season.

State funding formulas create the potential for competition among our country's school districts—hence the lack of transparency. For instance, if your state has a weighted student funding formula that links state special education aid to the percentage of students with disabilities, that might compel school districts to "overidentify" students for special education. Fixed-weight amounts, on the other hand, may motivate educators to minimize what's spent on special education programs.

Keep Your Eyes Wide Open:
The Complexity of Charter School Funding

Many parents choose charter schools thinking their child will have more personal attention in a more nurturing environment. This is true up to a point, but as I discovered through my own charter school experience, the charters get their funding from public schools—and the public schools are already struggling.

Think about this. Mark Weber, with a PhD in Education Policy from Rutgers Graduate School, and who is a teacher, blogger, and parent, has tried to clarify the funding systems behind charter schools. He reports this quote from Timothy White, a former board member for the NJ Charter School Association: "[Consider that] charters receive only about 69 percent per-pupil funding. The Ethical Community Charter School (TECCS) in Jersey City, for example, receives only 51 percent of the district per-pupil funding of $9,047 per pupil, compared to $17,859 per pupil for the district. Overall, Jersey City charters receive on average less than 55 percent of the district per pupil funding."[7]

Meanwhile, Weber believes "the Jersey City public schools have to do all sorts of things that the charters don't, like provide transportation, give support to private schools, place extraordinary special education students out-of-district, maintain facilities, and more. It's hard to justify charter schools requesting to receive equivalent funds if they aren't doing equivalent jobs."

As Weber points out, "One of the great secrets of charter school funding in New Jersey is that districts pass funds on to schools using a formula similar to the School Funding Reform Act's formula. Students are 'weighted' according to whether they qualify for free-lunch programs, have a special learning need, or are limited English proficient. The idea is obvious: These students need more funds because they are more expensive to educate. This is how we decide on state aid to schools in every New Jersey district.

"Since TECCS doesn't have as many kids who qualify for the federal lunch program, English as a second language, or have special needs as the Jersey City public schools do, it makes sense that the school doesn't receive as much per-pupil funding as the Jersey City district schools," Weber states. "But that also means that they don't have the same level of special education services available. So how do they serve the kids with these needs when they don't receive [the same amount of] federal funding?"

What Can You Do to Get the Funding You Need?

No matter how confusing these laws may seem, you can make change happen. We need your voice if our students are going to get the education they are legally entitled to by having services and programs funded to the levels needed. I've listed some easy, practical steps that you can take to start fixing our funding problems.

1. **Follow the Money Trail**

   How is your school district spending its special education dollars? The best way to find out is to attend your school district's board of education meetings. If you can't get out at night, go to the superintendent's office and ask for a transcript of the meeting notes. You can also watch a livestream or recorded coverage of board of education meetings online. Pay attention to the discussion of budgets.

   Because you're a taxpayer in your district, you are legally entitled to see a copy of the school district's budget. If you are refused these documents, you can file a Freedom of Information Act (FOIA) request. Find out how at https://www.foia.gov/how-to.html.

2. **Share Your Story**

   When you attend a board of education meeting, share your story of the struggles you and your child are facing. We owe it to our children to educate those who have little experience with learning differences.

   Make allies of your general education friends by sharing your story with them, too. Ask them to speak on your behalf at board of education meetings. We are a minority voice, and school officials are more likely to pay attention to an issue if they believe the larger school community is unified around it.

3. **Join a Civic Organization**

   Recently, I was part of a team that succeeded in pushing for an official audit of our school district's special education budget with the help of a civic organization. I never could have done this alone.

Our group, Jersey City Together, tackles issues like housing affordability, education, public safety, and criminal justice. It's an affiliate of the Industrial Areas Foundation, and you might have a local chapter near you, or another civic organization that can help you effectively air your concerns about special education funding.

4. **Share Local Stories of Failure with Your Legislators**
   Since funding issues begin at the federal level, we can inspire change by communicating directly with our senators and representatives. Let your senator know by email, letter, or in person that the school budget isn't big enough to uphold the federal government's promise to students with disabilities, and tell your senator to support the NEA's continued push to fully fund the federal commitment to special education. You can also contact your county's department of education and local legislators to learn more about how your area is spending and tracking special education dollars in real time.

EARLY INTERVENTION SERVICES: TOO LITTLE, TOO LATE, OR JUST PLAIN WRONG

In a February 2017 report, the National Center for Learning Disabilities (NCLD) found that one in five students have learning disabilities, but only about a third of these kids are diagnosed and given plans to help them.[8]

You can accurately diagnose dyslexia by age five. (For reference, most kids are fluent readers by age seven.) Only 6.6 percent of kids are identified with SLD by age six, but most kids can be helped if they are identified and given support, which can create a solid foundation of learning early that stays with them. Ola Ozernov-Palchik and Nadine

Gaab of Harvard Graduate School of Education define this as the dys-lexia paradox: the gap between the earliest time at which identification is possible and the time at which identification and treatment typically occur—which can preclude effective intervention.[9]

However, there are so many struggling readers who need help and aren't identified early. The fact that they don't get it soon enough means they're much more at risk for experiencing academic, social, and emo-tional difficulties in later grades. In fact, the NCLD reports that children who don't read well in third grade are four times more likely to leave school without a diploma, compared to proficient readers.[10]

Let's look at how this problem of early intervention begins and solu-tions to fix it.

The Problem Starts When Parents Bury Our Heads in the Sand

In this country, millions of kids do not have the ability to read. According to the National Assessment of Educational Progress (NAEP), one third of fourth-grade students can't read at even a basic level. That number decreases only slightly to 24 percent for eighth graders. How do we let these kids slip through the cracks?

Researchers, experts, teachers, and parents agree that identifying children with dyslexia early on, and providing intervention services as soon as possible, is the best way to keep kids on a path to academic success. When at-risk beginning readers receive intensive early reading intervention, 56 percent to 92 percent of these children achieve average reading ability.[11]

A common thread I found among the hundreds of parents I inter-viewed for this book was that their children were denied these services early on. Or, if they received services, they were too little, delivered too late, or the wrong kind.

How did we reach this dismal state of affairs? As always, the answer is complicated.

Sometimes, parents are the ones who deny that their children are struggling. I was one of them. As I described earlier in this book, I ignored red flags in my son's development that were crucial clues to his learning difference.

We may be in denial for a variety of reasons. I didn't want to believe that anything was off with my child because I didn't want him to experience the same painful school years that his dad had. I was scared to face any challenges to the world of possibilities I had imagined for my child. African American parents, whose children have historically been overidentified as having learning and behavioral issues, may resist evaluations because of the cultural mental health stigma, or the fear of giving educators an excuse to underserve their children.[12]

Most parents also don't know a lot about dyslexia. Two-thirds of parents believe that preschoolers who demonstrate difficulty in rhyming and mispronouncing words will outgrow it, according to an Emily Hall Tremaine Foundation poll.[13] But in reality, when these signs persist until third grade, they begin to form signs of a learning disabilities profile. In addition, parents whose first language isn't English may believe that their children are struggling in school because they're learning a new language, not because they have learning disabilities.

Educators may also resist identifying children with dyslexia, because they lack confidence in their own assessments or because the school has implicitly or explicitly discouraged it. Even though our education laws require schools to identify children with dyslexia starting in kindergarten through third grade depending on state regulations, they don't mandate that all students be screened, so many kids go for years without being tested or diagnosed. And, even when educators recommend children be evaluated for special education services, parents followed recommendations only 56 percent of the time.[14]

There are subtler factors as well. For instance, only 28 percent of parents and 39 percent of classroom teachers recognize frequent refusal to go to school as a possible sign of learning issues.[15] Pediatricians miss signs that might be indicative of dyslexia. For instance, toddlers who have signs of delayed developmental milestones such as walking late and talking late are more likely to present with learning disabilities, so push for an evaluation around five or six years old, when you can get an official diagnosis.

The problem continues when we don't screen our instincts.

Once everyone agrees that a child with reading struggles should be screened for learning disabilities, your school will probably evaluate your child using PAR (Predictive Assessment of Reading) or DIBELS (Dynamic Indicators of Basic Early Literacy Skills), a series of short tests designed to assess early childhood literacy. The skills assessed include phonemic awareness, alphabetic principle, accuracy and fluency, vocabulary, and comprehension. In Brooklyn, two schools are testing out the Shaywitz DyslexiaScreen, developed out of the Yale Center for Dyslexia and Creativity, with a price tag for the entire pilot program for both schools at two thousand dollars.

This screener comes before an evaluation, and you should push to have the school district do it early, in kindergarten or first grade. Each of the DIBELS tests takes only about two to five minutes to complete, and together they serve as an indicator of your child's overall reading status. These tests aren't intended to be in-depth or comprehensive measures of reading. Just like using a thermometer to take your child's temperature is one indicator of general health, these quick DIBELS tests provide teachers with information about your child's reading health.

If the screener results confirm that a more thorough evaluation is necessary, buckle up. The school might still fight the results from the test and not want to automatically provide an evaluation. This situation happened to me with my son Oliver (see his story in the Epilogue). But you should push for transparency of results and put other concerns you see into a request for the CST to evaluate your child.

Under IDEA legislation, states are given sixty days from the time a parent requests an evaluation to complete testing. States define sixty days differently—some by "calendar days" and others by "business days," but the important thing for you to note is that your district must perform an evaluation sixty days *after you request testing*, not sixty days after the initial screenings are performed. In any case, since the school year consists of 180 days, that still means your child could lose a third of the academic year struggling.

In another twist, the language of the test results is virtually impossible for the average person to understand, and the data collected won't really be enough for you to determine next steps. Trust me, it's super hard to understand the intricacies, so ask for help. Reach out to a professional who understands educational testing, such as a neuropsychologist, psychologist, or literacy expert, and if these people aren't available, post in some advocacy groups and maybe someone might be able to help.

We have to do a better job of diagnosing and helping children with dyslexia earlier. Learning disabilities don't suddenly appear in third grade. It takes children with reading difficulties four times longer to catch up with their peers if intervention isn't done until fourth grade, instead of late kindergarten.[16]

So let's be more proactive, people, and screen all children sooner for reading issues.

Nobody Really Knows if Response to Intervention (RTI) Really Works

If your child is struggling in school but hasn't been diagnosed with a learning disability or put on an IEP, what happens next?

In accordance with the laws we described above, funding streams are granted to the states from the U.S. Department of Education based on a prepared formula. The states then use their own formulas to distribute these funds to the different Local Education Agencies (LEAs) within the state. These formulas take into account factors like the number of students on IEPs and the free and reduced lunch counts or poverty percentage, and also determine their response to intervention (RTI) funding.

RTI isn't considered a special intervention; it's meant to involve general and special education working collaboratively. As we discussed earlier, there are three tiers of RTI: Tier I is for all students and occurs in general education class, while Tier 2 provides specialized small group instruction for students identified to be at risk for academic and behavioral problems. Tier 3 provides specialized, individualized instructional and behavioral support for students with more intensive needs. The point of RTI is to help students stay in the general education classroom and out of special education.

Does RTI work? The jury's still out. One large 2015 study showed that "students in the program who were supposedly receiving targeted interventions actually performed worse than their peers who weren't in an RTI process."[17] Others worry that RTI may allow the school district to delay screenings and more effective interventions like structured reading programs, meaning kids with dyslexia could fall even further behind. Make sure you call the school out on this commonly used excuse and push harder for reasons on delaying evaluation. The most common reason I have heard for delaying intervention is again lack of resources and support.

The real problem for parents is that, without a diagnosis and an IEP, there is no structured way for you to track your child's progress, as it is not required to be documented. There's also no stated end point, so RTI can go on forever, up to eighteen months, regardless of its effectiveness. Remember, each moment your child isn't getting an education delivered in the effective way is another wasted moment in your child's optimal development.

A Scattershot Approach

In general, one of the biggest obstacles parents are facing is the scattershot approach to early intervention services taken by most public schools. A report prepared by the education think tank Public Agenda found that most parents feel their schools "keep information about special education services close to the vest."

For many parents, getting a diagnosis is just the beginning. More than a third of special ed parents surveyed by Public Agenda said that it was "frustrating" to not get services even after "the school knew your child had special needs." About 43 percent said they had to "stay on top of the school and fight to get services."[18]

Most of the parents I spoke with said that even after their children were identified as having a specific learning disability (SLD) in reading and provided with IEPs, they didn't get intensive support. Many said their kids didn't get the right support at all, since so few teachers, and even reading specialists, are qualified to use the structured literacy programs shown to be most effective in teaching kids with dyslexia.

Another issue is that the time spent in these pull-out special education intervention sessions will be time your child misses in the regular curriculum. This could mean that your child will fall behind in academic subjects, not necessarily because of reading struggles, but because your child simply wasn't there when the teacher explained a key lesson or the class went over homework.

Finally, many of the intervention services provided by your school will be just plain wrong, especially if your school doesn't have a literacy specialist trained in reading programs that teach kids phonics and reading comprehension. (See the section on teacher training on page 214.) I spoke with many parents whose children were placed in small group special education pull-out intervention sessions with classmates whose issues ranged from attention issues to serious behavior problems, and even more parents whose children were being "helped" by teachers with absolutely no knowledge of how to teach kids with dyslexia.

HOW *YOU* CAN FIGHT FOR
BETTER INTERVENTION SERVICES

1. **Believe in Yourself as a Parent**
    Trust your instincts. If you suspect there is something wrong with the way your baby or toddler is develop-

ing, talk to your pediatrician and request early intervention services. These are paid for by the government and are free for your family before your child's third birthday. Your baby's brain grows fast, and the more support you can provide to your child early on, the better your child will do in school later. The Center for Parent Information and Resources is a place to start your search: https://www.parentcenterhub.org/services-ei/.

2. **Talk to Your Child's Doctor**

   Many pediatricians will be pressed for time during well-baby visits. Your doctor may breeze through a checkup unless you specifically express your concerns and ask if your pediatrician can screen your child for dyslexia. More pediatricians are using early screeners now. For instance, a start-up company called BabyNoggin is targeting pediatricians with a suite of mobile apps that can be used to screen children for delays in the development of motor skills, language, social-emotional abilities, and cognitive processing. You can ask your pediatrician what is the preferred method to keep track of these milestones so you have a common language and system to use for your visits.

3. **Find a Self Screener Tool**

   If your doctor is not moving at the speed you want, you can take on the screening yourself. There are many tools, such as the upcoming Early Literacy Screener app, created by Dr. Nadine Gaab in partnership with Boston Children's hospital. For age appropriate sceeners consult https://dyslexiaida.org/screening-for-dyslexia/

4. **Get Support from Other Parents**

   Talk to somebody with a child who struggles in reaching milestones like reading—a neighbor, a friend, or a friend of a friend. You can even go on social media and find advocacy groups for children with dyslexia—a great place to ask any questions you have.

5. **Dig Into What the Teacher Says**

   If your child's teacher says that your child's learning is "within range," dig into what this means if you have doubts. Find homework completed by one or more of your child's friends and compare assignments to see how your child's work aligns with the class progress. If it falls short, make note of these assignments and arrange a conference with the teacher to discuss in detail why you don't think your child's learning is progressing as it should.

6. **Ask an Expert to Walk You Through Evaluation Results**
   a. Press the school into doing a screener for dyslexia as soon as possible. Follow up to make sure it's scheduled. Once you know the date, make an appointment to talk with the evaluator and your child's teacher as soon as possible afterward to discuss the results. Keep an email chain going so that everything is documented.
   b. Make the school give you the hard data from the screener results, not simply data range. If they explain the results and you still don't understand them, ask an outside professional to meet with you, or go on a Facebook page for parents of children with learning disabilities and ask what the numbers actually mean.

c. Remember, you are your child's best advocate. This is the time to speak up.

7. **Don't Be Afraid to Retest**
There are a variety of screening methods out there, so if you don't agree with the results of one, ask for another, or find one you can use on your own to confirm or dispute the first results.

8. **Work with the Interventionist**
Most schools have an "interventionist," someone who is responsible for implementing interventions at your school. Ask for that person's name and schedule a meeting to find out their story, and kindly inquire if that person is qualified to teach children with dyslexia how to read. If not, ask them who in the school or in the district has had the required literacy training to do so.

9. **Synchronize Schedules for Intervention**
Your child's intervention support should happen during the same time activity is taking place in the general education class. Make sure in advance of your IEP meeting you ask for the CST to bring the class schedules to ensure that nothing your child enjoys is being missed. If you can't make this sync happen, try to negotiate for a time that you find is not productive for your child. For example, if they have sensory issues related to sound, you might want to skip music. Also, when possible try to have related services sync up to the subject matter. So if your child is working on writing support, it could be pushed into the science slot, when the joint planning is required on the IEP.

10. **Measure Progress by Letting Data Guide Your Way**

Don't assume that your child is learning simply because there are intervention services in place. When possible, look at the goals from the IEP and try to break them into bite-sized chunks that you can measure. For example, if they have reading goals, find out what Fountas & Pinnell level they are at now, and discuss where they should be in three months, six months, and nine months. Then ask for data points such as work products or samples of how your child has independently met these progress milestones. This is where schools try to skirt your novice abilities, so keep them honest.

11. **Communicate Directly with Your Child's Teacher**

As we saw in the previous section, one mom found that staying in close email contact with her child's teachers and communicating information about his learning needs proved far more effective than waiting for paperwork from the school's overwhelmed special education services division to reach the teachers. Another parent found it instructive to volunteer in her son's classroom to see firsthand how he was performing. Communicating with teachers also worked for me. When I asked my younger son's teacher point-blank in first grade whether she was qualified to teach my child the science of reading, and when she said "no," I was grateful for her honesty, because it meant I could bring that information to the school administration and request other, more effective reading instruction.

HOW YOU CAN HELP YOUR PEDIATRICIAN

One million children each year will enter schools with an undiagnosed disability,[19] and one in four children under age five are at risk for developmental delays.[20] The risk is doubled when parents live in poverty or have less than a high school education. We must do better when it comes to screening for disabilities and learning differences.

This means turning our pediatricians into allies. Predictors of dyslexia, such as smaller vocabularies, are detectable as early as age three, so why wait until children start school and begin struggling?[21] In her article titled "Pediatricians Have a Role in Early Screenings of Dyslexia," Dr. Molly Ness pointed out that "In a 2009 position paper negating visual deficiencies as the origin of dyslexia, the American Association of Pediatrics stated that pediatrics should be vigilant in looking for early signs of evolving learning disabilities."[22]

Pediatricians should perform basic literacy screenings as a routine part of well-child visits beginning around three. This will more likely be a regular occurrence if we, as parents, ask our children's health-care providers for information on reading development as part of our child's visits.

Your own pediatrician may hesitate to cause alarm early on, but if you describe your child's struggle to learn, or your family's history with dyslexia, your pediatrician will be more open to conversation on the subject. Ideally, he/she will suggest getting some baseline reports so your child at least can be watched more closely for problems in school.

TEACHER TRAINING:
TAKE YOUR FIGHT INTO THE TRENCHES

Overcrowded classrooms. Children who are homeless and hungry. Children with learning disabilities and behavioral issues. Kids acting out because they're being bullied or abused at home. Toxic levels of lead in the water. No air-conditioning. That kid who makes fun of your shoes. That other kid who set the trash can on fire. Slashed school budgets. Mountains of paperwork. Active shooters. Late-night grading. Standardized testing. With such dire working conditions, is it any wonder that our nation is suffering one of the worst shortages in history?

The General Education Teacher's Dilemma

When it comes to having children with disabilities in their classrooms, many general education teachers feel overwhelmed, or even unqualified. An IEP becomes just another tiresome item on their massive "to do" lists.

In one poll taken by the Emily Hall Tremaine Foundation, only 36 percent of teachers felt their education and training had prepared them to deal with learning disorders, including dyslexia.[23] Even with training, most teachers don't have the tools or time to identify and help struggling readers, according to the NCLD.

In addition, many teachers aren't familiar with the overwhelming number of studies demonstrating that the science of reading, proven through research, is the most effective way to teach *all* children how to decode written language—and that's what children with dyslexia *must* learn to do if they're going to become proficient readers.

As Tracy Thompson pointed out in an article she wrote for the *Atlantic*, "The Special-Education Charade," general education teachers are "overworked, stressed, and undertrained in the discipline techniques that are most effective with kids whose brains are wired differently."[24]

Teachers get copies of each child's IEP at the start of school, ideally, but they are lengthy documents, and each teacher likely has several to read. It doesn't help that IEPs are filled with jargon, making them difficult to parse.

Then, when it comes to implementing IEPs (not to mention 504 plans), many teachers are already so overstretched that even the most basic provisions—like printing out the class notes, when lesson plans are always changing, or offering individualized instruction when a classroom has twenty energetic students—are taxing. Instead of implementing accommodations on day one, it might be many, many days before they even finish reading the document, much less put accommodations into place. After all, it's a heavy load even in optimal conditions. Melissa Corto is the cofounder of Education Modified, an interesting company whose mission is to bring to life the IEP with software by trying to ease the load on teachers implementing special education documents. They have built research-based, online solutions that support teachers, improve student outcomes, and engage all stakeholders in the classroom delivery of IEPs.

A Critical Shortage

While a lack of general education teachers is bad enough, the dearth of qualified special education teachers has hit crisis levels. In addition to the many teachers who avoid special education because of increased responsibilities and paperwork, special education teachers exit the profession at higher rates due to burnout. About 75 percent of special education teachers leave their jobs within ten years of starting, while only 17 percent of teachers overall leave after five years.[25]

One of the biggest challenges is the amount of time special educators spend on paperwork, including conducting assessments, evaluations, and IEP meetings. It can take up to half of their working hours. According to the DOE's Study of Personnel Needs in Special Education fact sheet, special education teachers spend about five hours a week on paperwork—as much time as they spend on preparing lessons for students.[26] On average, over half of every special education budget is spent on meetings and paperwork.[27]

Closing the Special Education Teaching Gap

The demand for qualified special education teachers is increasing at a time when the Bureau of Labor Statistics already reports that the shortages are acute. "A whopping 82 percent of special educators and specialized instructional support personnel (SISP) from across the nation report that there are not enough professionals to meet the needs of students with disabilities."[28]

Given the severity of the shortage, certain school districts are forced to take extreme measures to staff their classrooms, like hiring novice teachers, or even interns, with little or no classroom experience.

Some states even recruit teachers from overseas. The U.S. State Department issued 2,876 J-1 "cultural exchange" visas to school employees in 2017, some to teachers effected by shortages.

The problem with this system, like with so much else in education, is a lack of transparency. For instance, agencies acting as matchmakers between overseas teachers and our nation's schools demand such a hefty fee from international teachers that their already modest pay starts to resemble indentured servitude. Many are so deeply indebted to recruiting agencies that they have little choice but to stay here for the full time allotted on their visa, even if they are unhappy with the job.

Several unscrupulous guest-worker schemes have been taken to court. For instance, in 2012, a federal jury awarded $4.5 million to Filipino teachers who paid a California placement agency up to sixteen thousand dollars in fees for their forty-thousand-dollars-a-year teaching positions in Louisiana. A jury found that the recruiter failed to properly disclose its fees to the teachers.[29]

One teacher I interviewed, Mrs. Cruz, also a native of the Philippines, had earned a master's degree in education and was working as a general education teacher in her country when her mother-in-law told her that agencies were recruiting teachers to come to the United States—especially those certified in special education, as Mrs. Cruz was.

The agency helped with her J-1 visa—a cultural exchange visa good for three years in the U.S.—and found her a job in rural Montana. She had to borrow twenty thousand dollars from the agency to process her documents, which she paid back in installments.

She currently works with children who have emotional, behavioral, and learning disabilities. Despite her master's degree, six years of teaching experience in the Philippines, and an additional special education certification, Mrs. Cruz said she "wasn't trained to teach children with specific disabilities."

Although she learned some strategies to help struggling readers, none of them were specifically for dyslexia. She researched training programs in structured literacy instruction, but there weren't any in Montana, and doing a program on the East Coast, where she could live with family, was also too costly. "I'd have had to pay that out of my own pocket, and one week of training was around fifteen hundred dollars," she said. "I asked the superintendent if the district could pay even half of that amount for my training, but they said they didn't have the money."

Fortunately, her mother-in-law is a special education teacher on the East Coast, and she was able to teach Mrs. Cruz how to use Orton-Gillingham in a sort of do-it-yourself boot camp.

"There's a big shortage of special education teachers in this country because a lot of the locals don't like doing the job," she said. "It's very stressful. Aside from the legal paperwork, we have to deal with some kids who have big behavioral issues, conduct IEP meetings with parents, and prepare individualized lesson plans for students, yet we're not paid any more than regular teachers."

Still, there are rewards. Recently she received a letter from a former student thanking Mrs. Cruz for teaching him to read. "It's a calling for me," she said. "I like seeing kids improve and knowing that I'm part of their success."

Her J-1 visa is only good for three years, though the school district can request an extension for another two years if they want her back. If that doesn't happen, Mrs. Cruz isn't sure what will happen to the children and parents who have come to rely on her.

"I'm really concerned about that," she said. "Who will teach these kids after I'm gone?"

Why Can't So-Called Specialists Teach Children with Dyslexia?

Special education isn't only about access. It's also about fidelity and quality.

In addition to hearing parents' concerns that there weren't enough literacy specialists in their schools, I also heard that the specialists assigned to work in small groups or individually with their children weren't actually trained in any of the structured reading programs designed for children with dyslexia. Keep in mind that SLD is the most common category covered under IDEA.

Yet how is it possible that, after all the research that's been done on reading, our teachers are so poorly trained?

As I explained earlier in this book, this is partly due to "the reading wars," as it's often described, between phonics-based approaches and whole-language approaches. Teacher preparation programs still fail to take into account the science of reading, as Emily Hanford pointed out in her October 2018 op-ed piece for the *New York Times*, "Why Are We Still Teaching Reading the Wrong Way?"

Once again, the problem starts at the top. In this case, the "top" is at our colleges and universities, where our educators are being prepared to teach in classrooms but are poorly schooled in the science of reading. They lack the necessary training to teach children with dyslexia, because for decades the whole-language approach has been entrenched in all of the curriculum materials put out by publishers and adopted by school systems.

However, new research shows that the phonics approach doesn't only work best for children with dyslexia, but for all children. Without structured, evidence-based phonics instruction, many students struggle to read and spell. A recent teacher survey from Decoding Dyslexia Oregon, for example, showed that 56 percent of teachers felt their teacher training prepared them poorly to identify or work with struggling readers.[30] And, according to the National Council on Teacher Quality, only 37 percent of elementary and special education teaching programs at the college level appear to be teaching scientifically based reading programs to pre-service teachers.[31]

Given the severe shortage of special education teachers, it's time that *all* teachers were trained in the science of reading, so that children learn to read using the method that is proven to work best, no matter who is teaching them.

Change Is Coming

One big success story is in Mississippi, where former Governor Phil Bryant, who struggled with dyslexia when he was in school, signed a bill that requires all kindergarten students and first graders to be tested for dyslexia. He went with his team to study classrooms around the state and determine what was causing so many Mississippi students to struggle in reading. His goal was to measure where students are, and then create a baseline of knowledge in the science of reading that all pre-service teachers should have before entering the classroom. What his team discovered was shocking: Those preparing to be teachers in Mississippi were spending a total of only twenty minutes on phonics.

That's right: twenty minutes over the course of four years of college.

In 2003, the state began requiring future elementary school teachers to take two early literacy courses, and in 2013 Mississippi passed a Literacy-Based Promotion Act.[32] Under this act, beginning in 2014, a student scoring at the lowest achievement level in reading on the established state-wide assessment for third grade wasn't promoted to fourth grade unless they qualified for a good-cause exception.[33] The purpose of this act was to make sure that no student with reading issues would be missed at this critical milestone.

Today, teachers in Mississippi spend 282 minutes learning how to teach phonics in four years of college, and in 2019, Mississippi was the only state in the nation to improve its reading scores. This wasn't a quick fix—in fact, it took fifteen years of big changes, starting at the government, college, and university levels—but this effort, as you can see in the scores, will more than pay off in the long term.[34]

As more and more programs incorporate these standards, more teachers will be properly trained and more qualified in teaching students with dyslexia. Ideally, your school district will be one of those that supports proactive teacher training, since reactive lawsuits against school special education services are common, wasting precious time and resources for both parents and schools.

Some college and university education programs now recognize that dyslexia is a learning difference that can be remediated through evidence-based reading instruction. The International Dyslexia Association recognizes those education programs and has been credentialing them since 2012.

HOW *YOU* CAN HELP TEACHERS
HELP YOUR CHILD

1. **Ask Your Child's Teacher about Preparation Programs**
   Both general education teachers and special educators should learn about phonics and the science of reading while they're preparing for their professional ca-

reers. Find out if your district has specialists trained and certified to teach reading instruction programs appropriate for children with dyslexia, like Orton-Gillingham or Wilson Reading System. Be sure your child has a teacher or specialist with this training.

2. **Track the Money Spent on Professional Development— and Raise Your Own**
Every school district has a budget for professional development and resources. Find out how much your district is spending on training teachers to work with children who have dyslexia, and what curriculum resources your district has that are dedicated to language-based learning difficulties. According to the Institute for Multi-Sensory Education, the cost to train a teacher in OG (including teacher materials costs) is $14.14 per student over 5 years.[35] Now that's a number you can bring to your board.

3. **Go Directly to the Literacy Specialist**
Ask the literacy specialist in your school how they were trained, and whether they would like more support learning programs. Approach them as an ally, not an enemy. Reading specialists are trained to help lots of kids, but they're not necessarily trained in successful methods for dyslexia specifically. It's not the teacher's fault. But the administration should be more informed.

4. **Offer to Be a Class Substitute**
One reason some administrators give for not allowing teachers to pursue professional development is time. If teachers attend a professional development workshop, they can't teach their classes, and the district will

need to find a substitute teacher, which some districts say is too expensive. If possible, offer to substitute for your teacher's class while he/she's getting trained in a phonics-based reading program geared toward students with dyslexia, or find a group of friends willing to share substitute days with you.

5. **Bring In Trained Literacy Tutors or Reading Specialists**
Some parents I interviewed were able to supplement their district's supply of trained literacy tutors by bringing in reading specialists to meet with their children after school, at lunch, or even virtually, to offer effective reading instruction. Some school districts won't allow outside tutors in the building due to liability issues, but there are online tutors that might be acceptable to your school as an option that helps everyone. Some more privileged districts are asking their PTAs to fund the training for OG specialists.

6. **Track Your Child's Progress**
Some teachers give children passing grades to push them through to the next grade level. Track your child's progress carefully and compare it to what classmates are doing. If your child's teacher gives passing grades for work that is obviously subpar, call them out. Show the teacher your child's papers and those you see around the classroom as the evidence of your child's failure to progress.

7. **Seek Out Organizations That Support Schools**
There are some organizations that bring in support, from extra tutoring to social emotional partners. For

example, David Flink is the founder of Eye to Eye, an organization that trains high school and college students with learning differences, including dyslexia and ADHD, to mentor similarly identified middle school students.

IS A NONTRADITIONAL EDUCATION PATH RIGHT FOR YOUR CHILD?

As you know from reading this book, after fighting tooth and nail with the schools in Jersey City to get the education my oldest son needed, I realized that they had no capacity to serve my child. Special education litigation is usually in high gear around fifth grade—a time period lawyers call the "wait to fail" where the discrepancy gap is so obvious the schools must grant students the services they actually need or pay for private placement.

I was determined to compel the schools to pay for my son's education. I felt like that was my right. So Fede and I made the tough choice to pull our son out in second grade (nowhere near the fifth-grade wait-to-fail time frame), and find a place where he could learn the right way the first time.

We found that place at the Craig School, an independent school that specializes in working with students with language-based learning disabilities. Around 50 percent of the kids in the Craig School are sent on their home district's tab after they have waited for the child to "fail." We were able to make the sacrifice to pay out of pocket to get our son there sooner, and I am so grateful that we could, despite the financial hit.

From the moment Matias walks into school to the moment he leaves, everything he experiences at this school is built for his brain: small class sizes, highly specialized teachers, and hands-on learning to enhance tactile capabilities. He makes folders and binders to help his organizational skills. The school also offers assistive technology, FM systems to block out noise, homework help, and amazing dance classes he loves.

His teachers are my idols. The school is extremely accessible for parent participation; I can chat with Mr. Furlong about composting in the garden, my son's favorite subject these days, or speak about his Orton-Gillingham progress with Mrs. Schilling, his language arts teacher. I can also ask for help to understand the latest report card with Mrs. Miller and Mrs. Imperatore, and Matias loves to brag about his status in math with Mrs. Stubaus. Most important for us, the Craig School uses cutting-edge research in dyslexia to determine the content they teach and the programs they use, rather than offering a special-ed stew of whatever resources happen to be handy or cheap.

Despite our rocky start, we're in a good place. Matias has mastered OG and can now decode in his sleep. He can do his homework on his own, organize it, and prepare for what's coming the next day. I know it isn't possible for most people to pay for private tuition, so I went in search of more equitable models that address the needs of our kids. We should not have to keep answering these mind-numbing questions that traditional models put up for discussion.

Is it worth fighting your school district so that your child can spend a few more minutes every week with a special education teacher who isn't even really trained?

Is it worth trying to tap the dry stone of your school district for more special education funds, when the district is already drowning in debt?

Are you willing to wait until your child fails long enough for the school to notice and agree to your repeated pleas for a private placement?

These are questions that most nontraditional schools have already answered. I have described a few of these models in the following pages. One thing they all have in common is a visionary leader with the patience, inspiration, and persistence to think outside the box. Students are nurtured and inspired to grow not only academically, but emotionally.

My methodology for exploring different models was not scientific, or on a grand budget. I simply followed leads from stories, news from our community, and places that my travels naturally took me. While the models below might not all exist in your neighborhood, I encourage you to reach out to the folks that run them and see what you can learn.

A Free School, Built Specifically for Kids with Dyslexia

New York's first public charter school focused on
language-based learning differences

Bridge Preparatory Charter School—Staten Island, New York

Bridge Preparatory Charter School is the first public school in New York designed for kids with dyslexia and other language-based learning difficulties, and one of only a handful of such schools nationwide. Just to give you some context, Staten Island is the least populated of all five boroughs in New York City; due to a lack of subway access, it is sometimes referred to as "the forgotten borough."

After seeing Staten Island public schools create programs for kids with autism and behavioral problems, parents of children with dyslexia felt they were being left out again, and began showing up at board of education meetings to speak up about their needs. Staten Island Borough president James Oddo formally met with parents, advocates, and students with dyslexia over the next few years to better understand the challenges they faced. In 2018, the State Board of Regents approved the proposal to establish the Bridge Preparatory Charter School to serve students with dyslexia.

The tuition-free school opened in 2019 with eighty-six first- and second-grade students, and is expected to grow to 242 students, in grades one to five, during the final year of the charter term, which is 2022–2023. Classes will serve no more than twelve students. The application process is open to all Staten Island residents, and available seats are filled by lottery. There is already a waiting list for admission.

Tim Castanza, executive director and founder of the school, literally went door to door with his team to let parents know that the school would be opening, so they could guarantee fair access to everyone who had a need.

What makes this school so special?

Let's start with the building itself, which has hallways designed to encourage multisensory movement breaks, with hopscotch outlined on the floors. The classrooms are named after famous people with dyslexia, like Whoopi Goldberg and Thomas Edison. And there's a sign that greets you as you walk in the door that pretty much sums up their philosophy: *"To get all, we focus on each."*

Tim said that he and his staff "make every decision based on what's best for the child," and it's clear that Tim wears his emotions on his sleeve. He has a tattoo on his forearm inspired by his time as a teacher, which shows he is the captain of the plane and there is no one else to blame but him. And he does inspire confidence in students, staff, and parents.

The school's collaborative teaching model allows for continuous assessments, benchmarking, ability-based grouping, and low student-to-teacher ratios to meet the needs at all student levels. It is also designed to support the development of key social skills we all need in the twenty-first century. Teacher-looping, which keeps the same teacher with students for an extended period of time, minimizes student anxiety as they transition between grades, and provides consistency for families and staff too.

What fascinated me most was that everything is kept in the classroom—targeted interventions, enrichments, and necessary learning extensions—unlike pull-out services, which can be jarring for kids. Students are grouped according to learning levels, and because the classes are small, the passionate teachers are able to deliver the right-sized lessons in small groups. I didn't even notice at first that they were multi-age groups, but it didn't seem to make any difference socially.

As for hiring teachers, there is a rigorous interview process. The teachers are enthusiastic about seeking additional support in the science of reading, and about putting in the extra time needed to learn these skills. And with an Orton-Gillingham Fellow on board who consults and trains, they're able to coach teachers in-house at all levels, with no time constraints.

The school uses project-based learning to teach ideas that kids are interested in, and connect with parents by meeting with them and demonstrating what's going on in the school.

Right now I don't have the patience or skills to cut through the invisible red tape needed to open a charter school in Jersey City, but if I did, I would call Tim and ask him to advise me. I was truly blown away with what I saw at the school. He gets emails daily from frustrated parents across the country looking to build alternative schooling options, so I have high hopes that there will be more schools like Bridge Prep around very soon.

Direct Instruction Schools: An Effective Combination of Individualization and Validation Critical for Our Kids to Learn

Open communication and close monitoring allow this format to work for all

Arthur Academy Public Charter Schools—Portland, Oregon

Like most other charter schools, Arthur Academy was the brainchild of a visionary leader, retired teacher and counselor Charles Arthur, a struggling reader himself. Ironically, it wasn't until he attended an International Dyslexia Association conference and saw a brain scan that he realized he had dyslexia. After twenty years in the classroom, Arthur, at age sixty, and his wife chose to open their first charter school with their son. By 2007, they had six schools up and running, with a proven track record of success. I saw the school in Portland for grades K–5.

Their instructional model is a phonics-based program that Arthur used when he was a special education teacher, and one that he found to be effective with beginning readers and older readers who'd been unsuccessful in the past. It's a structured, research-validated curriculum called "Direct Instruction"(DI).

These DI programs break general objectives down into small teaching progressions. The activities and examples for each lesson are carefully sequenced so they can be easily learned and incorporated into more complex, higher-level applications. Whatever students are learning is continually used and applied, so there's less need for review.

The lessons are presented in hands-on, interactive formats to make them easier to understand, and they add small amounts of new material to each lesson to make sure that the whole class moves up in unison. Those who fall behind repeat lessons. However, this doesn't happen often, since the curriculum they use, "Reading Mastery," is phonics-based. They have 99 percent of graduating kindergarten classes reading. Wow.

When I first saw this model in action, I thought it couldn't possibly work, because the environment seemed rigid and the classes had up to thirty kids, sometimes with only one teacher. However, the children are split into groups according to levels, and moved up when necessary. I asked the administration to point out the lower reading group so that I could pay attention to the instruction they received and how it differed from how other students were being taught.

What I learned was key to this success formula consisted of bite-sized material being delivered, and the amount of repetition in the lessons. I saw the repetition begin to spark comprehension in their minds by the end of each lesson.

While there weren't any small groups in the older classes, they did have a very engaged bunch of kids following along with the curriculum binder. The enthusiastic teacher was giving instructions about what was to come, and it sounded almost like a song. This is part of the multisensory delivery that helps the kids process the information. They answered back with the right notes. She went through the short lesson, then asked the kids to take an assessment on what they had just learned. She looked around the class and asked how they'd done on the test. Each child made eye contact with the teacher, one hand was raised in a self-noted flag of concern, the teacher noted who raised their hand, and the class proceeded.

After that class, I spoke with the director of the school and asked how this system worked to flag those who were not progressing. She smiled and said the kids graded themselves. If they are below 80 percent on the self-assessment test at the end of lesson, they know they must raise their hands, under the honor code. At the the end of each lesson, the teacher notes who is struggling, and enters the data point to monitor progress. If students are below standards, they make up the lesson in small group support throughout the rest of the day.

I saw the spreadsheet on every child, and it was impressive. Other industries rely on data. Why isn't student data driving more school decisions? Probably due to time and money constraints.

Imagine what your child's school would look like if you had self-reported data on what was working and what wasn't on a daily basis. Think about how much more effective our kids could be.

While the DI method might not work for every child, I was impressed by the leadership I saw. The teachers naturally conveyed enthusiasm for learning. They weren't part of any union, and the method was a lot of work if done correctly, but you could see the pure joy and excitement every day—in both the students and teachers. That's when you know true learning is taking place.

Microschools: A Small Classroom Environment Where Learning Is Driven by Students' Interests and Skills

Size of classes allows for high levels of personalization and time spent with a progressive curriculum aligned with state standards

Prenda microschools—Arizona

Sir Ken Robinson's TED talks highlight the value of creativity in unlocking human potential. He has often singled out public education as the chief culprit in dampening our children's creativity.

"We have built our education systems on the model of fast food," Robinson explained in a TED Talk delivered in 2010, adding that there are at least two ways to ensure a good meal when you're cooking for a crowd: "One is fast food, where everything is standardized. The other [is] customized to local circumstances. And we have sold ourselves into a fast-food model of education, and it's impoverishing our spirit and our energies as much as fast food is depleting our physical bodies." As we have seen, standardization can sometimes work. However, microschool formats like Prenda and Acton offer a healthy alternative to the fast-food model of public education.

The word "microschool" was coined by British education blogger Cushla Barry in 2010. It refers to small educational institutions—think "one-room schoolhouse" sort of small—that emphasize interdisciplinary, project-based learning led by trained professionals who steer conversations, rather than lecture. They build social skills such as communication and critical thinking, and tailor instruction to the needs of each individual student. Microschools offer mixed-age classes with fifteen students or fewer, and focus on meaningful, sustainable, whole student learning. There can be multiple classrooms in one branded microschool network.

Microschools have been on the rise as public-school budgets are slashed, and private-school tuition soars ever higher. This alternative model offers greater affordability and accessibility than a private school, due to the lower cost of their buildings and of technology. And the small class sizes allow for high levels of personalized instruction.

Microschools are not the same as homeschooling co-ops or private tutoring centers, because they are registered as state schools. This means that students in microschools must meet the compulsory state attendance requirements.

The Prenda network was founded by Kelly Smith, a former physicist and tech executive who moved home to Mesa, Arizona, and wanted to give back to his community. In 2013, Smith started volunteering at the public library, teaching kids computer programming. The classes were a big hit, and there was soon a huge demand for them.

As he watched kids work hard to build cool projects, Smith had an epiphany: Often they learned better when the adult helping them didn't know how to code. That set Smith on a new path into education research, and he developed his own model of education: Prenda.

His mission is to empower learners. His team does this by combining flexible environments with interesting teaching techniques. The curriculum is progressive, and the teachers are called "guides"—they're there to steer the student-led learning.

Sounds innovative, right? But for Smith, a learner is merely someone who chooses to learn, and every learner has the skills to learn whatever they want. He feels that our schools have literally beaten the learner out of our children, with rigid testing standards and burned-out teachers. Imagine how it feels for the one in five, who have never been empowered but are constantly made to feel "less than" because they struggle to do what so many of their friends seem to do naturally: read.

Because so many children with dyslexia are also bright, hands-on learners, their parents have been especially drawn to Prenda. As we saw earlier in one of our parent stories, Prenda has responded by developing a literacy program geared specifically toward children with dyslexia.

In Arizona, Prenda students meet 16–20 hours per week, and they spend five hours a week on non-academic activities. The school partnered with a charter school, which means they receive money from the state and support for special education.

On average, there are no more than ten children per Prenda school. Most guides meet with the students in homes or take over an office space. The guide's children attend for free, and guides earn an hourly amount for each child depending on location.

These guides aren't just people off the street. They are screened vigorously for alignment and life experiences that mirror Prenda values. And because Prenda is part of the charter network, students are required to take state tests, but the teachers aren't required to teach to the tests—a blessed relief. The early data shows Prenda students are performing well in state testing.

Socialization is the biggest question many parents have about alternative education models like microschools. I often get the same question, because my son's school is an hour from our home. In my experience, socialization isn't a problem. School takes up part of the day, but my son has friends in our community that he has known all his life, who have helped Matias form his identity and values.

Other parents who have chosen homeschooling or microschools say the same thing. Prenda students, for instance, have a core block of time called "collaborate," designed to hone their social skills. They also take outings together in the community.

For children with dyslexia, Prenda guides meet them where they are daily and give them the accommodations they need to learn. Unlike traditional schools, where parents aren't always encouraged to contribute ideas about curriculum or methodology, Prenda welcomes input. It's a truly collaborative approach to teaching and learning. If a parent brings in a new software program or teaching ideas, Prenda's typical answer is, "Why not?" and they will use it to see if it works for your child. They did this recently when a mom asked for new tools to be added to the reading program and they were able to add them the next day.

Kaity Broadbent, Prenda's content specialist, is a mother of four and a trained speech pathologist with literary expertise. As more parents of children with dyslexia began discovering Prenda, she decided that her best bet was to teach Prenda guides how to spot struggling readers and give them the basics to begin interventions.

Since Prenda has a start-up mentality, Broadbent built her own phonics-based reading system. She calls it "Treasure Hunt," and dresses up as a safari explorer to help kids learn to decode. She filmed all the videos and created an accompanying workbook and mini books only three months after having her fourth child—now *that's* dedication. And anyone can use it for a three-dollar materials fee—or, it'll be free in the fall of 2020, just contact Prenda.

CONCLUSION: HOW WILL YOU GET YOUR CHILD TO SCHOOL TODAY?

These alternative models are bright lights in a dreary landscape. But it takes strong leaders, with vision, to create them. You have to be willing to fight through the invisible red tape and play the long game.

It's tough and time-consuming for parents to think outside the box at first, especially when we're already exhausted from the daily struggle. But it's possible, and it may be well worth it. Maybe these innovative school models don't exist in your neighborhood yet, but I hope this book inspires you to look for one a reasonable distance away—or explore the possibility of replicating it with a group of like-minded parents.

To find the right educational solutions for your child, you're going to have to be the visionary, the courageous one, the one who takes risks and speaks up.

What's stopping you? Childhood can't wait, and neither should you.

FINAL THOUGHTS

From my mother's fight to get the education and career she wanted as a woman in the 1950s, I learned early on that access to education isn't always fair. There will always be people who will be quick to tell you that you can't do something, and those who believe that they are entitled to equality simply because they're wealthier or from a certain class or culture.

Sometimes you have no choice but to fight to be heard.

That's certainly true in education. I've seen through my own experiences that our country's public school system is broken, especially when it comes to serving the one in five children with dyslexia. The special education system is confusing, and the path to educating children with learning differences is littered with obstacles.

In advocating for my sons, I kept asking myself why they, and other children with dyslexia, aren't being treated equally. As we've seen in these pages, the problems start at the highest level with a federal government that's no better than a deadbeat dad when it comes to upholding its financial obligations, which leads to kids being invisible and not getting identified early enough and who are being taught by teachers who aren't trained in the science of reading at our highest institutions of learning. The lack of money means specialized teacher salaries are low, classrooms are crowded, and school administrators often have to make heartbreaking decisions about which children they will fail by not offering the services they so desperately need. How can the schools provide trained reading specialists, when they can't even get the kids to the campus and feed them?

Even when there is money, reams of invisible red tape mummify any clarity about budgets, and trip up possible innovations in education. Practical solutions that could be so easily implemented remain elusive, or are even deemed "impossible" by burned-out teachers and exhausted, overwhelmed administrators.

Dr. Shaywitz testified in front of Congress that "[we] have not a knowledge gap, but an action gap."[36] This has to stop, and we're the ones who have to stop it. As you know from reading this book, right now, two-thirds of all children with learning disabilities are never given the support they need, leading a large proportion of those kids to experience low self-esteem, academic struggles, and school failure. Struggles in school put children on the path to becoming adults who experience many hardships such as low self-esteem, unemployment, homelessness, or even prison.

It only takes a few months for a child working with a teacher trained in phonics to enjoy progress and even success in reading. If you find the right early interventions and put them in place sooner rather than later, you can help your child, and then you can share with other parents how you did it. They can then help their children and go on to offer advice to other parents.

Yes, even you—one parent, with one voice—can chip away at the problems children with dyslexia face every day, now that I've shown you some of the hacks and work-arounds gathered from this amazing group. I'm grateful I had the chance to learn these shortcuts through talking with the brave women who have gone before me in this fight.

The public school system is often obstructionist. The special education system is so convoluted that it can take parents years to figure it out and get the right support for their kids if they don't have mentors. It's easy for school officials to gaslight you into thinking you must be wrong about what your child needs if you don't have allies and mentors in this fight.

I was lucky. I had an educated mother, a supportive husband, a privileged background, and friends in education who helped show me how to stand up for what my sons needed. Now I want to provide the same sort of mentoring to other parents with this book. For my dyslexia fight club, I am creating "Glinda," an eAdvising product for parents of special needs kids, with this mentoring mission in mind. I believe parents need accessible, consistent, and affordable support in navigating the education system. But currently, this doesn't exist. Glinda is an online advising platform designed to match parents trying to navigate the school system and advocate for their children, with experienced parents and experts who can help light the way. You can learn more about it at www.helloglinda.com.

It doesn't take a hero to be an activist who fights for change. All it takes is love for your child, compassion for others, and a willingness to learn and spread your knowledge. Delay your Netflix series for five minutes and share a post that you found interesting, or talk your neighbors into joining you at a board of education meeting to discuss your school district's budget and policies. Each small action you take will be a step forward for you, for your child, and for all children in our country who need, and deserve, an equal education.

ONE LAST FIGHT: MY SECOND SON'S STORY

W e breathed a sigh of relief when Matias was finally settled into his school. It had been a long battle. I still felt guilty for not having seen the obvious signs that he needed extra help in school from the start, but at least he was happy in school and progressing academically. We felt blessed, too, that we didn't see any obvious signs of learning issues for our second son, Oliver, who was three years younger.

They're very different kids, both physically and emotionally. Oliver is super funny, outgoing, and energetic. He can charm a crowd and memorize countless facts about animal migration patterns. With a drama-free birth and typical development, we weren't initially worried about his ability to learn. However, I certainly knew more about what to look for this time around. We did wonder if his high energy level might be read as hyperactivity by his teachers, so we spoke with his pediatrician and agreed to keep an eye on it.

We decided to place Oliver in the charter school lottery, as we wanted a cheaper alternative to the private pre-K he was in. This might seem strange after our first experience with the charter system, but this would be a different charter school, and, like I said, we didn't see any problems at the time, so we figured it could work. He began at this new charter school as a pre-K 4.

* * *

The charter school seemed like a perfect match for Oliver at first. He fit in socially, and showed no signs of struggling with any of the work. We began to truly relax. Oliver's academic progress seemed to be in line with his classmates'. He was right on track.

However, just as a precaution, we decided to share our family history of dyslexia with Oliver's teachers, letting them know we were open to talking about any concerns they might have.

In pre-K 4 he was learning the basics and socializing well, and his vocabulary and memory were light years ahead of the other kids.

But the following year in kindergarten, as they started on reading skills, we were concerned with his ability to match sounds to letters in words. So we requested a dyslexia screener just to see where his skills were in comparison to the national average.

His screener came back with no flags. I couldn't get an exact number of where he fell in the range, but I spoke with his teacher, who agreed with the "no concern" conclusion. In summary, we would keep an eye on Oliver as he headed into first grade.

Just to be proactive, we brought in Mrs. Dawn, our master of OG tutoring, over the summer to give him a good foundation for first grade. It was convenient, as she was also providing support for Matias to make sure he didn't lose any ground before fall.

A SHARP TURN IN FIRST GRADE

In first grade, however, we began to see some obvious indications of learning and attention issues. This wasn't completely unexpected. First grade is when students are expected to read longer passages. They're also asked to read aloud, and mispronunciation is common.

By then, I'd already started researching this book and interviewing parents around the country about their own experiences, and I'd learned that *an alarming 40 percent of children who have dyslexia also have siblings who struggle to read.*[1] These numbers, and Oliver's clear signals of struggle, put me on the alert.

Before long, I felt like Bill Murray in *Groundhog Day*. As Oliver's school struggles intensified, we began seeing a side of him we'd never seen before. Instead of our happy, talkative, singing charmer, we had a son who dreaded school. His teachers reported that Oliver didn't want to take off his jacket when he arrived, and was hiding under the table when asked to read. Often, he sat all by himself, trying to work out the words on his own, clearly ashamed that he was struggling to read when so many of his classmates did so easily.

We needed to figure out the root of these problems. At our spring parent-teacher conference, we reviewed Oliver's work in detail with his teacher. It was heartbreaking to see that Oliver had missed almost all of the spelling words on a test, despite his fantastic memory. He had also begun reversing letters and was unable to match sounds to letters in a complex word. There was no question then that he needed support.

We asked his teacher to send this documentation to the CST and request an evaluation. She agreed.

A NEW CHALLENGE: BREAKING THROUGH
THE EVALUATION THRESHOLD

With Matias, the signs that he needed a formal evaluation were very clear. I thought it was equally obvious with Oliver, given his low test scores and his behavioral issues, which manifested as resistance to reading in class.

I consented to have a CST determine if Oliver was eligible for an evaluation. They used the Predictive Assessment of Reading (PAR) screener again. They also provided subjective classroom observations from the school's speech therapist. I showed up to the eligibility meeting thinking that this was going to be procedural, where they do family intake, explain the special education handbook and rights, and I would sign the paperwork for the evaluation. I thought with my family history and teacher's report it would be a seamless meeting.

To my surprise, it did not go smoothly. I was in utter shock when Oliver was denied an evaluation by the charter school because "he was screened for dyselxia using PAR, and was not flagged again."

What? How was it possible that a fifteen-minute screener and a few subjective measures would determine the fate of my child, who was obviously struggling?

I asked these professionals to present me with their rationale for denying an evaluation. They simply restated ranges from the screeners and subjective measures from classroom observations. I questioned the speech professional about what she had seen in the classroom. But she hadn't brought her notes to our meeting, and her independent recollection was unhelpfully vague, though the observations had taken place only two weeks before. That sounded very sketchy to me. I asked if they took the information his teacher submitted seriously, and they said the results were in Oliver's files.

They then offered me a parting gift of something I'd never heard of before, despite everything we went through with Matias. It was called "response to intervention" (RTI). Basically, they would begin providing assistance with decoding skills for Oliver in sessions twice a week. The good news here was that I knew the reading interventionist was highly trained in Orton-Gillingham. The bad news was that there would be no way to monitor progress or fidelity during this RTI.

Still traumatized from my combative experience with my first charter school three years earlier, I doubted that the school would be honest or transparent about his RTI. I wanted a formal, legal document such as an IEP. That way, if they failed to provide services, or if a teacher left or some other unforeseen event derailed things, I'd have recourse options.

Ultimately, I did the only thing I knew how to do when backed against the wall: tell my story with emotion. I explained in detail how it would affect Oliver and our family in the future if he didn't get the support he needed now.

This tactic failed. The head of the CST was sticking to her subjective evaluation and her social work credentials as justification of denial for an evaluation. She even said to me point-blank, "I know what you trying to do: get your son to go to the expensive private school that your older son goes to."

I was floored again. This, from a woman who fought the system for her own child, using my previous lawyer. I had no intention to get "legal," I told her. I simply wanted to make sure that I was documenting what steps were being taken to support Oliver, and advocating for my child, a procedure that had taken me years to learn. Something in my manner must have triggered her.

I had arrived at this meeting to sign what, in my mind, would be procedural papers to begin an evaluation, but ultimately I was kicked out the door with a "watered down" intervention plan and someone questioning my motives. I couldn't believe this was happening again. I wept all the way home, where I crawled into my bed and wondered what to do.

My only glimmer of hope was that the CST had agreed to have Oliver evaluated at the end of first grade to see what progress he made with RTI in the last three months of school. I wasn't confident that they could tell much within this time frame, but I felt I had no choice but to let it ride.

THREE MONTHS TO BREAK THROUGH

I wasn't about to wait for the school's end-of-year evaluation. My previous battle and research had taught me that the sooner we could help Oliver, the better his chances were of reading fluently and regaining his love of learning. As with Matias, I brought Oliver to outside experts. They agreed that the school district's denial of services was unjustified. I had paid yet again for more testing, adding more bills to the pile, but the good news was that I was now ready to battle at the end-of-year progress meeting.

This meeting took place in a bigger room, but it was crowded with administrators, teachers, and specialists, presumably since I'd been so openly disgusted at the way the school had pushed my concerns aside the first time. They contended that Oliver had made significant progress in the past three months, thanks to RTI, but I didn't see it.

Based on the results from the new testing I conducted with Lindamood Bell and the school's OT observation, he qualified for IEP evaluation. Phew. That three-month hustle had been worth it, and I couldn't have done it without everything I'd learned from Matias's journey. But of course, we weren't out of the woods yet.

STILL A LONG WAY FROM HOME

We had more evaluations conducted over the summer, and by the start of second grade, we had a diagnosis, qualifying Oliver for an IEP. They were hesitant to write the word "dyslexia," but I let that go. I had to pick my battles.

Now, having gone through the process the second time around, I still think it's crazy that schools want parents to sign the IEP on-site. Thank goodness I brought the IEP home and, after the long two-hour meeting, read it in detail, because none of the goals they listed in it were appropriate for Oliver.

When we reconvened, I asked the team how they had arrived at these goals, and was shocked to hear the reading interventionist admit that she had never written an IEP goal. The head of the CST told me that she could not write reading goals either, since she was a social worker and not trained to do so.

I asked "Who is performing this critical task, then?" They all looked around the room at one another. It looked as though they had simply copied and pasted the goals from a standard dropdown menu of second grade goals.

It took two more months for me to find the right goals for Oliver. What parent wants to do that? I was amazed that with ten professionals it seemed that there was nobody on the team who was qualified to write comprehensive and customized IEP goals. I had to get involved and figure out how to get effective goals for my son.

The school didn't know what to do with my pushback on these goals and objectives, so I truly admired their decision to call in a consultant to advise them on how to incorporate my revised goals into the IEP. However, she had never met my son, and I didn't know an outside resource was being brought into the conversation until I was asked for written permission from the consultant to share my goals document.

After one more contentious meetings to hammer it out, we finally agreed on a set of goals and expectations. We all learned a lot in this process and I believe the school is giving everything they can within their reach and resources. The extra attention and time Oliver has been given since then have really helped him gain self-confidence. He reads the street signs aloud as we drive, and is able to navigate on-screen game directions. He is popular with his peers, and has found outlets for his creative energy. His handwriting has greatly improved. He sings at the top of his lungs at the holiday spectacular, and I get warm and fuzzy knowing this fight was worth it, because my son is a happy, curious learner.

I wanted to tell Oliver's story to those of you who might have two or more children with different struggles. Just because you know one doesn't mean another isn't ready to introduce itself. Stay vigilant, trust your instincts, and understand your family history.

WHAT I LEARNED FROM OLIVER:

- Ask for a screener as well as the hard data that accompanies the results when you have concerns. Most states are required by law to have universal screeners in kindergarten to identify those students who are at risk for reading failure. Double check the laws in your state to make sure your child receives appropriate screening.
- Question the subjective nature of the observations that determine whether an evaluation can proceed. Consult independent professionals to see if they agree. Try to make a timeline as a way to monitor progress for an RTI.
- Send friendly reminders to teachers about the RTI, and make a form that's easy for your teacher to fill out to keep you updated. Make sure the interven-

tionists working with your child are trained specialists.

- Figure out who is writing your child's IEP goals and
  ask how they arrived at their conclusions. There are
  many sites and groups that discuss the ins and outs
  of IEP rigor.

ACKNOWLEDGMENTS

It has been a privilege and honor to be able to tell the stories of the Dyselxia Fight Club. Together, this community of family and friends made this all possible. So now let the members of this esteemed club be recognized in style. Let's begin with the OG's bloodline. To my mom and dad for teaching me to stand up for what's right, respectfully. To my sister, Jessica, for her never-ending listening and analytical skiils. To my family, mis corazones, mis amores. Without your patience fueling my passion, this book would not exist. To Fede, I truly value your vision and your support during this process. Your ability to create the space needed to write, edit, and do it all again was amazing. My partner in life, I love you. To Matias, you inspire me every day with your tenacity, grit, and ability to take on anything that is lucky enough to grab your attention. To Oliver, your fearless ability to share your humor and stories with the world will inform and entertain us for years.

To my Tiller Press/Simon & Schuster colleagues, starting with Sam Ford, who only says yes to the impossible. I have always looked up to your ability to craft amazing, spreadable stories. Thank you for having the confidence and candor to take on the impractical, an unknown author and book-publishing model. To Emily Carleton, the editor extraordinaire, how did you deal with such a novice? You taught me more than you'll ever know such as how to define sections and keep out extras. To

Theresa DiMasi, for asking the hard questions, such as "How did we get here?" To Scottie Ellis, for her innovative angles on research and recruiting, and producing an outrageous highlight reel of stories that will create change. To Michael Anderson who helped me audit, analyze, plot, and plan digital dominance. And the rest of the crew: Samantha Lubash, Laura Flavin, Matthew Michelman, Jeff Miller, Patrick Sullivan, Marlena Brown, Lauren Ollerhead, Morgan Hart, Stacey Sakal, and Norma Lippincott.

To Evelyn Frison, an ingenious force of nature who can see the forest through the trees. Your ability to keep me focused and moving forward was beyond brilliant. I couldn't have found the amazing characters and built *Invisible Red Tape* without you.

To Sebastian Bottazzini, my design mastermind, your ability to guide the look and feel of *Invisible Red Tape* with ease and grace was unbelievable. You created twenty versions of covers, ten logos, social media posts, and even T-shirts. My friend from Barcelona, thanks for being with me on yet another crazy journey.

To Daniela Medina Mate, thanks for your amazing content strategy and production skills. There would be no speeds and feeds without you. I appreciate your time and dilligence.

To Emily Pecot, my bold, beautiful friend who joins me in advocacy and resistance. Thank you for the site design and many other pieces you contributed to this project. Thanks to Nico and Caroline for web design 2.0.

To Jesse Rosenblatt, you are a master negotiator and have taught me everything about being a businesswoman. Thanks for keeping my best interests in your line of sight.

To Avery Roth, my coach who has helped me remove all the barriers to create my proudest piece of work. You helped me jump and find my true voice.

To The JC Crew, for picking up the kids from afterschool programs, play dates on Sundays, cooking meals, listening to real-time edits, and helping me find resources for the book. Marianela Fernandez, Pedro Giraldo, Mariana Rodriguez, Camilla and Lucas Rosario, Joanna Garnett Raeppold, Claudia Munhoz Irico, Lorenzo Irico, Cristel Suarez, Melinda Mangin, Tim Synder, Salomon Lopez, Angie Vazquez, Tyler Lee Burston, Angela Bennett Glock, and Melissa Lamb.

To my writing partners—Holly Robision, you were my ride or die on this journey. You can tell stories and write like nobody I know. Your craft in building a narrative and pulling it all together is magical. If I can only come out of this slightly as brilliant as you, I might be able to do this all again one day. To Mary Ann Sherman and the Jersey City Writers' Non-fiction Workshop, I started this process having no idea how to write a book, and with your guidance, Monday night meetings, and painstaking patience you taught me how to become an author. MAS, your brilliant PR skills and your painstaking attention to detail helped me with catalog copy, final edits, and framing of the story. To Greg Collins, for always being my snarky copywriting partner. Your skills as a writer still amaze me. To JJ Kaufman, for help on bios and web copy.

To Jersey City Together, for teaching me how to build collective power. Frank McMillian, for setting an example of finding common ground. To the Education Team members I admire: Brigid D'Souza, Jyl Josephson, Jim Nelson, and Emily Pecot.

To my key collaborators—Liz Deupree Barnes, Dawn Dennis, Jena Cordova, Elyssa Dole, Sam Silver, Decoding Dyslexia leaders, Renay Zamloot, Lorenzo Santos, Romy Nehme, Tad Jacks, Nicole Moon, and the Craig School.

Special thanks to:

Gabriel Flores, Melissa Garvey, Pete Young, Alex Taylor, Lauren Kanter, Justin Stewart, Katherine Kelly, Erin Patrice O'Brien, Allison Barkan, Meaghan Kennedy, Isabelle Swiderski, Miranda Howell, the Habitas Crew, the NationSwell Council, AndCo, Breakout, Matias's teachers, UltraWorking, Caveday, Pablo Cubarle, Carrie Cubarle, Phil Scott Jackman, and the Crema Crew.

ENDNOTES

PREFACE

1. Bonnie Rochman, "Is 10 Minutes Enough for a Well-Child Visit with the Pediatrician?," *Time*, September 19, 2011, https://health land.time.com/2011/09/19/one-third-of-pediatricians-breeze-in -and-out-yet-parents-seem-satisfied/.
2. "Brain Development," First Things First, https://www.firstthings first.org/early-childhood-matters/brain-development/.

SECTION I:
HOW DID WE GET HERE?

1. Sally E. Shaywitz, *Overcoming Dyslexia: A New and Complete Science-Based Program for Reading Problems at Any Level* (New York: Alfred A. Knopf, 2012), 3.
2. Dr. Albert M. Galaburda et al., "Developmental Dyslexia: Four Consecutive Patients with Cortical Anomalies," *Annals of Neurology* 18, no. 2 (August 1985): 222–33, https://doi:10.1002/ana.410180210.

3. G. Reid Lyon, "The NICHD Research Program in Reading Development, Reading Disorders and Reading Instruction: A Summary of Research Findings. Keys to Successful Learning: A National Summit on Research in Learning Disabilities," ERIC, The National Center for Learning Disabilities (website), 1998, https://eric.ed.gov /?id=ED430366.

4. "Dyslexia Information Page: What Research Is Being Done?," National Institute of Neurological Disorders and Stroke (website), https://www.ninds.nih.gov/Disorders/All-Disorders/Dyslexia-Infor mation-Page.

5. "International Dyslexia Association," International Dyslexia Association, n.d., https://dyslexiaida.org/.

6. "CST—Child Study Team," Special Education News, n.d., http:// www.specialednews.com/special-education-dictionary/cst---child -study-team.htm.

7. Richard Wagner et al., "Comprehensive Test of Phonological Processing | Second Edition," Pearson, 2013, https://www.pearson assessments.com/store/usassessments/en/Store/Professional-Assess ments/Speech-&-Language/Comprehensive-Test-of-Phonological -Processing-%7C-Second-Edition/p/100000737.html.

8. "What Is 'Early Intervention'?," Centers for Disease Control and Prevention (Centers for Disease Control and Prevention, December 9, 2019), https://www.cdc.gov/ncbddd/actearly/parents/states.html.

9. "OHI—Other Health Impairments," Special Education News, n.d., http://www.specialednews.com/special-education-dictionary/ohi ---other-health-impairments.htm.

10. Amanda Morin, "Understanding Response to Intervention," What Is RTI? (Understood, n.d.), https://www.understood.org/en/school -learning/special-services/rti/understanding-response-to-interven tion.

11. Susan Hall, "Is It a Reading Disorder or Developmental Lag?," Reading Rockets, n.d., https://www.readingrockets.org/article/it-reading -disorder-or-developmental-lag.

12. "Sec. 300.8 (c) (10)," Individuals with Disabilities Education Act, May 25, 2018, https://sites.ed.gov/idea/regs/b/a/300.8/c/10.

13. Understood Team, "3 Tiers of RTI Support," 3 Tiers of Response to Intervention (RTI) (Understood, n.d.), https://www.understood .org/en/school-learning/special-services/rti/3-tiers-of-rti-support.

14. "Identifying Struggling Students," National Center for Learning Disabilities (website), January 25, 2017, https://www.ncld.org /research/state-of-learning-disabilities/identifying-struggling -students/.

15. "Third Grade Reading Success Matters," The Children's Reading Foundation, n.d., https://www.readingfoundation.org/third-grade -reading-matters.

16. "Identifying Struggling Students," National Center for Learning Disabilities (website).

17. "Students Who Don't Read Well in Third Grade Are More Likely to Drop Out or Fail to Finish High School," The Annie E. Casey Foundation (blog), The Annie E. Casey Foundation, April 8, 2011, https://www.aecf.org/blog/poverty-puts-struggling-readers-in -double-jeopardy-minorities-most-at-risk/.

18. Lamk Al-Lamki, "Dyslexia: Its impact on the Individual, Parents and Society," National Center for Biotechnology Information, U.S. National Library of Medicine (website), July 15, 2012, https://www .ncbi.nlm.nih.gov/pmc/articles/PMC3529660/.

19. Matthew Lynch, "High School Dropout Rate: Causes and Costs," The Edvocate (website), August 2, 2016, https://www.theedadvocate .org/high-school-dropout-rate-causes-and-costs/.

20. Michael Sainato, "U.S. Prison System Plagued by High Illiteracy Rates," *Observer*, July 18, 2017, https://observer.com/2017/07/prison -illiteracy-criminal-justice-reform/.

21. "New Research Reveals Many Entrepreneurs Are Dyslexic," American Management Association (website), January 24, 2019, https://www .amanet.org/articles/new-research-reveals-many-entrepreneurs-are -dyslexic/.

22. Kate Griggs, "Connecting the Dots: Understanding Dyslexia," Made by Dyslexia (website), n.d., http://madebydyslexia.org/assets/down loads/made_by_dyslexia_connecting_the_dots.pdf.

23. "13% ROI Research Toolkit," The Heckman Equation (website), May 10, 2019, https://heckmanequation.org/resource/13-roi-tool box/.

24. "Identifying Struggling Students," National Center for Learning Disabilities (website).

25. Stephen Sawchuk, "Meet the Moms Pushing for a Reading Overhaul in Their District," *Education Week—Curriculum Matters*, April 3, 2019, https://blogs.edweek.org/edweek/curriculum/2019/04/meet _the_moms_pushing_for_a_reading_overhaul.html.

26. Jo Kroeker, "New Law Seeks to Prevent School Districts from Silencing Staff," *gtInsider*, September 19, 2019, https://www.ctinsider .com/news/greenwichtime/article/New-law-to-prevent-districts -from-silencing-14453606.php.

27. Louisa C. Moats and Carol Tolman, *The Challenge of Learning to Read*, Sopris West Educational Services, 2009.

28. "Phonics-Based Reading vs. The Whole Language Approach," Educational Connections, March 12, 2019, https://www.ectutoring .com/phonics-based-reading-whole-language-approach.

29. Emily Hanford, "Hard Words: Why Aren't Kids Being Taught to Read?," *APM Reports*, September 10, 2018, https://www.apmre ports.org/story/2018/09/10/hard-words-why-american-kids-arent -being-taught-to-read/.

30. Emily Hanford, "Why Are We Still Teaching Reading the Wrong Way?," *New York Times*, October 26, 2018, https://www.nytimes.com /2018/10/26/opinion/sunday/phonics-teaching-reading-wrong -way.html.

31. "Identifying Struggling Students," National Center for Learning Disabilities (website).

32. Sarah D. Sparks, "Study: RTI Practice Falls Short of Promise," Education Week (website), November 6, 2015, https://www.edweek

.org/ew/articles/2015/11/11/study-rti-practice-falls-short-of-promise
.html.

33. "Attention-Deficit/Hyperactivity Disorder (AD/HD) and Dyslexia,"
International Dyslexia Association (website), n.d., https://dyslexiaida
.org/attention-deficithyperactivity-disorder-adhd-and-dyslexia/.

34. Emma García and Elaine Weiss, "The Teacher Shortage Is Real,
Large and Growing, and Worse than We Thought: The First Report in 'The Perfect Storm in the Teacher Labor Market' Series,"
Economic Policy Institute (website), March 26, 2019, https://www
.epi.org/publication/the-teacher-shortage-is-real-large-and-growing
-and-worse-than-we-thought-the-first-report-in-the-perfect-storm
-in-the-teacher-labor-market-series/.

35. "Dyslexia in Schools 2019," Made By Dyslexia, n.d., http://madeby
dyslexia.org/assets/downloads/Dyslexia_In_Schools_2019.pdf.

36. Laura Stewart, "The Science of Reading: Evidence for a New Era of
Reading Instruction," The Superkids Reading Program, n.d., https://
www.zaner-bloser.com/reading/superkids-reading-program/pdfs
/Whitepaper_TheScienceofReading.pdf.

37. Christina A. Samuels, "10 Big Ideas: Special Education Is Broken,"
Education Week (website), January 8, 2019, https://www.edweek
.org/ew/articles/2019/01/09/special-education-is-broken.html.

38. "IDEA Full Funding: Why Should Congress Invest in Special Education?," National Center for Learning Disabilities (website), https://
ncld.org/news/policy-and-advocacy/idea-full-funding-why-should
-congress-invest-in-special-education/.

SECTION II:
THE STORY OF MY SON'S DYSLEXIA JOURNEY

1. Johannes Schumacher et al., "Genetics of Dyslexia: the Evolving
Landscape," *Journal of Medical Genetics*, February 16, 2007, https://
jmg.bmj.com/content/44/5/289.full.

2. Geri Coleman Tucker, "President Signs READ Act, Funding Research on Dyslexia and Other Learning Issues," October 17, 2019, https://www.understood.org/en/community-events/blogs/in-the-news/2016/02/25/president-signs-read-act-funding-research-into-dyslexia-and-other-learning-differences.

3. Bonnie Rochman, "Is 10 Minutes Enough for a Well-Child Visit With the Pediatrician?"

4. "The Importance of Screening," AAP.org, n.d., https://www.aap.org/en-us/advocacy-and-policy/aap-health-initiatives/Screening/Pages/The-Importance-of-Screening.aspx.

5. Jin Lee, "How Innovation Can Change the Course of Child Development," March 2018, TED video, https://www.ted.com/talks/jin_lee_how_innovation_can_change_the_course_of_child_development.

6. Lisa Chedekel, "Study Finds Racial Disparities Among Developmentally Delayed Toddlers in Early-Intervention Programs," Boston University Medical Campus, March 22, 2011, https://www.bumc.bu.edu/2011/03/22/study-finds-racial-disparities-among-developmentally-delayed-toddlers-in-early-intervention-programs/.

7. "Identifying Struggling Students," National Center for Learning Disabilities (website), January 25, 2017.

8. "The State of LD: Understanding the 1 in 5," National Center for Learning Disabilities, May 2, 2017, https://www.ncld.org/news/newsroom/the-state-of-ld-understanding-the-1-in-5.

9. Elizabeth Stearns et al., "Staying Back and Dropping Out: The Relationship between Grade Retention and School Dropout," *Sociology of Education* 80, no. 3 (July 2007): 210–40, www.jstor.org/stable/20452707.

10. Miriam Kurtzig Freedman, *Special Education 2.0: Breaking Taboos to Build a New Education Law* (California: School Law Pro, 2017), 153.

11. Dana Fattore Crumley and Jackie Gharapour Wernz, "Back to Ba-

sics: Rowley, Endrew F, and the Chevy vs. Cadillac Analogy," *Special Education Law Insights*, February 19, 2019, https://www.specialed lawinsights.com/2019/02/back-basics-rowley-endrew-f-chevy-vs -cadillac-analogy/.

12. Valeria J. Calderon et al., "Confidence in U.S. Public Schools Rallies," Gallup (website), September 14, 2017, https://news.gallup.com/poll /219143/confidence-public-schools-rallies.aspx.

13. "Dyslexia in Schools 2019," Made By Dyslexia, 2019, http://made bydyslexia.org/assets/downloads/Dyslexia_In_Schools_2019.pdf.

14. Evans v. Board of Education of the Rhinebeck Central School District, 930 F. Supp. 83 (S.D.N.Y. 1996), https://law.justia.com/cases/federal /district-courts/FSupp/930/83/1963891/.

15. Christina A. Samuels, "Special Education Is Broken."

16. "Title I Funding Gap," National Education Association (NEA) Title I Funding Gap, 2019, http://www.nea.org/assets/docs/Title-I-Funding -Gap-by-State-FY2019.pdf.

17. National Education Association (NEA) Title I Funding Gap by State for Fiscal Year Ending 2019 (ESEA Title I, Part A Grants to Local Educational Agencies), https://www.nea.org/assets/docs/Title-I-Funding -Gap-FY2017-with-State-Table.pdf.

18. David Cantor, "NYC Charter Schools Get 20% Less Funding than Traditional Schools, Study Says," August 30, 2017, https://www .the74million.org/article/nyc-charter-schools-get-20-less-funding -than-traditional-schools-study-says/.

19. T. A. Fiore et al., "Charter Schools and Students with Disabilities: A National Study (Final Report)," U.S. Department of Education, 2000, https://eric.ed.gov/?id=ED452657.

20. Robert B. Brooks, "Nurturing Islands of Competence: Is There Really Room for a Strength-Based Model in the Treatment of ADHD?," The ADHD Report 9, no. 2 (April 2001): 1–5, https://doi .org/10.1521/adhd.9.2.1.19075.

SECTION III:
THE OUTRAGEOUS HIGHLIGHTS REEL

1. "Understanding Response to Intervention (RTI) and Multi-Tiered System of Support (MTSS)," The University of Kansas School of Education (website), October 2008, https://educationonline.ku.edu/community/what-is-response-to-intervention.
2. Brian M. Rosenthal, "Denied: How Texas Keeps out Tens of Thousands of Children out of Special Education," *Houston Chronicle*, September 10, 2016, https://www.houstonchronicle.com/denied/1/.
3. Ibid.

SECTION IV:
SAVVY SOLUTIONS TO PERSISTENT PROBLEMS

1. Caralee Adams, "Class Size Crunch: What's More Vital to Classroom Success, a Great Teacher or Lower Class Size?," Scholastic, 2010, http://www.scholastic.com/browse/article.jsp?id=3755248.
2. "Child Poverty," National Center for Children in Poverty (website), n.d., http://www.nccp.org/topics/childpoverty.html.
3. "IDEA Full Funding: Why Should Congress Invest in Special Education?," NCLD, n.d., https://www.ncld.org/news/policy-and-advocacy/idea-full-funding-why-should-congress-invest-in-special-education.
4. "Background of Special Education and the Individuals with Disabilities Education Act (IDEA)," National Education Association (website), n.d., http://www.nea.org/home/19029.htm.
5. Tammy Kolbe, "Funding Special Education: Charting a Path That Confronts Complexity and Crafts Coherence," National Education Policy Center, June 25, 2019, https://nepc.colorado.edu/publication/special-ed.
6. Brigid D'Souza, "A Closer Look at Jersey City's School Tax Rate,

Part 1: the Public Data," Civic Parent, October 15, 2019, https://civicparent.org/2019/10/15/a-closer-look-at-jersey-citys-school-tax-rate-part-1-the-public-data/.

7. "Will The Charter School BS Ever Stop?," April 13, 2015, https://jerseyjazzman.blogspot.com/2015/04/will-charter-school-bs-ever-stop.html.

8. "Executive Summary," National Center for Learning Disabilities, February 1, 2017, https://www.ncld.org/research/state-of-learning-disabilities/executive-summary.

9. Ola Ozernov-Palchik and Nadine Gaab, "Tackling the 'Dyslexia Paradox': Reading Brain and Behavior for Early Markers of Developmental Dyslexia," *Cognitive Science* vol. 7,2 (2016): 156–76.

10. "Students Who Don't Read Well in Third Grade Are More Likely to Drop Out or Fail to Finish High School," *Casey Connects*, The Annie E. Casey Foundation, April 8, 2011, https://www.aecf.org/blog/poverty-puts-struggling-readers-in-double-jeopardy-minorities-most-at-risk/.

11. J. K. Torgesen, "Lessons Learned from Research in Students Who Have Difficulty Learning to Read," in: P. McCardle and V. Chhabra, eds, *The Voice of Evidence in Reading Research*. Baltimore, Maryland: Paul H. Brookes Publishing Co.: 2004.

12. Paul L. Morgan et al., "Are Minority Children Disproportionately Represented in Early Intervention and Early Childhood Special Education?," *SAGE Journals*, December 1, 2012, https://journals.sagepub.com/doi/abs/10.3102/0013189x12459678.

13. "Measuring Progress in Public & Parental Understanding of Learning Disabilities," Tremaine Foundation, September 2010, http://inter.jwhowarddesign.com/ewebeditpro5/upload/TremaineReportofCompleteFindingsSeptember2010.pdf.

14. "Identifying Struggling Students," National Center for Learning Disabilities (website), January 25, 2017, https://www.ncld.org/research/state-of-learning-disabilities/identifying-struggling-students.

15. Ibid.

16. Susan Hall, "Is It a Reading Disorder or Developmental Lag?," Reading Rockets, n.d., https://www.readingrockets.org/article/it -reading-disorder-or-developmental-lag.

17. Rekha Balu et al., "Evaluation of Response to Intervention Practices for Elementary School Reading," National Center for Education Evaluation and Regional Assistance (website), U.S. Department of Education, November 2015, https://ies.ed.gov/ncee/pubs/20164000 /pdf/20164000.pdf.

18. Jean Johnson and Ann Duffett, "When It's Your Own Child: A Report on Special Education from the Families Who Use It," *ERIC*, 2002, https://eric.ed.gov/?id=ED471033.

19. Lynn A. Karoly, M. Rebecca Kilburn, and Jill S. Cannon, "Early Childhood Interventions: Proven Results, Future Promise," RAND Labor and Population, 2005, rand.org/content/dam/rand/pubs /monographs/2005/RAND_MG341.pdf.

20. "Birth to 5: Watch Me Thrive!," ACF, n.d., https://www.acf.hhs.gov /ecd/child-health-development/watch-me-thrive.

21. Ao Chen et al., "Individualized Early Prediction of Familial Risk of Dyslexia: A Study of Infant Vocabulary Development," Frontiers in Psychology, February 21, 2017, https://www.ncbi.nlm.nih.gov/pmc /articles/PMC5318442/.

22. Molly Ness, "Pediatricians Have a Role in Early Screening of Dyslexia," International Dyslexia Association, October 2018, https:// dyslexiaida.org/an-invitation-to-pediatricians-for-early-dyslexia -screeners/.

23. "Measuring Progress in Public & Parental Understanding of Learning Disabilities," Tremaine Foundation, September 2010, http://inter.jwhowarddesign.com/ewebeditpro5/upload/Tremaine ReportofCompleteFindingsSeptember2010.pdf.

24. Tracy Thompson, "Why Special-Education Programs Are So Frustrating for Parents," *Atlantic*, January 3, 2016, http://www

.theatlantic.com/education/archive/2016/01/the-charade-of-spe
cial-education-programs/421578/.

25. Melissa Ferry, "The Top 10 Challenges of Special Education,"
    Friendship Circle—Special Needs Blog, February 1, 2012, https://
    www.friendshipcircle.org/blog/2012/02/01/the-top-10-challenges
    -of-special-education-teachers/.

26. "SPeNSE Fact Sheet: Study of Personnel Needs in Special Educa-
    tion," U.S. Office of Special Education Programs, n.d., https://edu
    cation.ufl.edu/spense/files/2013/05/Paperwork.pdf.

27. Jean Johnson and Ann Duffett, "When It's Your Own Child: A Re-
    port on Special Education from the Families Who Use It.," ERIC,
    2002, https://eric.ed.gov/?id=ED471033.

28. "About the Shortage," NCPSSERS, n.d., https://specialedshortages
    .org/about-the-shortage/.

29. "Filipino teachers still awaiting $4.5M from federal lawsuit,"
    KSLA News 12, updated August 12, 2017, https://www.ksla.com
    /story/34680055/filipino-teachers-still-awaiting-45m-from-federal
    -lawsuit/.

30. "Teacher Preparedness Survey – Fundamentals of Literacy," De-
    coding Dyslexia Oregon, n.d., http://www.decodingdyslexiaor.org
    /teacher-preparedness-survey/.

31. "Strengthening Reading Instruction through Better Preparation
    of Elementary and Special Education Teachers," NCTQ Databurst,
    August 2018, https://www.nctq.org/dmsView/Strengthening_Read
    ing_Instruction_Databurst.

32. Stephen Pruitt, "OPINION: Four ways Mississippi is teaching more
    children to read well," The Hechinger Report, November 21, 2019,
    https://hechingerreport.org/opinion-four-ways-that-mississippi-is
    -teaching-more-children-to-read-well/.

33. "Literacy-Based Promotion Act," Mississippi Departmenr of Educa-
    tion, http://www.mdek12.org/OEER/LBPA.

34. "2019 Literacy Summit: Presentation Resources," Mississippi De-

partment of Education, September 13, 2019, https://www.mdek12
.org/node/4087.

35. The Institute for Multi-Sensory Education, https://www.imse.com/.

36. Kyle Redford, "Dyslexia Action: Denied and Delayed," *HuffPost*, updated December 6, 2017, https://www.huffpost.com/entry/dyslexia
-action-denied-an_b_5950008.

EPILOGUE:
ONE LAST FIGHT: MY SECOND SON'S STORY

1. Nelson Dorta, "Is Dyslexia Genetic?," Understood, n.d., https://www
.understood.org/en/learning-thinking-differences/child-learning
-disabilities/dyslexia/is-dyslexia-genetic.